...atkins, line coach; Bob Groseclose, backfield coach. Back row (l. to r.): Shorty ... sophomore coach; Tommy Morris, B team assistant ... ach; Nat Gleaton, soph assistant and head ba...

...agles Ey... ...rown Against Tyler

JACK HOLDEN
...rter-News Editor

If the Eagles can take this one they'll be the No. 2 team in the history of schoolboy football in the state. Only Waco, with five championships and a tie for another, would be out front.

It's chapter three in the success story of Charles (Chuck) Moser, Abilene Eagle coach. The former star Missouri guard has had his team in the finals two of his three years in Abilene and has seen those teams win 26, lose three and tie one.

...30 seconds on a scoring pass. If Saturday's game is anything like ... should get value received.

Weather forecasts indicate the ... clear and cool ... There will be plenty of seats left for the customers in the 37,000-seat stadium ...

Except for weight, the Abilene line should match Tyler. The ...

...ead Holds Miami ...ad Despite 70

...igh Game Bowling

PROBABLE OFFENSIVE LINEUP

ABILENE			TYLER
Weight	Player	Pos.	Player
170	[illegible]	LE	[illegible]
185	Rufus King	LT	[illegible]
180	Stuart Pastle	LG	Haskin Wilson
180	[illegible]	C	Jim Davis
170	[illegible]	RG	[illegible]
153	Homer Rosenbaum	RT	Billy Sims
193	Jerry ...	RE	Mickey Trimble
141	David Bourland	QB	Charles Milstead
175	Glynn Gregory	LHB	Joe Leggette
169	Henry Colwell	RHB	Kenneth McGuire

Warbirds

How They Played the Game

Tony — This is the
Abilene I come from —
Michael Grant

Warbirds

How They Played the Game

Michael Grant

Dust Jacket and Interior Design: The Printed Page, Phoenix, AZ, www.theprintedpage.com

ISBN: 0-9749662-0-7

Printed in the United States.

Lone Star Sundries
(619) 660-1447
warbirds@lonestarsundries.com

In Memory of
Coach Moser

Acknowledgments

WHATEVER THE PROJECT, Meredith Grant is my eternal strength. John Odam told me to write the book and saying no to John is like beating the Abilene Eagles. Bob Cluck and I have been best friends since 1955 and know more about each other than will be told here. When I told him about this project, he said, "I will help." And he did, and so did his wife Marilyn, also a dear friend and a great link to sources in the Abilene High administration. Eddie Baldwin is another old Eagle brother who remembered what it was like even better than I did. Gerald Galbraith, whose name appears time and again in this book, was most generous with his support and advocacy, as was his cousin Gervis Galbraith, both Eagle stars in 1956-57. Gervis was also Dub Galbraith's older brother, and if it had not been for Coach Moser this book would have been dedicated to Dub, but that's another story. Lynn Nichols gave me wonderful access to materials in the museum he created in the very hot loft above the Abilene High auditorium. Joe Humphrey, another old classmate, was almost as enthusiastic as John Odam (this is a high compliment) about the project and provided invaluable official background to the story. George Nichols helped me understand the book as a business deal, which took Moser-quality coaching. Tom Perini told me what it took to get a book published. Sue Diaz and Sandy Briggs provided invaluable publishing information. Molly Cline was an inspiration in her connection with all things Abilenian. Rufus King doesn't know the inspiration he provided simply by meeting me for lunch one day. David Bourland after almost 50 years actually remembered the rule blocking for 4 Straightaway which is one reason why he was so good in 1955. The Abilene Public Library was most patient with a man copying more than 350 pages out of microfilm files. Wayna Polk, Flashlight advisor at Abilene High, was a savior with the visuals. Finally, this book was written by a Texan who sees and thinks about and loves Texas in a certain, constant way that I always have, and so in the evocation of place, all the words were weighed with Nancy Birdwell in mind, the only person I ever met who I thought was more Texan than me.

Michael Grant
Feb. 21, 2004

Table of Contents

Introduction

> *"When the One Great Scorer comes to write against your name, he marks—not that you won or lost—but how you played the game."—Grantland Rice*

ON AUTUMN FRIDAY NIGHTS in Texas, the One Great Scorer is a busy deity. In brilliant metropolitan concrete bowls and in rural settings where the lights are barely strong enough to cast a player's shadow, thousands of Texas high school boys (and an occasional girl) go at each other on the football field for personal fulfillment and the glory of their schools and towns.

Unless it's a tie, one school wins and the other loses but the Scorer pays no mind to that. His only care is how you played the game. Still, most of the time there was a predictable correlation between the Scorer's judgment and the final score. It was possible to receive the Scorer's highest marks and still lose, but it didn't happen often.

Thus there were two compelling reasons to begin each season with how you played the game. In Texas high schools, football was not and is not an extracurricular activity. Football is a class in physical education, whose curriculum credits are as necessary for graduation as credits in English and math. In fact football was a very long class. It always began by mid-August, and in some places players started receiving mimeographed instruction from their coaches, their "teachers," as early as July 1.

Of course there were lots of X's and O's, that are central to how you play the game. But it hardly ever began with X's and O's. A few coaches might settle for that, but most understood that their first job was to extract from a 16- or 17-year-old boy a commitment to achieve a goal. That was a far more difficult teaching assignment than the belly series or 5-2 defense, and coaches took inspiration where they found it, in convincing a boy that an afternoon at the lake was not as good in the 100-degree heat as putting on 15 pounds of football gear and slamming into each other for three hours.

If the boy accepted that commitment, there was a good chance he would learn what it felt like to win, and winning, he was promised, was a feeling that would serve him well in building a successful life. Not one, but thousands, of coaches have told their teams in August: "Men, football is like the game of life." Of course it became a cliché and fuel for mockery, but it was a true cliché nonetheless.

Winning was a powerful attraction. Not many 16-year-olds would submit to twice-a-day football practices in order to prepare themselves to lose. Coaches talked about winning, and what it took to win, constantly.

But the coaches knew that every weekend there would be as many losing teams as winning ones. The best they could do was prepare their teams to give them the best *chance* to be the team that won. If their boys won, the coaches knew they would like the lesson. It was equally important that the boys who lost would feel like they learned something, too. It was the only way they could improve.

Some coaches developed great skill in articulating that truth to their players. Others could rely on the literary sports writer, Grantland Rice, for inspiration, even if they couldn't recall the Scorer quote verbatim. "Boys," they would say proudly in both locker rooms, "you did your best."

Doing your best. What does it take to do your best? First of all, you have to do good. Good, better, best, we all learned in English class. Best is the superlative of good, but good is where it starts.

There are two main ways to do good. You do things good, and you do good things. That is where not just football, but all athletics, start. Before they ever pick up a ball or get into a stance, athletes are taught to do things good and do good things. Many of these they are given to do; others they are encouraged to do. Get in good shape.

Don't smoke. Don't drink. Have good eating habits. Have good study habits. Make good grades. Be a good citizen.

If you do things good, you will get better. If you keep getting better, you have a chance to be the best. All over Texas, in rich huge districts and poor tiny ones, those were the first lessons of the season, and they did comprise a good textbook for preparing for the life beyond athletics. Then finally, when you go on the field, make the best use you can of all these good things. As long as the deity is the One Great Scorer, and not God, you could almost call football Sunday School taught on grass and not get in too much trouble with the U.S. Constitution.

Year after year, thousands of times over, the lessons were taught and learned and a team went into a game with its best chance to win. But every Friday night, someone won, and someone lost. Then in one Texas town, a team started to learn from a new coach how to do things good and do good things. He was a man who understood that principles were principal to any success on or off an athletic field and he was exact and unrelenting in teaching the value of values. Studying him now evokes a nostalgia for that time when principle and values were unabashedly traditional in the American dialogue. With these lessons and his meticulous knowledge of the game, he provided his players their best chance to win, and on Friday night they won. And won. And won. And won, won so much they made history and set lasting examples for coaches everywhere to give their players about how to be good, and maybe better, and maybe the best. This book is about that coach and that team, and the reason for the book is their winning streak. But its content is about how they played the game.

'A Very Respectable Season'

IN THE FINAL GAME of the 1952 football season, the Abilene High School Eagles, led by the passing of senior quarterback Jimmy Dan Bourland and the defensive play of junior tackle Bobby Jack Oliver, defeated the San Angelo Bobcats, 26-6, at San Angelo, in their traditional Thanksgiving Day battle.

A win over bitter rival San Angelo, 87 miles southwest of Abilene on U.S. 277, was always satisfying. And it was the Eagles' seventh victory against three defeats for the 1952 season, earning them a third-place finish in District 1-AAAA, by consensus the most rugged district in Texas high school football. A respectable season, Abilenians rationalized.

That same day, the defending state Class AAAA champion Lubbock Westerners beat the Amarillo Golden Sandies, 40-13, to complete a second straight undefeated regular season and repeat as District 1-AAAA champions.

Abilene, 170 miles west of Dallas, was the easternmost team in the district. Other teams in sprawling District 1-AAAA stretched from West Central Texas up the Caprock to the Panhandle. They were Lubbock, Amarillo, San Angelo, the Midland Bulldogs, the Odessa Bronchos, the Borger Bulldogs and the Pampa Harvesters. In 1952, Abilene, with a strong defense but a sporadic offense that only scored 120 points all season, collected wins over Fort Worth Arlington Heights, Sweetwater, Borger, Amarillo, Midland, Odessa and San Angelo and lost to Breckenridge, Pampa and Lubbock.

As the Eagles once again hung up their football gear and moved indoors to basketball, Lubbock High swept through the state football playoffs and defeated Baytown, 12-7, to repeat as state Class AAAA champions. It was only the second year that Texas high schools played to a state championship in classes – AAAA, AAA, AA and A – based on school enrollment. Cities with only one high school, like Abilene, in Class AAAA, had populations in the 40,000-75,000 range. Abilene's population of about 60,000 was not as large as Amarillo or Lubbock, but larger than Midland, Odessa and San Angelo. The district's "small" cities were Borger and Pampa.

They were all working-class cities, with economies based on oil, agriculture and ranching, and the boys growing up to play football knew about work. In the 1950s, in Texas, the legal driving age was a very young 14, because so many families needed their young men to operate trucks and other farm and ranch equipment.

After the 1952 season, Pete Shotwell, head coach at Abilene High since 1946, decided to leave coaching after a legendary career that spanned 37 years. But he didn't want to leave athletics, and he saw a need. Abilene had experienced significant growth during and after World War II, and there were more elementary schools and two junior highs with a third planned to open in 1955, plus a black elementary school and a black high school, Woodson High. But there was no centralized physical education system. To Abilene school administrators, Shotwell, or "Shot," as he was affectionately known, made a proposal to create a new administrative position that would oversee physical education and health education in the growing Abilene schools system.

It would give him official authority over a program he had already helped create, elementary school football. Football, in uniform, was played as a strictly recreational program in all the city schools. By 1950, boys as young as fourth grade in Abilene could start playing organized football, in city school leagues, that played to championships and awarded championship trophies and jacket patches.

At its regularly scheduled meeting on Feb. 2, 1953, Abilene Superintendent of Schools A.E. Wells presented Shotwell's proposal to the Abilene School Board. The Board voted unanimously to accept the proposal and transfer Coach Shotwell into the newly created position at his old head coach's salary of $6,500.

The next day at the top of the front page of *The Abilene Reporter-News,* sports writer Fred Sanner's story began: "The 37-year active coaching career of Prince Elmer (Pete) Shotwell came to an end Monday night when the Abilene School Board created the position of co-ordinator of health and physical education and, in a unanimous vote, transferred him from head football coach to the new position.

"The School Board, after hearing Coach Shotwell, the only man in Texas schoolboy circles who has won state championships at three different schools, request that the transfer be made, unanimously agreed that there was a definite need for such a co-ordinator and that 'Shot' was the ideal man for the position."

More than a few readers of the paper that morning, after three straight "respectable" seasons, may have thought the position ideal for the man because it preserved Shotwell's dignity as it simultaneously opened up the Abilene High coaching job to new and younger blood.

Shotwell, in a career that began in 1920, won state championships at Abilene in 1923, at Longview in 1937, and a co-championship (with Port Arthur) at Breckenridge in 1929. In his second stint at Abilene, beginning in 1946, Shotwell's Eagle teams won 43, lost 26 and tied 3. His 1949 team won the district championship with a record of 7-2-1 and lost to Highland Park in the state quarterfinals. Amazingly, in 34 years as a high school coach, none of Shotwell's teams ever finished below .500 for the season.

"Shotwell will retain his present duties," Sanner wrote, "until a new head coach has been hired, a task which the School Board hopes to accomplish as soon as possible."

THE TASK TOOK LESS than two weeks. Applications flooded in, 20 in all, from all over the state and even a couple from out of state. And there was one more name recommended to the board. Abilene High track coach Bob Groseclose told Abilene Superintendent A.E. (Poly) Wells about a young, successful coach from the Rio Grande Valley. Groseclose, who had worked at Alice High School, had coached against this man, Chuck Moser, who was head coach at McAllen.

Wells agreed to telephone Moser and, if he was interested in the job, invite him to Abilene for a visit. But there was a complication. Moser had already left McAllen, had been hired as head coach at Corpus Christi Miller High School, had bought a house and moved in. But he had not signed a contract, and he asked Doris, his wife, what she thought. She said he'd better go check out the Abilene opportunity or every time he lost a game at Corpus he'd regret it.

Moser flew to Abilene, and Supt. Wells, a shrewd man, asked a couple of football players to show Moser around the school. They were Bobby Jack Oliver, the 215-pound tackle, and halfback Jim Millerman, who Moser had heard of even in McAllen. Moser joked that he didn't see much of the school because he couldn't take his eyes off the big tackle and the swift halfback. For those and other reasons, he liked Abilene, and the Abilene authorities liked him. Moser submitted the 21st application for the position.

But Wells told Moser the Abilene board probably wouldn't make a decision until the third or fourth week of February. Moser said he had scheduled spring training to start the following Monday, Feb. 16, at Corpus Christi, and once it began, he was going to stay there. At midweek, Moser returned to Corpus Christi.

The Abilenians saw something in Moser that called them to action. On Friday, Feb. 13, 1953, the Board of Education of the Abilene City Schools met in a called special session in the superintendent's office at 12:30 p.m. Those present were W.E. Fraley, board president; Morgan Jones, Jr., vice president; Mrs. George H. Swinney, secretary; board members Bert Chapman, Roy Skaggs and Ollie McMinn; A.E. Wells, superintendent; and Charles Romine, Abilene High principal.

The meeting was called for the purpose of discussing applicants for the position of Head Coach at Abilene High School. The list of applicants was trimmed to six finalists. After three and a half hours of discussion and consideration of the applicants, Mr. Chapman, a partner in the Wright-Chapman Pontiac dealership in Abilene, made a motion that the position be offered to Charles Moser of Corpus Christi at a salary of $7,000 per year on a three-year contract. Mr. Skaggs, a Taylor County judge, seconded the motion, and the motion carried unanimously.

After the meeting, Wells telephoned Moser and offered him the job. Moser accepted. The story was on the front page the next morning, Feb. 14:

> "Charles H. (Chuck) Moser, who guided McAllen to the Class AAA state semifinals last year, was named new head football coach at Abilene High School Friday afternoon by the School Board and given a three-year contract at $7,000 per year.
>
> "The 34-year-old Moser, who only recently had moved to Roy Miller High School of Corpus Christi when Bob Harrell left there to become coach at San Angelo, was chosen from a list of 21 who received serious consideration for the post vacated by the transfer of veteran P.E. (Pete) Shotwell to co-ordinator of health and physical education in the Abilene school system."

In selecting Moser, the Abilene board passed over Ty Bain of Kilgore, Gene Corrotto of Tulsa Central High, Owen Erekson of Brenham, Jay Fikes of Littlefield, Guy Gardner of Borger, William H. (Bill) Hinton of San Angelo, Al Johnson of New Mexico Western College, Johnnie Kitchen of Austin, Gene McCollum of Port Neches, Al Milch of Sul Ross College, Fagan (Moon) Mullins of Anson, M.O. (Mike) Murphy of Stephenville, Marion L. Priddy of Gainesville, Theo Rigsby of Alice, T.M. (Pete) Roach of Mineral Wells, W.P. (Bill) Sheffield of Lufkin, Elmer Simmons, assistant coach at the

University of Houston, John Tomlin of Port Arthur, John Whinnery of Dumas, and Gordon Wood of Stamford.

ON SUNDAY MORNING, Feb. 15, 1953, Abilenians had their first look at the new coach, in a two-column photograph of a ruggedly handsome man on the second page of the Sunday *Reporter-News* sports section. The formal photograph, of the type that would accompany a resume, showed a man with dark hair and eyes, prominent brow and chin, a football player's flattened nose, and an amiable grin showing slightly crowded teeth.

Moser was a native of Chillicothe, Mo. He played college football at the University of Missouri of the Big Six Conference, under coach Don Faurot, where he was a 172-pound center. He was an All-Conference selection in 1939 and as a senior was recognized as the top scholar in athletics in the entire Big Six Conference. In addition to his B.A. in physical education and biological sciences, Moser later (in 1952) received his M.A. in educational administration.

Moser's biggest play in college was instrumental in Missouri's first-ever Big Six Conference title under Faurot, in 1939. Missouri had Oklahoma backed up on its own five-yard line, and the Sooners had to punt. Moser blocked the punt. The ball was snagged by Missouri end Bob Orf, who fell into the end zone for the touchdown that won the game, 7-6, and sent Missouri to the Orange Bowl.

Moser coached at Lexington in 1940-41, then entered the Army Air Corps and trained as a navigator at Kelly Field in San Antonio. Through his roommate, who was dating her roommate, Moser met blonde, fair Doris Woodley, of Sabinal, Texas, an undergraduate at the University of Texas. They were married on Oct. 25, 1942.

Moser almost didn't stay in Texas at all. He was discharged from the Army in 1946 with the rank of major, and his intentions were to return to Lexington, a mining town where in 1941 he had posted a 9-1 record. But Mrs. Moser wanted to stay in Texas. Her husband listened, but told her he was not likely to find a head coach's job in Texas, where he was a stranger in high school coaching circles.

So it was up to people who did know Moser in other, sometimes unlikely, circles, starting with Mrs. Moser's college roommate. While visiting the Mosers in San Antonio and learning of their indecision, she said she thought the small Rio Grande Valley town of McAllen was looking for a head coach.

His wife urged him at least to inquire, and Moser did. He wrote a letter to the McAllen schools superintendent. The superintendent happened to be a University of Missouri alumnus who remembered Moser as a player. The superintendent invited Moser for an interview. In McAllen, the Mosers found they had at least one ally, a Methodist preacher in McAllen who had lived next door to Doris Moser's parents in Sabinal. Moser, a Methodist, got the job.

In his seven years at McAllen, Moser's teams finished second in the district five times. In the 1952 season, the Bulldogs won the District 8-AAA championship and defeated San Antonio Edison, 28-6, before falling to the Temple Wildcats, 36-14 in the semifinal game. Missouri coach Faurot, interviewed by *The McAllen Monitor,* said: "I would rather have Moser coach one of my boys on a losing team, than most coaches coach them on a winning team."

In nine years of coaching, including his first job at Lexington, Mo., Moser's record was 63-21-3. In his last three years at McAllen, his teams lost only four games. Then came the call from Corpus Christi Miller, and then from Abilene.

"The general opinion," wrote sports editor Al Ward in *The Monitor,* "was that McAllen was losing probably its best coach ever."

Chuck and Doris Moser had two daughters, Janie and Glenn, who were 7 and 2 when the Mosers moved to Abilene.

Moser was to assume his Abilene duties by March 1. In fact he arrived early enough to schedule the beginning of spring training for March 2. His office was a 10-foot-square room in Eagle Gym. The high school, a four-story classic of 1920s brick educational architecture, faced South First Street, a busy artery which was also U.S.

Highway 80, carrying motorists from San Diego to Savannah. Beyond South First were the Texas and Pacific railroad tracks, which divided Abilene into north and south sides. Downtown was a few blocks east.

The gym was at the back of the school, at a right angle, and its three arched entranceways faced the corner of South Second and Peach streets, where a quiet residential area began. The gym, like the rest of the school, was of buff brick. Above the entrance was a stone pediment in which was chiseled the title, "Abilene Eagles Nest," and above the pediment was a huge, carved eagle.

Moser brought in only one new assistant coach and in so doing gave Abilene High a second man who had been a head coach. Hank Watkins was head coach at nearby Donna when Moser was at McAllen. Every Sunday Watkins came over to the Mosers' house and the two men talked football. Moser asked Watkins to come to Abilene as his line coach, and Watkins agreed.

"You give me a good quarterback and a good line coach, and you will win some football games," Moser said.

~

FIRST AND FOREMOST, CHUCK MOSER was organized. His first activity in his Abilene High office was preparation and distribution of blue-mimeographed policies and procedures, for players, the coaching staff, for coaches at the city's two junior high schools, North Junior and South Junior, and for administration of the football program in the elementary schools.

For players, these were the general rules:

1. No smoking or drinking.
2. Home at 10, except on Friday and Saturday (12).
3. Do not eat between meals.
4. Take care of injuries (show coach always).
5. No dates the night before a ball game.
6. You must be enrolled in four subjects and passing three subjects in order to be eligible to play the next week.

7. Turn your eligibility slip into coach's office by Thursday, 8:30 a.m.
8. Show your teachers and school the highest kind of respect.
9. Make every practice a good one.
10. We need boys with the right spirit and hustle.
11. Please don't steal from your school or teammates.
12. We expect *every boy* to abide with all the rules.

There were rules for the dressing room:

1. Read the bulletin board each day.
2. Hang up equipment each day.
3. No fighting or horseplay. Save your energy for the field and act like a gentleman.
4. No cussing.
5. Stay out of the equipment room.
6. Do not wear football shoes inside the dressing room.
7. Keep your equipment clean.
8. Always clean and polish your shoes the day before a game.

There were rules for the practice field:

1. Be on time.
2. *Do not sit down.*
3. Run and hustle when you hear the whistle.
4. Do not cuss (keep your poise and don't lose your temper).
5. Do not leave the field (this means water).
6. Save conversation with spectators until after practice.
7. On the field, always be in full uniform, including helmet.
8. Walk across track, then run to the field and start to work.

There were rules of the game; not an actual rulebook, but two mimeographed pages of 32 rules that Moser titled, "Rules Everyone Should Know." Chuck Moser's No. 1 rule on the list: "The ball is never dead until the referee's whistle kills it. Play till you hear the whistle."

And there were rules of common sense. Moser demonstrated to his players how to dry their feet after a shower, to avoid athlete's foot. "Take good care of your feet," he said. "Wear good, clean socks. Watch for signs of blisters. Be sure your shoes fit and are laced tight and high."

About diet, he instructed his players to drink as little as possible in hot weather before eating. They should eat foods that provided energy, such as eggs, meat, breakfast food, fruit, vegetables, potatoes (not fried), and graham crackers and honey. He was a particular fan of graham crackers and honey. Stay away, he said, from pastries, doughnuts, popcorn, nuts, fried food and carbonated drinks.

Moser backed up his rules with penalties, ranging from extra sprints after practice to missed playing time and demotion or dismissal. His players would learn the penalties soon enough. They already were forming the idea that he didn't miss much.

~

OLIVER AND MILLERMAN and 43 other varsity candidates reported for the first day of spring training on Tuesday, March 2. About 100 other B and sophomore team players reported to coach Groseclose. The varsity practiced on fields east of the football stadium in Fair Park, two miles from the high school on Barrow Street south of South 7th.

Fair Park was a huge rectangle, extending from South 7th to South 10th Streets, and from Ross Ave. on the east to Catclaw Creek on the west. It was a busy place, shaded by native mesquite trees. Fair Park Auditorium, on the east side, hosted plays, concerts and performances by numerous Texas western swing bands. The Abilene Zoo was in Fair Park and attracted visitors and school groups from towns all around the Abilene area. Recreational buildings across a wide picnic area from the zoo were crowded every day of the summer with kids playing basketball or taking part in summer programs. There were concrete tennis courts on the west side near the creek. High school and college students went to dances at the Roundhouse, a round brick structure, like a low silo, built by the Works Progress Administration across Barrow from the stadium's north end.

Fair Park Stadium was tucked into a crook in Barrow Street, where the street bent to the west south of South 7th, following Catclaw Creek. The stadium could seat around 10,000, in bleachers that once had been a part of the old Texas Christian University stadium in Fort Worth. There was a six-lane running track, but the stadium site was so compact that the backstretch ran beneath the east-side bleachers. It added a touch of suspense. Track fans watching the leaders disappear beneath the bleachers at the south end never knew who might be leading when the runners emerged from the north end.

East of the stadium were playing fields and a dirt oval track used for motorcycle and stock car racing. Inside the oval was a field where the Eagles practiced. Players drove in cars from the high school and suited out in the stone field house under the scoreboard at the stadium's south end.

The field house was very small, so Moser met with his players in an area under the east bleachers, where he had set up benches and hung a blackboard on the side of an equipment shed. Among the 45 varsity candidates sitting on the benches were seven lettermen: ends Twyman Ash and Bob Gay; tackle Bobby Jack Oliver; guard Dick Orsini; backs Jim Millerman, Wendell Phillips and Hal McGlothlin; and quarterback Don Harber.

Like every other one in his career, Moser began the Eagles' first practice session with a chalktalk. "I see great value in skull practice briefly before every practice," he said. Moser told the players what he intended to accomplish in the 30 days of training that would end with a Spring Training Game on April 1. He said the first week would be all fundamentals. He said players who didn't perform would be demoted to the B team, and promising B team players promoted in their place. He said they were going to work hard, because football was a hard game, requiring players to "put out all the way."

"If some of you don't agree with me," he said, "you'd better head on into the shower now and save us the trouble of sending you in later on."

Moser's voice was a low baritone, almost a bass, and melodic, a reverberation that seemed to start deep in his throat. And in his speech there were eccentricities. When he said "little," it came out "liddle." When he said "Odessa," it came out, "Uhdessa." He could yell, but he never did, quite. Instead, he was intense, and his players would learn to fear that intensity even more than temper, because it was so direct, and personal.

With a couple of exceptions, Moser had no idea who could play, and who couldn't. Equally important, he didn't know who *wanted* to play.

He did know that he would carry about 40 boys on the varsity, and that no more than 22 of them would be seniors. He knew he was looking for players who would hustle, and who would hit. Above all, he was looking for players with spirit. Moser believed three things were needed in order to have a successful team. The first was spirit. Spirit required closeness, among the players but also between the players and the coaches. Moser was already teaching his coaches techniques to develop team spirit; most involved simply making each boy feel important.

The second need was a good quarterback. Moser had five criteria for his starting quarterback, in this order: he must be well liked; he must be the hardest worker on the squad; he must be smart; he must be quick; and he must be a good passer.

With his first three criteria, Moser could have been describing the leader of a gang. That was exactly the idea. "Boys want to be members of a gang," he said. "We just want it to be the right kind of gang." A gang, Moser knew, was bigger than any of its individual members, and that was the way he wanted his players to feel about their football team. Every gang had its leader, and the Eagle gang's leader was the quarterback.

The third need was good assistant coaches. All good assistant coaches, Moser said, had one quality in common: they could develop aggressiveness, yet be loved by the players. Moser believed in increasing his assistants' pay whenever possible, and in giving them credit whenever possible. He believed in giving assistants responsibility. And he mimeographed all of the football material and gave assistants copies, so each assistant would know what the head coach wanted.

Moser also had two cardinal rules for coaches. First, the coach must have a purpose for everything that he does. Second, the coach must have enthusiasm for anything he does.

~

ALL OF THESE THINGS, even more than X's and O's, were being taught to the players, and the coaches, in those first Eagle practices under Moser in March of 1953.

With Moser on that first day of spring practice were Hank Watkins, line coach, the only new assistant that Moser brought in; Bob Groseclose, B team coach and varsity track coach; Shorty Lawson, sophomore team coach and assistant baseball coach; Wally Bullington, assistant line coach; and Nat Gleaton, sophomore team coach and varsity basketball coach. Another assistant, B.L. "Blacky" Blackburn, would coach the B team but he was also the varsity baseball coach and busy with those duties.

Every coach and team manager had a mimeographed schedule of the day's practice. The managers were crucial in Moser's system. There were four team managers, all students, and one of them, always a senior, was selected by Moser to be head manager. The practice schedule allowed the managers to have the practice field set up so the team, or the team in units, could move smoothly from one drill to the next. Moser insisted on organized workouts with no wasted time. The managers also ran the locker room before and after practice, took care of equipment problems before, during and after practice, ran the training room, taped ankles, managed supplies, washed uniforms and towels, and accounted for footballs and other coaching paraphernalia after every practice.

The importance of managers in Moser's system was personified by Billy Jack Rudd, who was a junior manager in 1953 and would be appointed head manager in 1954. "You know," Moser said, "I'm not so sure if Rudd wasn't the one that started the whole thing. He would do anything for anybody, and he was so gung-ho he made me more gung-ho."

The first week of spring practice was devoted to fundamentals: blocking and tackling and, for the backs, running and passing. For Moser, both blocking and tackling began with one fundamental technique. He demonstrated the technique himself, at the same time illustrating for his assistants one of the principles outlined in his mimeographed policies for coaches: "A coach should teach football just like he would teach spelling. You must teach, drill and test. If you are conducting a 10-minute drill, it is best to teach (talk, demonstrate, and explain). Then do, do, do the drill, and some days give a little test."

In this instance, Moser became the blocker against an assistant coach defender. The trajectory, he said, squaring himself into a crouch before the defender, was always "in and up." You want to drive into the defender with your head up so that your forehead meets his chest right on his jersey numbers. With force that was not all pantomime, Moser stepped quickly into the defender, making the described contact, that knocked his black baseball cap sideways. Then, he said, drive *up,* into the defender's chin. And he drove up, again with a force kinetic enough to knock the assistant coach backward a few steps.

As the players, in small groups, went through the drills, Moser and his assistants saw quickly enough who would hit and who would hustle, and who *wanted* to hit and hustle. No one sat down, and no one ever took off his helmet. Those were in the players' rules. The practices moved quickly from one session to another. When the whistle blew, players ran from one part of the field to the next drill. That also was in the rules. In Moser's instructions to his coaches, he said he wanted short, snappy workouts because they helped build team spirit.

Observers took note. *Reporter-News* sports columnist Don Oliver wrote: "We know one thing for sure, win, lose, or draw, they'll be the hustlingest ball club that has represented Abilene in a long time. Those that don't hustle won't play for Chuck Moser very long."

FALL DRILLS BEGAN at the end of August for the 1953 season, with the first game at home, at Fair Park Stadium on Sept. 11 against the Highland Park Scotties of Dallas. Moser knew roughly that his starting lineup would be Twyman Ash and Bob Gay at ends; Bobby Jack Oliver and Dan Boyd at tackles; Dick Orsini and Frank Liles were the guards; Mac Starnes was the center; halfbacks were Jim Millerman and Wendell Phillips; the fullback was Jim Briggs; and the quarterback was Don Harber. Harber was a senior. Moser always wanted a junior and a sophomore quarterback on the varsity as well. The junior was H.P. Hawkins; the sophomore was David Bourland.

Most of the boys, driving to Fair Park Stadium for practice, had their AM car radios blaring, and a few of them might have realized they were listening to a Top 10 song written by an Abilenian. Slim Willet, whose real name was Winston Moore, was an erudite man with a degree in journalism from Hardin-Simmons University. But he made his living in the country music business, writing unique but forgettable songs about West Texas oilpatch life like "Toolpusher from Snyder" and "Rig-Movin' Man." He wrote one song, though, that made the big-time: "Don't Let the Stars Get in Your Eyes." The crooner Perry Como recorded it, and it became a Top 10 hit in 1953, along with "No Other Love" (also by Como), "Til I Waltz Again with You" (Teresa Brewer), "How Much is That Doggie in the Window" (Patti Page), "Song from Moulin Rouge" (Percy Faith), "Vaya con Dios" (Les Paul and Mary Ford), "I'm Walking Behind You" (Eddie Fisher), "You You You" (the Ames Brothers), "Rags to Riches" (Tony Bennett) and "Pretend" (Nat King Cole).

During the hated, hot, two-a-days of late August, most of the Eagles' attention was directed to running Moser's offense and defense. His offense was the split-T, with seven linemen spaced evenly across from end to end, a quarterback under center, the fullback behind the quarterback, and halfbacks on either side of the fullback. The splits were precise. If Moser wanted an 18-inch gap between the guard and tackle, he meant 18 inches, not 15. And the splits changed, from play to play, depending on the defensive lineup. A split might be 12 inches on one play, and 24 inches on another.

Moser's version of the split-T was called the "belly series," so called because its basic play sent the fullback straight into the line. The quarterback placed the ball into the fullback's belly and either gave the ball to the fullback, or pulled it out and gave it to a trailing halfback off-tackle, or the quarterback could fake that handoff as well and keep the ball around end. The belly series was being used by many college coaches, most notably Bobby Dodd at Georgia Tech, who was given most credit for developing it.

Moser also brought with him an innovation called "rule blocking." Each play had its own blocking rule for each player, most importantly each lineman. The player, having memorized the rule, knew what to do on each play irrespective of how the defense lined up. For "4 straightaway," a dive play that sent the right halfback straight into the line between right guard and tackle, the right guard's rule was: "On, In, Out, Linebacker."

If the defender was directly "on" the guard, the guard blocked him. If there was no one "on," then the guard looked inside, between him and the center. If there was a man there, the guard blocked him, taking the appropriate split to get the best blocking angle. If not, the guard looked outside, between him and the tackle. If there was no one "out" to block, then the guard went for the linebacker. When all the rules for each player were put together, every defender in every possible defensive alignment was accounted for. It was elegant simplicity. The end, tackle and guard off side, away from the play, were expected to block downfield. If Moser had a pet peeve, it was failure of the off side linemen to get downfield and block. At the bottom of his 32-item list of "Rules Everyone Should Know," Moser appended four personal rules founded on his own experience: "What Wins Games: 1. The desire to win; 2. Downfield blocking; 3. Faking; 4. Maximum effort by every player on every play."

Moser and Hank Watkins also taught the linemen a technique called "false" or "influence" blocking, to negate a weight disadvantage. Rarely did an Eagle lineman weigh over 185 pounds, and occasionally they would line up opposite a defender who was a good football player and who also weighed 200 or more. When that happened, the Eagles were taught to "influence" the defender. To move a defender to the blocker's right, the blocker would want the defender on his right shoulder. If the defender were strong enough to fight through the block, the Eagle blocker would drive in with his left shoulder and the defender, reacting, would actually fight in the direction the blocker wanted him to go. Then the blocker simply squared up, pivoted, and drove the defender to the right.

Moser's basic offense included straight-ahead dive plays by either the fullback or halfback; a fake to the fullback and an off-tackle handoff to the trailing halfback; a fullback power play at tackle; end sweeps by the halfbacks or fullback; a couple of inside trap plays (a guard pulling to "trap" an unsuspecting defender on the other side of the center); a couple of misdirection, or "counter," plays; and play-action passes to the ends or halfbacks. All the plays were run to either side. Players were tested on the plays and blocking rules, and those who didn't pass, didn't play.

The week of the first game, Moser had his team work out a couple of times under the lights at Fair Park Stadium. He said his team was "ready," but it had lost one of its key players, the big tackle Oliver, who had hurt a shoulder. Starting in his place would be 183-pound James Smith.

The Eagles would start the first game with an offensive line averaging 177 pounds, five pounds fewer than the Scotties. The Scots of Coach G.B. Morris had 11 lettermen to Abilene's seven. For the

Eagles, there was one record at stake: their new head coach had never lost a season-opening football game. Ticket sales, said Abilene High assistant principal J.H. Nail, were slow.

~

THE PLAYING AREA AND sideline bench areas at Fair Park Stadium were enclosed in a chain link fence. Players emerged from the stone field house—Eagles from the east door, visitors from the west—and walked across the running track, then through gates at either corner of the fence behind the south end zone.

The Eagles' colors were black and gold. In the Shotwell era, the Eagles wore all white: white pants and white jerseys with black numbers and three narrow stripes, one black and two gold, around the upper sleeve, and they wore gold helmets with a black stripe.

Moser's Eagles walked out of the field house and toward the field on the evening of Sept. 11, 1953, wearing black pants, and white jerseys with black military-style numbers and single, wide, black stripes starting at the neck on either side, crossing the shoulder pads and extending down the length of the sleeves to the cuffs. The helmets were gold with a black stripe. The jersey design was one that Moser had worn with his teammates at the University of Missouri, and that his McAllen teams (whose colors were purple and gold) also wore.

The backs and ends, meanwhile, were wearing "low-cuts." During the week, in practice, all the players wore high-top shoes that laced up above the ankle that gave more protection against ankle injuries. For games, Moser had his skill or speed players switch to low-cut cleats, that were lighter. As they came through the chain-link gate onto the field, all the Eagles' shoes were highly shined. It was in the rules.

About 5,500 spectators showed up. This was a "new" Abilene Eagle football team, and from the stands the Abilenians watched them closely. When they had the ball, the Eagles gathered in what was called a military huddle: two ranks, linemen in the front rank, hands on knees, and behind them, standing upright, the backs and ends. In the huddle, the white jerseys and wide black sleeve stripes gave the Eagle team a distinctly symmetric look. The huddle faced the defense and the quarterback faced the huddle, called the play and gave the snap count that would start the play, for example, "4 Straightaway, on one, on one. Break!"

With a clap of hands the Eagles broke the huddle and trotted briskly (the Eagles didn't walk anywhere) to the line of scrimmage in a straight-T formation, looked at the defense, remembered their rule blocking, and adjusted their splits to get the best blocking angle. The ready position was hands on knees. Don Harber, the quarterback, stepped under center and started the count, which was always: "Down! Set…Hut! Hut! Hut!" Harber's command, "On one," meant the play would start on the first "Hut." Given the situation, he might elect to start the play "On two," or even choose a quick count like "Set," or even "Down."

In Fair Park Stadium, the fans could hear Harber's count. "Down," he began, with a downward inflection. At the command the Eagles dropped into a three-point stance, right hand down, and again the jersey stripes presented a symmetric, unified look that may have made movie fans remember the choreographer Busby Berkeley. "Set…," Harber continued, giving the word a rising, anticipatory inflection, and then "Hut!" and the Eagles charged, the Eagle linemen away from the play sprinting downfield to block, and all the Eagles ran until the whistle blew. It was in the rules. In fact it was their first rule. Then they trotted briskly back to the huddle. Abilenians saw a team that knew what it was doing, and that moved with a sense of purpose, and also of unity.

The Eagles, with their first touchdown, gave the crowd a quick sample of Moser's style, which was equal parts flair and discipline. But it wasn't on offense. It was a punt return.

Midway through the first quarter, the Scots had to kick. Moser called for a "left" punt return. Not one, but two, Eagles, Jim Millerman and Don Harber, dropped back to receive the punt, Millerman on the right and Harber on the left. A "left" return meant that Millerman, the better runner, would return the punt, no matter who caught it. Millerman caught it at the Eagle 41 and turned toward Harber, 15 yards away on the other side. The players crossed, and Millerman faked a handoff to Harber. Had Harber caught it, he would have handed off to Millerman. It took mental discipline; the player catching the ball had to remember always to cross in front of his teammate, so that his body would conceal the handoff, or the fake.

The Eagle blockers, meanwhile, were peeling into an evenly spaced "wall" down the left sideline, a maneuver that they had practiced time and again. Millerman ran behind the wall untouched 59 yards for the Eagles' first touchdown under their new coach.

It was an ordinary situation into which Moser had built several options. It could go either left or right. Either Millerman or Harber might wind up with the ball, and they could switch sides, Harber on the right and Millerman on the left. Later in the game, it was Harber keeping the ball on the crisscross, returning a punt from the Eagle 45 to the Highland Park 38. *Reporter-News* sports editor Jack Holden, covering the game, called it "deceptive."

Halfback Wendell Phillips ran 58 yards to score on a belly handoff to the halfback off-tackle; Harber threw 38 yards to end Joe Vick for a touchdown; and Phillips ripped eight yards through the line for the final score as Abilene won, 28-13.

"Those scrapping Eagles," Jack Holden wrote in his Sunday column, "were the talk of the town Saturday. It was one of those games which thrill the spectators: long runs, fancy punt returns and a long pass or two sprinkled in.

"The blocking alone which the Eagles exhibited will win some games this fall," Holden continued. "The Abilene rushers tore up the Dallas line much of the time. Most pleasing, however, was Abilene's downfield blocking, a trait which Eagle elevens have been short of on many occasions for the past few years."

~

REGIONAL RIVALRIES THAT HAD developed over four decades remained fierce even after the schools became divided into competition classes by enrollment. Such was the case with Abilene and two smaller cities, Sweetwater, 44 miles west on U.S. 80, and Breckenridge, 60 miles east on U.S. 180. Even after Abilene became AAAA and Sweetwater and Breckenridge AAA, the two teams remained on the Eagles' non-district schedule.

Sweetwater was next, and Holden urged his readers "not to build hopes" based on the Highland Park opener. "The team will be in better shape," he wrote, "if they just go out and do their darndest every Friday and be satisfied with the results."

Sure enough, Sweetwater's Mustangs, who had become a powerhouse in Class AAA, tied the Eagles, 13-13. The following week, however, Abilene beat Breckenridge, 19-6, ending the Class AAA Buckaroos' 14-game winning streak.

Breckenridge was the Eagles' last non-district game. They opened play the following week against Borger, the team figured by most to finish last in District 1-AAAA play. Lubbock, the defending district and state champion, was favored to repeat as district champion, followed by Pampa, Amarillo, Odessa, Abilene, San Angelo, Midland, and then Borger.

The Eagles thrashed the Bulldogs, 60-0. No one could remember an Abilene Eagle team scoring 60 points in a game; it was half as many points as they had scored in the entire 1952 season. Halfbacks Phillips and Ronnie McDearman sparked a 33-point first-half explosion with touchdown gallops of 52 and 64 yards. Subs mopped up in the second half. Soph halfback Henry Colwell scored on a pass from junior quarterback H.P. Hawkins, senior halfback Hal McGlothlin scored twice, and Hawkins threw a second TD pass, this time to end Frank Etter.

The Eagles were seen as a young, inexperienced team improving quickly under a new and innovative coach. Hopes were indeed building as the Eagles awaited the powerful Odessa Bronchos and their gifted quarterback, Carl Schlemeyer.

Hopes at Fair Park Stadium, overflowing with 12,000 fans, roared into the night sky as Abilene scored twice to take a 14-0 lead in the first quarter. But Odessa struck back thunderously in the second period. The Bronchos went 50 yards in three plays to score their first touchdown, then hit again only two minutes later after recovering an Eagle fumble at the Abilene 34.

Fumbles killed two promising Eagle drives, one at the Odessa eight, in the third quarter. With strong defense, Abilene nursed its 14-13 lead deep into the fourth period, once stopping an Odessa drive at the Eagle two. Abilene had to punt after that stand, and Odessa got the ball again at the Eagle 47. Schlemeyer immediately went to the air and the Eagles were slapped with an interference penalty that put the ball at the Abilene 25.

From there it was all Schlemeyer. He completed two passes and carried twice, the second carry for one yard into the end zone for the winning touchdown.

The final score was 19-14, and the Bronchos were grateful to escape.

"I think we ought to be especially thankful for this one," Odessa coach Cooper Robbins told his team.

"There's nothing much to say," Moser said in the Eagles' quarters. "We lost the football game."

The next week, at Pampa on a cold, muddy field, the Eagles lost again, 7-6. With their district record now 1-2, it appeared as if the Eagles might be on their way to another "respectable" fourth-place finish. Instead, they ran the table.

First they knocked off a good Amarillo team, 32-7, gaining 487 yards rushing, the most ever allowed by the Sandies. Then they did something an Abilene team hadn't done since the first Truman Administration. They beat the Lubbock Westerners, for the first time since 1947. And they beat them in Lubbock, the first home loss for the two-time state champions since 1950. And the Eagles shut them out, 28-0, only the second shutout for a Pat Pattison-coached Westerner team. The victory moved the Eagles into second place, behind unbeaten Odessa, in District 1-AAAA.

Next were the Midland Bulldogs, who went down, 39-13. Finally, on Thanksgiving Day at Fair Park Stadium, Abilene routed old rival San Angelo, 61-0. Subs played the entire second half, scoring 34 points, including three touchdowns by Colwell, the sophomore halfback. Still, San Angelo coach Bob Harrell, the man who Moser so briefly replaced at Corpus Christi Miller, said to an Abilene assistant, "Coach Moser will live to regret this day."

~

THAT WAS THE POINT when heads started to turn. The perennial middle-of-the-pack Eagles suddenly were finishing second in the district, with a record of 7-2-1, an even more than respectable season. But that wasn't it, really. What coaches around the district saw was what the Eagles did in the last four games of the season. They had outscored four tough District 1-AAAA opponents, 160-20. Scoring 60 points against Borger was one thing; scoring 61 against San Angelo was something else. People were wondering what might happen if Abilene were to play district champion Odessa again. Eagle line coach Hank Watkins put it plainly. "I wish we had another crack at those suckers," he said. Odessa went on to reach the state championship game, but lost there, 33-7, to Houston Lamar.

What the Abilene varsity achieved was mediocre, compared to the Abilene B team, composed of juniors and sophomores, and varsity subs who hadn't played on Friday night. Moser tried to schedule all his B team games on Saturday because varsity subs who didn't play could then play in the B game. Sophomore quarterback David Bourland, who didn't play at Pampa or Midland on Friday night, would ride back to Abilene with an assistant coach, get home about 3 a.m., and play in the B game on Saturday. "You need the playing time," Moser said.

In the middle of the season, the Goldthwaite varsity managed to score a touchdown against the Eaglets, in a 39-6 loss. And that was all. The Eaglets shut out their other eight opponents and in an unbeaten season scored 277 points to the opposition's 6. Coaches throughout the district sensed something starting to stir in Abilene.

ON NOV. 13, 1953, at Fair Park Stadium, the South Junior High School Coyotes completed an undefeated ninth-grade season by defeating the North Junior Broncos, 31-12.

Moser paid close attention to the ninth grade teams, who played road games as far away as Brownwood, Colorado City and San Angelo. They played all their home games at Fair Park Stadium, just like the Eagle varsity, on Thursday nights before crowds as large as 4,000. In his mimeographed policies to junior high coaches, Moser said, "I realize that the junior high program is about the most important part of our football program. Any way I can help you, let me know."

Both South and North teams that night were running Moser's offense. "We should all use the same numbering system for our plays, same basic plays and teach the same fundamentals," he had pointed out in his policies. "Our training rules should be about the same. (Ours are enclosed.)"

Starting for North Junior in the season finale were ends Jimmy Zacharias and Stuart Peake; tackles John Busby and Rufus King; guards Boyd King (Rufus's brother) and Erwin Bishop; center Ronny Tate; fullback Cleon Jones; halfbacks Harold "Hayseed" Stephens and Wilford Millsap; and quarterback Danny Yeary.

Starting for South Junior were ends Bobby Freeman and David Jones; tackles Kenny Schmidt and Bufford Carr; guards Hubert Jordan and Darrell Varner; center Jim Rose; fullback Guy Wells; halfbacks Butch Adams and Jimmy Carpenter; and quarterback Glynn Gregory.

WORD ABOUT THE EAGLES went out from West Texas and by August had settled brightly in the minds of the statewide media. The Eagles were ranked No. 1 statewide in Class AAAA in the first preseason poll and were picked by many to sweep through 10 regular season games and three playoff games to the state championship undefeated.

Chuck Moser didn't like it much.

"Because last year's team came along at the end of the season," he told the *Reporter-News,* "a sports writer in Dallas says we will win all 13 (games) this year. And since a man in Dallas says so, many other sports writers say so.

"Here are a few things that the people of Abilene should know:

"1. We don't like being put on the spot. I've never found a coach that did.

"2. The gentleman in Dallas knows less about our team than most people in West Texas. In fact I doubt if he knows one Eagle player's name.

"3. I read in the Port Arthur paper where we had 24 lettermen returning. That is not accurate, we have 14 lettermen returning and we lost by graduation 16 grand boys. Nine of these seniors are going to college on athlete scholarships.

"4. I read in another paper where our line will average 195 pounds. Actually the line that looked best in spring practice averaged 179 pounds. In fact our team will be lighter this year than last year.

"5. I have heard a good many other inaccurate statements about our Eagles. There are, though, a few things that I am rather sure about:

"We'll have the best practice fields that the Abilene Eagles have ever had the privilege of practicing on. We are very thankful to the Parks Board and Mr. Fikes, superintendent of parks; and to Ben Bradford, caretaker of these fields.

"We'll have a fine group of cheerleaders this year. They have the true Abilene spirit and are practicing at 6 o'clock every morning at Fair Park.

"We'll have a better printed program at the games this year, including pictures of the Eagles, the band, etc.

"We'll have a football preview Sept. 7 at Fair Park. This will give the people of Abilene a chance to see all three college teams and the Eagles introduced. Their scrimmages will help the Taylor County crippled children.

"We will have 40 Eagles on our A squad, and I will tell them Aug. 27 (the first day of practice) the same thing I told them last year on the first day of practice: 'Boys, our first goal is one thing and one thing only...beat Highland Park Sept. 10."

~

AT COACHING CLINICS, CHUCK MOSER told audiences: "We believe you make a team between Christmas and September. At this time our goal is to develop four things in each boy. These four are speed, hardness of his body, agility, and closeness between the boy and his coach."

Within that context, Moser identified "two phases in a year for football players: spring practice and fall practice. We try to have a goal or purpose for each of these phases."

The purpose of spring practice:

1. Teach fundamentals. Kicking, offense, defense.
2. Find personnel. Find which boy can play which position best both offensively and defensively. "We truly try not to change them in the fall from one position to another," Moser said.
3. Experiment with new plays, new ideas, or a new defense, "especially in the last week. Football should be fun," Moser said.

The purpose of fall practice:

1. Teach fundamentals.
2. Meet any situation that arises in a game.
3. Condition (be able to play at maximum effort on every play).

The 1954 Eagles were the first team to pass through the Christmas-September cycle under Moser. As it turned out that fall, Moser would still need to move boys around to put them in their best positions. But the three purposes were constant, and throughout the fall, game by game, all of Moser's practices were governed by them. Fundamentals got the teaching emphasis on Monday, with introduction of the scouting report and game situations for the week. Tuesday through Thursday the emphasis moved more and more toward team drills until, on Thursday, the Eagles spent 90 percent of their time working as a team.

Moser's Monday practices were always the same. They began with skull practice, first as a team for 15 minutes and then another 15 in offensive and defensive units. "I see great value in skull practice," Moser said. It was a pure teaching session, complete with chalk and blackboard. Then the team moved to the field for 10 minutes of pre-practice, loosening up, quarterbacks throwing, then the team coming together for five minutes of calisthentics and agility drills and, always, a push-up for every point that last week's opponent had scored.

The afternoon's first drill followed, and it was as fundamental as you could get: players in groups of threes spread across the field, rotating, becoming a ball carrier, then a tackler. They lined up three yards apart and at the whistle they charged and collided in loud reports of pads and helmets and effort and they drove at each other and fought and yelled until the tackler had the ball carrier on the ground. This was the famous "Oklahoma nutcracker" drill, despised by 95 percent of all who ever played the game. But always, a strange thing happened. As the 10-minute drill went forward, the boys became caught up in it. Boys making the best hits were identified and paired up until the best two or three hitters of the day were acknowledged by a grinning head coach and players yelling as a team.

To Moser, the drill was like teaching spelling. "We as coaches are just teachers," he said, and the first part of the nutcracker was punctuated with teaching: position, technique, proper point of contact, follow-through. "Then do, do, do the drill," he said, which was the heart of the 10 minutes. "Then give a little test." And the test was the closing competition, to find the best, and each player wanted to pass that test. They didn't learn anything about spelling. But it told Moser who could hit, and who wanted to.

Following the nutcracker was 40 minutes of unit defense (line, linebackers, secondary) and 10 minutes of team defense. Practice then shifted to offense, with 10 minutes of fundamentals (blocking, this time), 15 minutes of unit offense (linemen, backfield), 15 minutes of team offense, then 10 minutes of kicking and 10 minutes of conditioning. "Conditioning" was wind sprints across the field, one sideline to the other, 53 yards, and there were usually 10 or 12 of them, at the end of a two-hour and 45-minute practice. Moser also told his coaching clinic audiences the four things that, in his mind, won football games, including maximum effort by every player on every play. The wind sprints had their purpose and the players, their tongues dragging in the grass, knew what that purpose was.

AS IT TURNED OUT, the Eagles would start the season much weaker than Moser had supposed. On Thursday, Sept. 2, one week into two-a-day preseason drills, end Bob Gay and fullback Ronnie McDearman, both lettermen from 1953, abruptly left the team, and left town for parts unknown. Gay was a starting end in 1953 and a two-year letterman, while McDearman was among the leading rushers in District 1-AAAA. Both had made second-team All-District.

Apparently it was an impulse decision, made some time after noon on Thursday. Both had made the Eagles' morning workout, and McDearman at noon had asked his father to come watch the second practice, that was scheduled under the Fair Park lights Thursday night.

But by the time that practice started, both boys were gone, in Gay's car. Gay's mother, Mrs. H.L. Gay, said the boys had about $100. Mrs. J.C. McDearman said Ronnie had just been paid for some summer work. Mrs. Gay was "at a loss" to explain the boys' actions, but felt they would return to Abilene in time for the first day of school Tuesday, Sept. 7.

"I don't think they know themselves where they were going," she said. "But I think they'll be back by Sunday."

Moser said he knew no reason why the players left. McDearman had been slowed down by a leg injury suffered in spring practice but would have played a lot, Moser said. Team manager Billy Jack Rudd said the boys left town about 7 p.m., telling him to tell Moser "they weren't mad at anybody but just thought they'd take off."

Tuesday arrived, and the start of school, but the boys had not reappeared. No one seemed to know where they were. Moser did what any coach would do. He promoted letterman senior Hollis Swafford into Gay's starting spot at right end, and he restored depth to McDearman's position by moving the sophomore, Glynn Gregory, to fullback.

IF MOSER WANTED out of the state spotlight, his team didn't help him much. Weakened or not by the loss of two key lettermen, the Eagles trounced Highland Park, 40-0, in the 1954 season opener Sept. 10 at Fair Park before a crowd of 8,000. The Eagles rushed for 256 yards and starting quarterback H.P. Hawkins and his sub, junior David Bourland, combined to complete 8 of 11 passes for 98 yards and a touchdown.

Starting halfbacks Jim Millerman and Henry Colwell each scored twice, and second-string fullback Jack Self led all rushers with 80 yards on 13 carries.

On Tuesday, the day the *Dallas Morning News* state rankings came out, Abilene was even more firmly entrenched in the No. 1 spot. Three other District 1-AAAA teams, Lubbock, Midland and San Angelo, also were in the top 10 statewide.

The Eagles had a bye the second week. Then powerful Sweetwater fell, 13-0, in a rugged defensive struggle in which the Mustangs actually outgained the Eagles, 193 total yards to 168. Millerman and Colwell scored, both on two-yard runs, and guard John Thomas and sophomore defensive end Stuart Peake led a defense that let the Mustangs near, but not into, the end zone.

Then came Breckenridge, at Abilene. It was the first big schoolboy game of the year, billed as the top game in the state, pitting the top-ranked team in AAAA against the second-ranked AAA club. More than 10,000 fans showed up at Fair Park Stadium.

Breckenridge drilled the Eagles, 35-13. The Buckaroos, with far fewer players than Abilene, did it with speed and stamina, scoring four unanswered second-half touchdowns to turn a tight game into a rout. Led by backs Dick Carpenter, Jakie Sandefer and Bennett Watts, the Buckaroos of coach Joe Kerbel amassed 312 yards rushing to a paltry 95 for the Eagles. The Eagle defense, that hadn't allowed a point in the first two games, was brought crashing to earth.

It was a blow. The Dallas sports writer had been wrong. Abilene apparently wasn't all it was cracked up to be. The Eagles were not going to win all 13 games. Those aspirations had vanished already, in only the season's third game, beneath an unstoppable green wave from the little town of Breckenridge.

There are thousands of people, living in Abilene and around the world, who remember the Breckenridge loss. But they don't remember it because it was Breckenridge, which was just a name, a convenient bookmark. It is possible that some Abilenian who was there that night, in the next several years went back to the minutes after that game and lived them again, remembering what it felt like to lose, putting that feeling into the context that only history could provide, a context beyond the power of anyone to reasonably imagine at the time. That night, the thousands of Abilenians filing silently out of Fair Park Stadium knew only that they were disappointed by the ease with which the Buckaroos had beaten the Eagles, and remembered they weren't supposed to get their hopes too high. The date was Oct. 1, 1954.

Superintendent of Schools A.E. Wells. He knew what the 21st applicant wanted to see, so he asked Bobby Jack Oliver and Jim Millerman for a favor.

Twenty coaches applied for the Abilene job, then Abilene assistant coach Bob Groseclose told Superintendent A.E. Wells about a young coach at McAllen.

February 13, 1953

The Board of Education of the Abilene City Schools met in a called session in the superintendent's office at 12:30 p.m. Friday, February 13, 1953. Those present were:

W. E. Fraley	President
Morgan Jones Jr.	Vice-President
Mrs. Geo. H. Swinney	Secretary
Bert Chapman	Member
Roy Skaggs	Member
Ollie McMinn	Member
A. E. Wells	Superintendent
Charles Romine	High School Principal
Fred Sanner	Reporter News

Head Coach Selected

The meeting was called for the purpose of discussing applicants for the position of Head Coach in Abilene High School. After lengthy discussion and consideration of more than twenty applicants, Mr. Chapman made a motion that the position be offered to Charles Moser of Corpus Christi at a salary of $7,000.00 per year on a three year contract. Mr. Skaggs seconded motion and motion carried unanimously.

Signed: Mrs. Geo. H. Swinney

Approved: February 23, 1953

W. E. Fraley
President of the Board

February 23, 1953

The Board of Education of the Abilene City Schools met in regular session at 7:30 p.m. Monday, February 23, 1953. Those present were:

W. E. Fraley	President
Morgan Jones, Jr.	Vice President
Mrs. George Swinney	Secretary
Bert Chapman	Member
Ollie McMinn	Member
Roy Skaggs	Member
Mrs. Thos. E. Roberts	Member
A. E. Wells	Superintendent
Earle Walker	Reporter News

Minutes from the Feb. 13, 1953, meeting of the Abilene School Board.

Photos and documents courtesy of Abilene High School and Gerald Galbraith.

This is the photo that appeared in the Reporter-News *on Feb. 15, 1953, that gave Abilenians their first look at Abilene High's new coach.*

Chuck Moser's tenure at Abilene High started in a 10-by-10-foot office in Eagle Gym, with blank paper and a blue-ink mimeograph machine from which issued "Rules Everyone Should Know," and "Training Rules."

Rules Everyone Should Know

1. The ball is never dead until the referee's whistle kills it. (play till you hear the whistle)
2. The horn or gun doesn't stop the play. (Always finish the play.)
3. Fair catch--When the safety signals with his arm over hishead. (He can't run, don't hit him--it is 15 yards)
4. Do not interfere with a man catching a punted ball unless it is rolling toward you, cover it however. Never touch a punted ball Inside the 10 yard line, it is a touchback.
5. After a safety the ball is put in play by a kick-off from the 20 yard line.
6. A field goal should be played just like a punted ball, you can block it and run with it.
7. We must always have 7 men within one foot of the ball on offense.
8. You can block the passer after he throws the ball, but you can't tackle him.
9. Do not touch the punter unless you can block the kick.
10. Only ends and backs are eligible to receive a forward pass. QB's, guards, and tackles can not go over 1 yd. past the line of scrimmage till the pass is thrown; any one is eligible for a lateral pass.
11. A lateral pass is a free ball, any offensive player can run with it, defensive players can intercept a lateral and run.
12. Substitution:
    a. There are 5 time outs per half.
    b. Any substitution made while the clock is running and before the referee leaves the ball, costs one time out, but we don't get it. The clock starts when the ball is snapped.
    c. If a substitution is made after 5 time outs or after the referee leaves the ball, it costs 5 yds. and the clock starts when the referee leaves the ball.
    d. When the ball changes hands, after a kick-off or any time when we can sub as many as 11 players.
    e. Any player who leaves the field must remain out at least one play.
13. Defensive holding is when you are not trying to get the ball carrier.
14. A back cannot crawl with the ball, and no teammate can shove or push him.
15. When you block on offense you must have your arm in contact with your jersey, this is not true on a side body block.
16. Clipping is blocking i
17. You have 25 seconds be
18. A kick off is a free b you fall on it in the
19. After the center adjus one can interlock thei
20. No offensive player ca the offense off sides.
21. It is unsportsman to c opponent by counting o
22. Incomplete pass--Stops
    Time out called
    Measurement for a firs
    Any kind of score
    Penalty
    Ball goes out of bound

TRAINING RULES

1. No smoking or drinking
2. Home at 10:00, except on Fridays and Saturdays-11:30
3. Do not eat between meals
4. Take care of all injuries (show coach always)
5. No dates the night before a ball game

Rules in the dressing room

1. Read the bullentine board every day
2. Turn you equipment in each day
3. No fighting or horse-play
4. No cussing
5. Stay out of the equipment room
6. Save your ebergy for the feild and act like a gentleman
7. Do not wear shoes inside the dressing room
8. Keep your equipment clean
9. Always clean and polish your shoes the day before the game

Rules for the game

1. Be on time
2. Do not sit down
3. Run and hustle when you hear the whistle
4. Do not cuss-(keep your poise and don't lose your temper)
5. Do not leave the field (this means water)
6. Save conversation with spectators until after practice
7. On the field, always be in full uniform, including helmet

General

1. You must be enrolled in four subjects and passing three subjects in order to be elgible for play in the next game
2. Show your teachers and school the highest kind of respect
3. Turn your eligibility slipin the coach's gym office by Thursday 8:30 A.M.
4. Make every practice a good one
5. We need boys with the right spirit and hustle
6. No not go to the doctor without Coach Moser's permission
7. Please do not steal from your school or teammates
8. Do not miss practice without telling coach first

WE EXPECT EVERY BOY TO ABIDE BY ALL THE RULES

Take care of your body. -----dry well between your toes and hair after showering. Take good care of your feet. ----Wear good, clean socks. Watch for signs of blisters. Be sure your shoes fit, and are laced tight and high

FOOD ----Drink lots of milk, in hot weather drink as little as possible before eating. Eat foods that give you energy as: eggs, meat, breakfast food, fruit, vegetables, potatoes, (not fried) graham crackers and honey. Do not eat between meals---malts, pasteries, doughnuts, popcorn, nuts, fried food, and cokes. (these foods are not rules but only suggestions)

Coach

"Rule blocking" gave every Eagle player his blocking assignment against every possible defense.

	1 2 Counter	2 1 Trap	4 3 Trap	42 & 12 41 & 11 Wedge	42 41 Trap	36 25 Y	36 25 Y Otto
WE	S	H Z	H	H	H	H Do not use split rules	H
WT	H or SLB 4-5 Across	MLB 1st up Gap 8 (In)	In S Z	LB Pursuit	S Gap 8 (In)	In S	In S
WG	On In Out Pursuit	Trap 5-2W (Up)	Trap	Wedge Center	Trap	Trap	Pull non-hookable end
C	On or L, R	Set up or L, R	On or L, R	Wedge 2 Holes	Set Up or L, R	On or L, R	On or L, R
SG	Out Over 5-2W (On) 4-5 Or Post	Center or Set up	In Post	Wedge Center	Center or Set up	On In MLB Pursuit 7-2 don't use split rule	1 7-2 (LB)
ST	LB 5-2W (Out) Or On In Out	Across	In Center LB	Wedge Guard	1st up	On In LB Z 4-5 (Up)	Z Z
SE	On Pursuit Or H Z Gap 7-8 (In)	S	LB Across	S	Hook Up Across Z Gap 8 (S)	Out	3 use pro, Step Block
LH	Block HB	Cut Back	Cutback	Run 36 Belly	Block H Corner		
RH	Block S	Block H	S	Run 36 Belly Block H Corner	Flair	Flair	Flair H S
Full	Cut Back	Flair	Run at own End	Cut Back	Cut Back	S	Pursuit
QB	Fake Pass	Fake Pass		Close splits on 11-12 Wedge			
	No Good Gap 8 4-4 Good 7-1 Z	Poor 5-2W 4-4 Good LB go fast	Do Not No one inside our tackle Good 4-5 Even	Good At men up	Poor 5-2W 9 man line GOOd In gaps few LB	Poor 5-2W 7-2 Good G's man penetrates	Poor 7-2 4-5 In Good End can hook end, or man on him.

Halfback Jim Millerman scored the Eagles' first touchdown under their new coach on Sept. 11, 1953, at Fair Park Stadium against Highland Park. It wasn't a play run by the offense, but a 59-yard punt return.

Homecoming Queen Ann Hills riding high in the 1954 Homecoming parade.

Odessa High student officers presented the Victory Bell to the new district 1-AAAA champion Abilene Eagles at a pep rally in the auditorium.

The Eagles' Henry Colwell breaks into the clear in the 1954 state championship game. Blocking are No. 66 John Thomas and an unidentified Eagle clearing out No. 42 with a downfield block.

Chuck Moser and Eagle tri-captains Jim Millerman, John Thomas and Twyman Ash present the 1954 state championship trophy and game ball to Abilene High principal Escoe Webb.

1954

Oct. 8, 1954

PEOPLE WHO SO EASILY remember the Breckenridge game probably don't remember at all the equally historic foe the Eagles played the following week.

It was a week that began with pushups and castoffs.

EVERY WEEK, WIN OR LOSE, Moser had his varsity at the beginning of practice do push-ups for every point scored by the opposition the previous Friday.

After Breckenridge, that meant 35. Sometime between the end of the game on Friday night and the first school bell on Monday morning, every Eagle realized what the score would mean for them, not in the minds of sportswriters or the expectations of the town, but down on the ground in full pads with helmet on. Thirty-five. Following that would come the kind of practice that a good Moser team faced after a humiliating loss.

Then Bob Gay and Ronnie McDearman showed up. The media played down the details, but rumor said they had been to California. There was a popular saying among young Abilenians: "Everything starts in California and reaches Abilene two years later." Maybe that was the call. Maybe it was the glamour of the movies at the Paramount downtown. Television had arrived in Abilene in 1953, and the local kids quickly saw there was a world out there quite different from the one they knew. Whatever it was, the boys had had their hour of rebellion and now were home, safe and sound.

And they wanted back on the football team. The odds were against it. One of Moser's rules made it clear: "We expect *every boy* to abide with all the rules." There was nothing in the rules to accommodate a boy missing four weeks of practice and three games to indulge an impulse to go to California. Moser certainly already knew he would not let Gay and McDearman rejoin the team; all the others would lose faith in what it meant to be a member of the gang. But he must have also seen a strategy that would actually reinforce the code in the players' minds. At the chalktalk before practice, Moser told the team what Gay and McDearman had asked, and he said he would leave it up to the team to vote yes or no.

"But," the coach said, not trying, or unable, to hide his emotion, gestured angrily and barked, "I vote *NO!*"

By all accounts, no one on the team took an eye off Moser, or made a sound. Gay and McDearman were friends and peers of Hawkins and Ash and the others, and essentially good kids, but the team vote was a very quick and quiet no. When after a few moments the chalktalk began, it was a different Eagle team than had arrived at the stadium that afternoon for practice. Arguments have been made that that moment under the bleachers was where the streak actually began. The 35 pushups waiting ahead became less like punishment and more like the first page of a new resolve. After what had happened, the Eagles knew they were doing the pushups as a team.

NO MATTER WHAT ELSE he and his coaches had on their minds Saturday and Sunday, by Monday morning, Moser and his staff had ready for the players thick scouting reports on Friday's opponent, a very important game because it was the first in District 1-AAAA play. With teams like Midland and San Angelo rampaging unbeaten through non-district schedules, Moser knew that even one loss in district play could assure another "very respectable season."

The scouting report was information assembled from game films and from the scout work brought back by Blacky Blackburn, Shorty Lawson, Wally Bullington and Tommy Morris. When it was completed, the mimeographed report given to the players might be as many as 15 pages thick. On the first page were diagrammed by position the starting offensive and defensive lineups for the next opponent, including each player's name, weight, and jersey number. One or two stars were placed by the names of the opponent's best players, on offense and defense, with a comment or two about them.

If by Wednesday the Eagles couldn't pass a test on those lineups, including weights and numbers, they didn't play on Friday. Also on the first page was Moser's statement about what the Eagles would have to do "to win the football game."

The report continued with diagrammed offensive formations used by the opponent and plays run out of those formations. Tendencies were also shown, that is, which plays the opponent could be expected to run in specific situations. Next came a rundown on the opponent's defensive formations and variations, or "stunts," the team might use out of those formations. Next came plays the Eagles would use against those defenses. All of this was testable.

The scouting report handed out on Monday, Oct. 4, was on the Borger Bulldogs.

In three games, two of those losses, the Bulldogs had completed only three passes. So the Eagles would concentrate on stopping the run. Fullback Jerry Selfridge was a 180-pounder who had beaten out the 1953 starter, Calvin Marsh, who was still in the starting lineup at a halfback. The quarterback was Johnny Baskin, who only weighed 138, but had scored three touchdowns running and was noted as being effective running wide on keeper plays.

There were psychological factors. The Bulldogs, including seven lettermen, remembered the 1953 game in Borger, won by the Eagles, 60-0, and the media was playing up the "revenge" motive. Jack Holden of the *Reporter-News* said, "The stage will be ready for an upset Friday night." Issues facing the Eagles were more complex. They had lost respect in the Breckenridge whipping, dropping to third in the state Class AAAA rankings (behind Port Arthur and Baytown) and stirring up doubt in the minds of the Abilene faithful: Holden referred to them as "a still-developing flock of Eagles." On the other hand, the rejection of Gay and McDearman no doubt had an impact, but no one could yet say what kind of impact it might be.

∽o∽

OFFENSIVELY, MOSER PROMOTED three new players to starting positions. Junior Sam Caudle, 165, took over for 174-pound Jim Tatum at right guard; junior Elmo Cure, at 175, stepped in for 190-pound Joe Taylor at center, and Jack Self, 165, replaced 180-pound Jim Briggs, who had been fumble-prone, at fullback. Briggs remained a starter, however, on defense, at linebacker. The rest of the starting lineup against Borger: ends Twyman Ash and Hollis Swafford; tackles Jack Crumpler and Cullen Hunt; guard John Thomas; half-backs Jim Millerman and Henry Colwell; and quarterback H.P. Hawkins.

It rained during the week, but the Fair Park Stadium field was in good shape. Ticket sales were slow. About 5,500 showed up, and it was no time at all before their hearts were in their throats. Borger won the toss and elected to receive. Obviously they had scouted the Abilene-Breckenridge game and knew the damage that Buckie quarterback Bennett Watts had wrought. On the Bulldogs' first play from scrimmage, the quarterback Baskin broke free on a keeper and headed upfield. He ran 61 yards before Briggs, the Eagle linebacker, hauled him down at the Abilene 10-yard-line. In the stands, relief and fear spun around each other. Was this another Breckenridge?

But the Eagles stopped them there, and after a slow start, took control of the game. Halfback Jim Millerman scored on a one-yard run at the end of the first quarter, then in the second, quarterback H.P. Hawkins threw touchdown passes of 20 yards to Millerman and 10 to halfback Henry Colwell. Sub quarterback David Bourland ran 78 yards to the end zone on a busted pass play just as the half ended, but the play was called back for offsides.

Abilene was penalized a whopping 10 times for 60 yards in the game, but Hawkins threw a 46-yard TD strike to Colwell in the third period and sub halfback Phil Bailey ran 26 yards on the first play of the fourth quarter as Abilene won, 34-7. After Baskin's early run, Borger managed only 61 more yards in offense for the night. Hawkins was five of 10 passing for 100 yards and three TDs, and Colwell was the leading rusher with 103 yards, 94 of it in the first half. Subs played most of the second half for Abilene, which was a pattern with Moser. He wanted everybody to play, but he also looked at actual game conditions as the best possible practice opportunity. The second team, in effect, was scrimmaging Borger's first team. As the Abilene sports writers said, it was never too early for the second team to start practicing for 1955.

Abilene 34, Borger 7
Oct. 8, 1954

Oct. 15, 1954

ODESSA QUARTERBACK ED TYLER was not Carl Schlemeyer, the passing great who brought the Bronchos back from the brink of defeat in Abilene in 1953.

But you couldn't tell it from the statistics. There were big stars by Tyler's name in the scouting report on Monday, for his 26 completions in 61 attempts for 384 yards in four games. And he was getting better. In Odessa's 19-7 victory over Lubbock on Friday, Tyler had passed for 204 yards, a phenomenal performance for a high school team in 1954.

He was the man Abilene had to stop if the Eagles were to defeat the Bronchos for the first time since both had become members of District 1-AAAA in 1951. If Abilenians after the Breckenridge debacle had been nervous about Borger, they had good reason to fear Odessa. It was a big game, the biggest of the year to date in the district. More than 20,000 were expected at the stadium in Odessa. The Eagle Booster Club chartered a train to take more than 600 adults and students the 200 miles to the game.

Certainly the Eagles were ready for a rematch against the defending district champion, a club that by the end of the 1953 season they felt confident they could beat.

Odessa had two losses, but one of them was a 13-12 decision to Port Arthur, the state's top-rated Class AAAA team. (Abilene remained third-ranked in the state, after the win over a weak Borger team.) The Bronchos had also lost 14-0 to Highland Park, a team the Eagles had handled in the season opener, which brought hopes up.

Moser thought his defense would have to win the game, first by stopping or slowing up Tyler, and then by controlling the line of scrimmage against the run. Odessa halfback Tom Taylor, 170, was averaging 5.8 yards every time he carried the ball.

Against the pass, Moser had faith in his secondary. Millerman, Colwell and David Bourland were all smart and fast and quick enough to cover receivers, either in a zone system or man-to-man, long enough to let a pass rush reach the quarterback. The coach decided to blitz Tyler, that is, bring the linebackers into the pass rush instead of the usual tactic of dropping the linebackers into pass coverage. Moser believed strongly in taking away the other team's confidence as early as possible in the game, and the key in this game lay in making Tyler look for the rush instead of his receivers.

⁂

OFFENSIVELY, MOSER DECIDED to run straight at a big, mobile Odessa defense, anchored by three 200-pound linemen, that had held Lubbock to 118 total yards, including only 33 on the ground. The Eagles would run first and pass second. If the running game were successful, it might set up a good play-action pass to the halfbacks for the quarterback Hawkins, who had burned Borger for three TDs through the air.

The coach left Caudle and Cure in the starting offensive line, though both were considerably lighter than the players they had replaced. The rest of the lineup was unchanged, though sub quarterback and defensive back Glenn Belew broke an arm in practice and was lost for the season.

As the game began, the Eagle strategy appeared to work both offensively and defensively. On dives and belly-series handoffs, Millerman, Colwell and fullback Jack Self tore time and again into Odessa's big line for steady gains. Defensively, the Eagle linebackers and light but quick linemen—Sam Caudle, Glenn Woods, Cullen Hunt, Jack Crumpler, John Thomas, Twyman Ash, Bob Hubbard, Stuart Peake, David Steinman—penetrated successfully enough to throw the quarterback Tyler off-balance, and the Abilene secondary was doing its usual competent job.

But it took a break before anyone could score. Abilene defender Hubbard fell on an Odessa fumble at the Broncho 41-yard line late in the first quarter. The Eagle offense hammered to the Odessa 10, where Hawkins crossed them up, pitching out to Millerman on a sweep, who scored standing up. Hawkins' PAT made it 7-0 as the first quarter ended.

The Eagles got good field position again late in the second quarter on another Odessa mistake, this one a flair pass from Tyler that was ruled a lateral. The ball was not caught, hit the ground and almost rolled out of bounds before Colwell fell on it at the 50.

With play in the final minute of the half, the Eagles abandoned the slam-bang attack and Hawkins went straight to the air. His first effort fell incomplete, but the second one found Millerman in full stride for the 50 yards and the score.

IT WAS THE SAME SITUATION as 1953, when Abilene had led Odessa at the half. Like history repeating itself, the Bronchos came out after the half and started whittling furiously away. They did it mainly on the ground, after Abilene's success harassing Tyler. The Bronchos, who had only two first downs in the first half, drove 67 yards to their first touchdown, scored by halfback Leroy Scott on a nine-yard run with four minutes gone in the third quarter.

Abilene couldn't move after the kickoff and Odessa began another strong march downfield, reaching the Eagle 15 before Scott was stopped short of the necessary yardage on a fourth-down run. The Eagles took over. Deep in their own territory, with a 14-7 lead over an energized opponent, the Eagles might have been expected to try to hammer out first downs. Instead, on the first play, Hawkins hit Millerman on a play-action pass, and the shifty halfback eluded three or four defenders and went 85 yards to the end zone with 1:52 remaining in the third quarter.

The Bronchos came back, driving to the Abilene 25 early in the fourth period, but then Bourland intercepted a Tyler pass in the end zone. Abilene took the ball at the 20 and this time mounted a march that ate up all but four minutes of the quarter. Odessa got the ball back but went four-and-out, and that was the ball game.

The Eagles' rushing attack was a model of balance, with Millerman gaining 55 yards, Colwell 53, and Self 45. And the rush set up the pass, the old thunder-and-lightning approach. The Eagles had tried just five passes in the game. Three were incomplete. The other two went for touchdowns, covering a total of 135 yards. Tyler, constantly harassed by not only the Eagle linemen but also the linebackers, connected on only three of 14 passes for a total of 52 yards. It was a textbook example of a game unfolding in the way the coaches had drawn it up.

Throughout the game, the night air over the Odessa stadium reverberated with the echoes of a bell ringing. It was a railroad bell that had once sat astride a big Santa Fe steam locomotive. Now it sat mounted in a wheeled red-and-white carriage on the Odessa sideline, identifying the Bronchos as the reigning champions of District 1-AAAA. All the other teams in the district heard the bell only once a year, and none of them heard it without thinking how fine that bell would sound in their own stadiums. The Eagles were certainly thinking about it, on the ride home.

Abilene 21, Odessa 7
Oct. 15, 1954

Oct. 22, 1954

THE VICTORY OVER ODESSA had an interesting effect on the state Class AAAA rankings that came out Oct. 19, Tuesday. It dropped Abilene from third to fifth, behind Port Arthur, Baytown, Midland and Waco.

Midland had risen by virtue of two straight wins over tough District 1-AAAA opponents, San Angelo and Amarillo. In fact the unheralded Bulldogs were the district's only undefeated team, at 5-0, halfway through the season. They had just hammered a good Amarillo team, 35-14, and Chuck Moser called Wahoo McDaniel, the Bulldogs' fullback, the best runner in the state.

Abilene, with the one loss to Breckenridge, stood at 4-1. In their four victories, the Eagles had surrendered only 14 points. Two of those victories were shutouts, over Highland Park and Sweetwater, and neither Borger nor Odessa had managed more than a touchdown against the Eagle defense. People were starting to point to the Abilene-Midland game, at Midland Nov. 19, as the District 1-AAAA game of the year.

But the Eagles had only one goal, as Moser pointed out in Monday's Fair Park chalktalk, and that was to defeat Pampa.

And to do that, the Eagles had to count on their strong defense to do something with the Harvesters' high-striding offense. In close, high-scoring losses to Amarillo and San Angelo, the Harvesters had scored 28 and 34 points respectively, and the ground game, led by all-state candidate Harold Lewis, had amassed 1,411 yards, compared to the Eagles' total of only 931. Lewis alone had 724 yards and 10 touchdowns. And against Amarillo, a second-string halfback, Dickie Mauldin, came in when starter Bill Fulenwider was injured and promptly ripped off runs of 68 and 70 yards.

"They've scared every team they've played," said *Reporter-News* Sports Editor Jack Holden.

PAMPA WAS ANOTHER Panhandle town, like Borger north of Amarillo, and it was a 300-mile bus trip from Abilene. The highways were all two-lane, even the major routes like U.S. 80 and U.S. 66, and travel proceeded at the pace of the slowest vehicle until there was room to pass. No one who got behind a slow truck on these highways would ever call Texas flat again. In 1956, President Eisenhower signed the Federal Interstate Highway Act. The multi-lane interstates were envisioned as a Cold War national security measure, for the quick transport of men or materials. For West Texans, it meant simply a dream the day would come when U.S. 80 through Parker County could be traversed in less than three hours.

For those Panhandle games, the visiting team always departed on Thursday. The distinctive, black and gold Eagle bus, a 1947 Flxible and its venerable driver Bert Berry, would get the team (a few players rode in cars with assistant coaches) to Childress Thursday afternoon in time for a short workout, then it was on to Pampa or Borger or Amarillo to spend the night before the game. Abilene had only one Panhandle trip on the 1954 schedule, to Amarillo Oct. 30.

Harold Lewis came down with the flu early in the week, but the rangy 178-pound fullback was with the team when it left Pampa for Abilene on Thursday. Several Eagle starters were also battling colds during the week but all were ready to go by Friday. Moser's offensive starters had stabilized with Twyman Ash and Hollis Swafford at ends, Jack Crumpler and Cullen Hunt the tackles, John Thomas and Sam Caudle at guards, Elmo Cure the center, Jim Millerman and Henry Colwell the halfbacks, and H.P. Hawkins at quarterback.

The one uncertain position was fullback, where Jim Briggs and Jack Self had alternated, and now Moser had moved sophomore Glynn Gregory to the position. Self would get the start against Pampa.

As the game began, it was not the Eagle defense, or the Pampa offense, that lived up to notices, but the Harvester defense that appeared determined to deny its billing as the team's weak link. The Eagle offense struggled, once giving up the ball at the Harvester nine, but as the first quarter ended Millerman capped a 64-yard drive with a short touchdown run.

Abilene added six more points a couple of minutes later with a maneuver that was becoming an Eagle trademark. Pampa couldn't move after the first Abilene score and punted to the Eagles' twin return men, Millerman and Colwell. They crisscrossed at the Abilene 37, Colwell wound up with the ball and followed a perfect wall 63 yards down the sideline for the score two minutes into the second quarter.

Pampa came right back and, penetrating the Eagle defense for the first time in the game, moved 60 yards to a touchdown. Lewis's three-yard run cut the Abilene advantage to 14-7 with six minutes left in the half.

BUT THEN SOMETHING STARTED to happen that was reminiscent of the 1953 Eagles. In this sixth game of the season, the Eagle offense abruptly slid into gear. Line coach Hank Watkins' linemen were fast and very quick off the ball and hit blocks with impact and efficiency. And Moser's teams had already become known for getting downfield to block. Millerman and Colwell were big hard-running backs with speed, and both fullbacks, Self and Briggs, were good straight-ahead power runners who could block. The quarterback Hawkins was running the belly series and play-action passes with the precision that Moser demanded. The result could become demoralizing, and quickly.

Before the end of the half, the Eagles had scored twice more, on off-tackle runs of nine and 42 yards by the left halfback Millerman, the 42-yarder coming with 30 seconds left in the half. As the teams went to the locker rooms, Millerman had 104 yards rushing and had scored three touchdowns.

By the end of the game, the Abilene offense had generated 506 yards of total offense, including 380 yards on the ground. The final score of 41-7 might have been worse if the Eagles hadn't fumbled five times.

As it was, with a 28-7 halftime lead, Moser played the second and third teams throughout the second half. He played the whole team whenever he could, which was becoming often. He stressed the importance of developing depth on his football teams and he also wanted his younger players to gain game experience for the seasons to follow. His starters, meanwhile, remained relatively fresh for the week ahead. That was important, because most of the Eagle starters played both ways, on offense and defense.

Moser also knew some of his younger players were very talented. The sophomore Gregory had played quarterback in junior high and on the AHS B team before being promoted to the varsity and shifted to fullback. And of course he played both ways. In the Pampa game, playing safety on defense, Gregory intercepted a Harvester pass at the Abilene 12 late in the first half and returned it 46 yards to set up Millerman's last TD of the half. Then in the fourth period, Gregory at fullback took a handoff and ran 76 yards to the Pampa two-yard line. On the next play, he got the score.

Abilene's last touchdown was scored by another sophomore, Jimmy Carpenter, who took an intercepted pass back 31 yards.

The Eagle defense, meanwhile, shut down the vaunted Pampa ground attack with 72 yards. Lewis, the all-state candidate, had only 43.

Abilene 41, Pampa 7
Oct. 22, 1954

Oct. 30, 1954

THE UNIVERSITY INTERSCHOLASTIC LEAGUE was the governing body of Texas high school football. Since the UIL established official state championship playoffs in 1920, only two teams had won three straight state championships: Waco in 1925-27 and Amarillo in 1934-36.

Amarillo boosters thought it would be appropriate to recall that era with a 20th anniversary salute to the 1934 Golden Sandies during the Abilene game, played on a Saturday afternoon for the occasion, and it just might inspire the 1954 Sandies to play better than their 3-3 record against the Eagles. The team with its legendary coach Blair Cherry sat on the Amarillo bench during the game and was honored at halftime.

But if anyone appeared to be inspired on this gorgeous, windy Panhandle afternoon, it was the Eagles. The final score was 47-0. It was the Sandies' worst beating ever in their own stadium. The Eagle offense, which had roared into high gear against Pampa, flattened the Amarillo defense with 26 first downs and 389 yards rushing. Nine separate Eagle backs contributed to the yardage total. Quarterback H.P. Hawkins tried only four passes but completed three for 97 yards and two touchdowns.

The Eagles' defensive speed and execution, meanwhile, wrecked what had been a potent Amarillo offense, limiting Sandie runners to 112 yards. The gold-shirted Sandies completed only three of 16 pass attempts for 16 yards. Nobody could remember an Amarillo team getting beaten that badly. Jack Holden of the *Reporter-News* reported that Blair Cherry left before the game was over.

Actually the game was over at the half, but Cherry did hang around for the ceremony. Fullback Jim Briggs, returning to the starting lineup, bulled straight ahead four yards for Abilene's first touchdown after a short Amarillo punt into the wind. A little later from the Amarillo three, Briggs plunged straight ahead again, but this time Hawkins pulled the ball back from Briggs' belly and gave it to right half Henry Colwell slanting into left tackle and the Eagles were up 14-0 at the end of the first quarter.

IT WAS A BEAUTIFUL, clinical demonstration—as if the Eagles wanted to show the '34 Sandie state champions something—of the belly series, that was initiated with the fullback diving more or less straight ahead. If the play was going to the left, in the case of Colwell's touchdown, Briggs headed for the hole between the center and left guard. Hawkins took the snap and pivoted left to give the ball to Briggs going by. That's how Briggs scored the first Eagle touchdown. Or Hawkins could fake to Briggs, pull the ball out, step down the line and give the ball to the right halfback, Colwell, crossing behind and angling toward the hole between the left tackle and end. If they ran the same play to the right, it would be the left half Jim Millerman taking the handoff into the hole between the right tackle and end. The fullback handoff was called 41 or 42 Straightaway and the halfback handoffs were either 25 Belly or 36 Belly.

Or they could do something else. In the second quarter, with the running game chewing up yardage, Hawkins faked again to Briggs into the middle of the line, then stepped back and threw to Colwell, streaking between the frozen Sandie safeties, for a 54-yard score that made it 21-0 at the half. Hawkins threw the relatively short over-the-middle-pass into the teeth of a typical Panhandle wind.

Hawkins connected for his second passing touchdown with end Hollis Swafford, who was playing on a tender ankle, for 33 yards midway into the third quarter. The score came on the next play after another Amarillo punt was knocked down by the wind. Hawkins' PAT try was blocked, but with the score 27-0, Moser sent in the substitutes. Halfback Phil Bailey scored fourth-quarter touchdowns on runs of seven and two yards, and sophomore Jimmy Carpenter closed out the scoring with a nine-yard run on an end sweep.

Millerman led the Eagle rushers with 73 yards. Fullback Briggs averaged almost 10 yards a carry on only six trips, a performance with which Moser was particularly pleased. The coach had begun to get the player ready for a special assignment, and he had to see if the player was ready for it. In aviation, pilots have a saying: you have to stay a mile ahead of the airplane. Moser coached that same way. He would insist to his players that Amarillo was the only game that mattered, but part of his mind was always working beyond the horizon.

NEWSPAPER ACCOUNTS SAID the 47-0 result was the talk of the Panhandle from Lubbock to Borger for days after the game. Amarillo people said to Abilene people after the game, "How did Breckenridge ever beat you?"

Certainly the most interested spectator at the game that day was Thurman "Tugboat" Jones, coach of the Midland Bulldogs. The Bulldogs had escaped a squeaker in Pampa the night before, edging the Harvesters, 20-14, with the Harvesters threatening right to the final gun. The team had gone back to Midland, and his usual scouts were in Amarillo, but Jones was not about to miss a chance to see this Abilene team that the Bulldogs would play in less than three weeks, no doubt for the District 1-AAAA championship.

In the pressbox as the score climbed to 40-0, Jones waved a hand at the field and said, "It makes you worry a little when you know you have to play a team like this." He said his still undefeated Bulldogs had done as well as they had "just on spirit," and that on paper they could not match up with the Eagles.

Amarillo Globe sportswriter Dick Collins, assigned to write a story about the 1934 team, sat with the alums on the sidelines during the game. The best he could do about a comment on the game itself was to hear an old player say the 1954 Sandie band was much better than the '34 version. And *Globe* sportswriter Putt Powell, a nice man who bled Sandie gold for four decades, had to stand and take it from his peers after predicting the inspired Sandies would play their game of the year and beat the Eagles.

But it was the Eagles who were smiling as Bert Berry steered the Eagle bus out of the parking lot for the long ride home. They had won four in a row.

Abilene 47, Amarillo 0
Oct. 30, 1954

Nov. 12, 1954

THE EAGLES WERE ON a terrific roll. In their last two games, against Pampa and Amarillo, the Eagle offense had piled up 88 points, 49 first downs and 992 yards of total offense. The Eagle defense had held the two foes to a total offensive output of 302 yards and a single touchdown.

A shame to waste such momentum on an open date.

But there it was. Nothing to do on Friday night, Nov. 5, but go to the movies or cruise the hamburger hangouts. Television had arrived in Abilene in 1953, KRBC-TV broadcasting on Channel 9, but high school kids with access to cars didn't stay home for that on Friday night.

Gasoline was about 20 cents a gallon, the big V-8 engines were still a year or so away, and four boys (or girls) could cruise until curfew if everyone chipped in a quarter for gas. A typical loop took the cruisers downtown, up Cypress past the Queen and Majestic theaters and on past the first-run house, the Paramount (admission: 25 cents), to see who was standing in line, and then out to Sayles Blvd. and up to South 14th to hit Smitty's and the Dairy Delite. It wasn't only the upperclassmen. In Texas in the 1940s and '50s, the legal driving age was 14, because so many kids needed to drive tractors and farm trucks. It was perfectly ordinary for a football player to begin his sophomore year at Abilene High with a driver's license in his pocket.

On nights such as this, high school kids, even the athletes, had more than football on their minds, as Chuck Moser was well aware. If one of his players missed curfew, or broke some other training rule, Moser knew it. If one of his players was dating a girl, Moser knew who she was. He knew he couldn't do much about these things, except let the players know that he knew, which after a few extra wind sprints was usually enough.

HE COULDN'T KNOW how easy he had it, in Abilene in the autumn of 1954. American post-war mainstream culture, and the companies that marketed to it, was still adult-oriented, and in goods and services, movies and entertainment, the kids wore and watched and listened to the same things as their parents because that's all there was. It was very much a youth culture that convened at the movies and in the hamburger joint parking lots, but the movie was "Three Coins in the Fountain," and Perry Como, Doris Day, Rosemary Clooney, Eddie Fisher and Patti Page sang practically all of the music coming out of the car radios from Abilene's two stations, KRBC and KWKC.

But already, on that Friday night, Nov. 5, farther east and south out of the reach of Abilene antennas, there was in the air the first example of a sound that would change not only music, but everything. And in Hollywood, a movie starring Glenn Ford was being shot that in less than a year would create teen pandemonium in the Paramount Theater.

The Abilene kids that night did listen for a football score on the radio, and when it came, Lubbock had been trimmed by the San Angelo Bobcats, 13-6. The Westerners, state Class AAAA champions in 1951-52, had lost their third district game against only one victory, and that over lowly Borger. In a week the Westerners would arrive at Fair Park Stadium, and, wasted momentum or no, Abilenians thought this Lubbock team was a good way to get back into action after an open date.

They were right. The Eagles won easily, 35-7, before a Homecoming crowd of about 7,000. It was also Fathers' Night, and fathers of the Eagle players sat on the sideline and wore cards with their sons' jersey numbers.

Moser was not particularly happy with the Eagle offense, particularly the passing game, and he blamed sloppy practices.

"I don't know what was wrong with our passing," Moser said, "unless we just didn't work on it much last week."

THE EAGLES COMPLETED only four of 12 passes for 101 yards and had two intercepted. But the Abilene offense didn't need much production, when the Eagle defense shut down the Westerners with only three first downs and 84 total yards of offense for the night. Sixty-eight of those yards came on one play, a second-quarter touchdown pass from Lubbock quarterback Gehrig Garrison to halfback Jim Berly. In the second half, the Westerners couldn't collect a single first down and never crossed the 50-yard line.

Abilene fullback Jim Briggs had a second straight strong game, and that was most important to the coach. Briggs led all rushers with 97 yards and scored twice, once on a 27-yard run and also when right half Henry Colwell, about to be tackled, lateraled to Briggs who went 19 more yards for the score.

Sophomore Glynn Gregory added another touchdown on a fullback play, a 13-yard burst on a power play over left tackle in the first quarter. Halfback Jim Millerman scored on a six-yard run and quarterback H.P. Hawkins tallied his first running touchdown of the season when he couldn't find a receiver and scrambled 20 yards.

The subs got their usual playing time in the second half and were plagued by motion and offsides penalties, but the Eagles were back on track, 5-0 in district play, and the big game at unbeaten Midland coming up. On Tuesday, when the state rankings came out, Abilene was No. 3 in Class AAAA, behind Galveston and Pasadena. Midland was No. 4.

Abilene 35, Lubbock 7
Nov. 12, 1954

Nov. 19, 1954

IN ABILENE, TEXAS, in the autumn of 1954, there were separate facilities, wherever they were required, for the black population. Water fountains, restrooms, waiting areas, a part of town, all identified by the same label: "Colored." Downtown stores, restaurants and movie theaters were closed to blacks, to whom the Abilene media commonly referred as "Negroes."

It is intriguing to wonder how the Eagles might have fared against other teams if those other teams had black players. None did, of course, but if they had, that meant Abilene could have had some pretty good black players too, like Robert Kelley and Louis Kelley, who played for the Woodson Rams, the Colored high school down in Colored Town on the east side below the railroad tracks. Woodson and black high schools in the other cities played in their own league. The Rams, whose colors were green and white, did play some of their games at Fair Park Stadium, but that was as close as the Kelleys or any of those high school kids could come to wondering what it would be like to be an Abilene Eagle. White kids liked to go to the Woodson games because it was good football and Woodson High had a small but joyous band.

The education codes, unlike the social (written and unwritten) codes, didn't say anything about any of the other races: Hispanic, Asian, Indian. Not many of them did, but any of those could attend white high schools and play white high school football. So it was that the biggest obstacle between Abilene and a district championship came to be a Midland High School fullback who couldn't get served in any number of establishments. His name was Edwin "Wahoo" McDaniel. He was a Choctaw Indian, and Chuck Moser thought he was the best running back in the state.

"He reminds me of Kyle Rote (the famed Southern Methodist halfback)," Moser said before practice on Monday. "He doesn't beat you with the long runs, but he's good for five to 10 yards almost every time he carries."

And the 180-pound McDaniel had averaged more than 20 carries per game in Midland's 8-0 season. In only eight games he had already passed the 1,000-yard mark. In Midland's 41-13 victory over Borger on Saturday, McDaniel had picked up 186 yards on 26 carries. "He's a hard-running back, hard to stop," said Moser, "and is the top boy offensively in the state."

⁂

MOSER WAS ALSO LEERY of McDaniel's running mate, halfback Tommy Johnson, who in eight games had carried for 674 yards. As a team, Midland had out-gained the Eagles by 617 yards on the ground. Moser also thought the light but effective Midland offensive line was "the best blocking line in the district. It's especially strong in the center. They've got the most consistent offense in the district."

The Bulldogs, like the Eagles, didn't pass much, but quarterback Willie Brooks had gained almost 500 yards through the air.

Against McDaniel & Co., the Eagles would present a defense that had held seven opponents to a touchdown or less. Only Breckenridge had scored more than once against the Eagles, and five District 1-AAAA opponents had scored only 28 points.

The 1954 Abilene Eagles had talent and speed on both offense and defense, but a main key to the team's developing success in its almost two years under Moser was his ability to prove to his players the enormous value of the first hit.

He had taught them the technique, in both blocking and tackling, of squaring up, starting low, driving through, and finishing high. It was like hitting a baseball cleanly, with velocity. It was all in the wrists. There was a click and almost no other sensation, yet the ball flew a long way. A good block felt like that, and a good tackle. The Eagles learned that in practice and then in games: a clean hit, with velocity, and very little other sensation as you drove through the player to the finish.

The other player, meanwhile, felt, well, hit, and there was a feeling of flying, and not much he could do about it. And of course there was a direct link between physical momentum—one player driving through, the other flying back—and emotional momentum.

"If you hit your man the first time like that," Moser said, "then the next time and the rest of the game, it will be easier."

⁂

THE PLAYER THE COACH wanted hit hardest and cleanest was Wahoo McDaniel, on his very first carry of the game. It was the first thing Moser told his defense on Monday. Sam Caudle, John Thomas, Cullen Hunt, Glenn Woods, Bob Hubbard, David Steinman, Freddie Green, Twyman Ash, all the Eagle defensive starters. If they hit McDaniel like that on his first carry, he would remember it, and it would shift momentum not only between individuals but between teams. From that moment before practice on Monday, McDaniel had a bulls-eye on him and it made for a very long three days for the fullback portraying McDaniel on the scout team.

Then there was fullback Jim Briggs. Moser wanted to say to his team, and to Briggs, by the Midland game, "They've got Wahoo McDaniel, but we've got Jim Briggs." Moser always wanted to meet strength with strength. Briggs first had to prove he was ready for the role, and he had, with his performances in the Amarillo and Lubbock games.

Thus the week's practices were structured to build fire in the bellies of the Abilene defenders, and in fullback Jim Briggs, and collaterally in the center, Elmo Cure, and two guards, Caudle and Thomas. Moser's praise for Midland's offensive line, particularly in the center, was no doubt genuine, but it had another purpose too. Time after time in practice, quarterback H.P. Hawkins gave the ball to the first man, Briggs, in the belly series, behind the blocking of Cure, Caudle and Thomas.

And Moser made it a point during the week to talk to the newspaper about his team's defense.

"I don't believe I've ever coached a better tackling team than this one," he said. "There are two things about this team that stand out. We don't have a great football team, but our tackling and our unselfish spirit are outstanding."

Memorial Stadium in Midland was sold out, a standing-room only crowd of 12,500 expected. Midland school officials sent 1,000 adult and 1,000 student tickets to Abilene; most were gone by noon Monday. The Eagle Booster Club sold 750 tickets on its special Texas

& Pacific train to Midland. With an Odessa loss and a San Angelo tie the previous week, the winner of this game would be undisputed district champion and proceed to the state playoffs.

IT WAS CLEAR AND CRISP at the kickoff. The Eagles scored first, only three minutes into the game, after a 52-yard march. Briggs got the touchdown on a short straight-ahead blast. After the kickoff, the Bulldogs mounted a modest drive that ended at the Abilene 47 as McDaniel was hit hard and often by the Abilene defenders. On nine of his 22 carries during the game, he was held to only a one- or two-yard gain, and once he was stopped for minus yardage.

Abilene scored again just at the close of the first quarter when junior safety David Bourland picked off a Willie Brooks pass and returned it 73 yards behind beautiful blocking for a touchdown that, after Hawkins' PAT, made it 14-0.

In the second period, Midland, starting from its 33, drove all the way to the Abilene 5 before the Eagles stopped McDaniel & Co. on downs. The Eagles then mounted a spectacular 95-yard drive for their third score.

The highlight of the drive came when Hawkins pitched back to soph fullback Glynn Gregory who headed right on an apparent sweep. But Gregory, the ex-quarterback, pulled up and lofted a wobbly pass that end Twyman Ash caught for a gain of 46 yards, to Midland's 16-yard line. It would be Abilene's only completed pass of the night. Five plays later, left half Jim Millerman swept right end four yards for the score and Abilene appeared to be in control at 21-0 with two minutes left in the half.

But Midland came roaring back. From its 13, the Bulldogs moved quickly to the Abilene 37. From there, with less than half a minute left to play before the half, Midland coach Thurman "Tugboat" Jones knew he had to go to the air. Quarterback Brooks fired for right end Jim Owens, who this time caught the ball between Eagle defenders and stepped across the goal line with only 10 seconds left on the clock. At the half, it was Abilene 21, Midland 7.

The third period was scoreless, but late in the period Midland cranked up a drive from its own 13 and punched into Eagle territory as the fourth quarter began. McDaniel's six-yard scoring burst at 1:15 into the fourth drew Midland to within a touchdown and gave the Bulldogs' home throng reason to hope.

But the Eagles were too tough and hung tight to the momentum edge established early. Briggs and Millerman, who finished with 88 yards, were running powerfully behind typical blocking. Starting with good field position from the Midland 49, Abilene drove toward the clinching touchdown. Hawkins eventually got the touchdown on a one-yard keeper. Midland drove once more, reaching the Abilene 30, but the Eagles stopped them there on downs and ran out the clock.

THE NEW DISTRICT 1-AAAA champion Abilene Eagles carried Moser off the field.

"A great ball club," said Midland coach Tugboat Jones. "I couldn't name anyone in particular."

Abilene held statistical edges typical of a hard-fought 28-14 victory. The Eagles had 20 first downs to 17 for Midland and outgained the Bulldogs on the ground, 279-174. The Eagles had only thrown three passes, completing one, the fullback pass from Gregory to Ash, for 46 yards. One way to beat the district's most consistent offense was to keep it off the field and keep the clock running. So the Eagles kept running the ball, piling up first downs, playing ball control and eating up the clock. There were only three penalties in the entire game, all on Abilene, totaling 15 yards.

The Midland locker room was a place of a dead purple-and-gold dream of an undefeated season and a district championship. Several players cried, including big tackle Lee Woods. As other players moved to console him, another Midland player stood up and barked: "Let him cry all night if he wants to. We lost it, didn't we?" The player was Wahoo McDaniel.

McDaniel had chalked up 129 hard yards on 22 carries, a testament to his greatness. But Briggs, Abilene's fullback, had gained 149 yards on four fewer carries, a phenomenal average of 8.3 yards per carry.

"Jim came through for us when we needed him most," Moser said. Abilene students and fans milling outside the locker room after the game were calling him "Wahoo" Briggs.

Abilene 28, Midland 14
Nov. 19, 1954

Nov. 25, 1954

ON SATURDAY MORNING, the Abilene Eagles woke up and got out of bed in their mainly modest houses across the city with the feeling that they were the football champions of District 1-AAAA.

The feeling was unique, one that only a champion can feel, and it was a new feeling, a level of success that morning that to young men at 16, 17 and 18 was completely original and never to be forgotten.

By Sunday they knew they were going to play Austin High School of El Paso in their bi-district game and that the game would be played at Fair Park Stadium on Saturday afternoon, Dec. 4.

San Angelo to them might have become an afterthought, if it wasn't San Angelo, and if the Eagles weren't now district champions, with that new reputation to uphold.

The Eagles and Bobcats would meet in the regular season's last game, their traditional Thanksgiving Day blood rivalry, this year to be played at 7,200-seat Bobcat Stadium. Never mind records or circumstances, the stadium was already sold out, and it was the Bobcats' Homecoming game.

The Orange and Blue came into the game with their best record since 1944: six victories, one loss (26-21 to Midland) and a bizarre pair of identical 21-21 ties in their last two games, with Amarillo and Odessa.

They also were carrying a big Abilene grudge. In the 1953 game at Fair Park Stadium, the Eagles had beaten the Bobcats, 61-0. After that game, San Angelo coach Bob Harrell reportedly said to an Abilene assistant, "Coach Moser will live to regret this day." It didn't matter that halfback Henry Colwell, then a sophomore second-stringer, led all rushers with 126 yards and scored three touchdowns, or that senior tackle Bobby Jack Oliver played fullback once in the second half and actually carried the ball on fourth down. Even if Moser had sent the cheerleaders in, between Abilene and San Angelo 61-0 was 61-0.

⁂

THERE WAS IRONY as well. It was Harrell whom Moser replaced briefly at Corpus Christi Miller early in 1953, after Harrell left Miller to take the San Angelo job. And Moser was at Corpus barely a week before being contacted by Abilene.

The Eagles had unusual difficulties getting ready for the game. Several starters, including Colwell and fullback Jim Briggs, hero of the Midland game, were down with the flu. And Doris Moser's father died. Moser missed practices to go to Waco to attend the funeral. Players and coach were all back in time to get on the Eagle Bus on a beautiful Thanksgiving morning for the short 87-mile trip down U.S. 277 to San Angelo.

It didn't take long after the kickoff to learn that the grudge wasn't helping the Bobcats any, and that the distractions hadn't hurt the Eagles. Abilene simply took up where they left off in 1953. By the end of the first quarter, it was 20-0, and Harrell was wondering about a team that could out-score his own very respectable team, 81-0, over five consecutive quarters.

What's worse, the Bobcats were beating themselves. Halfback Norman Marshall ran the opening kickoff back 40 yards but then fumbled the ball, that was recovered by Eagle defensive end Stuart Peake at the Abilene 41. A little later, halfback Jim Millerman set up in a flanker right, then came back left on a reverse and scored from 28 yards out.

Four and a half minutes later, the Eagles were back again, deep in Bobcat territory. This time Millerman took a pitch from quarterback H.P. Hawkins, swept around right end, and went 24 yards to the end zone to make it 14-0.

~

IN THE SCOUTING REPORT, Moser had told his team that to win the football game, they would have to stop or slow down San Angelo's very good passing attack. San Angelo had led District 1-AAAA in passing, but quarterback Marvin Lasater was having no luck against Abilene's talented secondary and typical pass rush. It was three-and-out for the Bobcats, and before the end of the quarter the Eagles had scored again, this time on Henry Colwell's one-yard plunge.

In the second period, Abilene's second- and third-stringers started going in. By the end of the game, all 37 on the traveling squad had seen action, including no less than 16 offensive backs. Colwell returned a punt 44 yards early in the second half for the Eagles' last score and the substitute backs accumulated yardage and experience for the remainder of the game. Third-string fullback Jack Self was the leading rusher with 82 yards on 10 carries, including a 61-yard jaunt. Millerman had 61 yards on eight carries, Briggs had 55 yards and Colwell 39.

San Angelo threw a lot, attempting 20 passes, but only three were complete for a total of 29 yards. The Bobcats lost three fumbles and had a pass intercepted and their total offense for the afternoon was 93 yards. The Eagles accumulated 379 yards in total offense, 254 rushing and 125 passing, on eight completions in 15 attempts. Penalties, 11 in all for 115 yards, most of them in the second half, hurt the Eagles.

For all the build-up between old rivals, the game turned out to be nothing more than a nice tune-up for the state playoffs. While 27-0 wasn't 61-0, it had been unnervingly easy.

Abilene 27, San Angelo 0
Nov. 25, 1954

Dec. 4, 1954

WHEN IT WAS NEW, the Eagles' Nest, as the gym was called, may have accommodated the entire Abilene High student body. But by 1954, it was too cramped for the kind of throng that filed into the auditorium on Friday, Dec. 3. All the pep rallies were in the auditorium, but this one would be different, and thunderous.

Abilene High players, students, and teachers filing down the aisles saw, positioned in the middle of the stage, the Victory Bell, its carriage crepe-wrapped in Eagle black and gold. Just at the crown of the bell was a tuft of red and white, representing the Odessa Bronchos, come to surrender the bell to the new champions. The bell held an iconic command of the space, and at any given moment all eyes were on it.

Odessa High Student Council President Bobby Mitchell led a delegation of 23 Odessa student officers, cheerleaders and faculty sponsors who escorted the bell to Abilene. Mitchell, outlining its history, said the 150-pound brass bell had first been presented to Amarillo High School in 1940 by the Santa Fe Railway Co.

In the years since, it had represented district champions in Amarillo, Pampa, Lubbock and Odessa. (Abilene had won a district championship in 1949, but in a different district, before the creation of the AAAA classification.)

In a telegram, Santa Fe vice-president G. R. Buchanan said: "The Victory Bell is regarded as an emblem of good sportsmanship, keen competition and fair play and is an impetus to the fine spirit, rivalry and competition existing among teams of the district."

Mitchell officially presented the bell to Abilene High Student Council President Steve Marshall. Don Kirkpatrick, captain of the Odessa High Bell Team, then stepped forward and presented the bell's clapper to Don Burks, Abilene High's newly selected Bell Team captain. Burks formally accepted it, then bent toward the bell and with Kirkpatrick's guidance, fastened the clapper into place as the crowd watched and waited. It was very quiet in the auditorium.

Burks stepped back, stood up straight. Then he reached for the handle, set the bell into motion, and it rang.

THE AUDITORIUM ERUPTED, an instantaneous, sustained roar, going on and on, the clear ringing of the bell the only discernible noise above the roar, ringing and ringing as Burk and others kept the bell rocking in its carriage for a long time.

At the end of this, Eagle tri-captains Twyman Ash, Jim Millerman and John Thomas presented the gold District 1-AAAA championship trophy to Abilene High Principal Escoe Webb. The bell hardly stopped ringing through the rest of the pep rally, the sound reaching even a few cynics, who that afternoon maybe couldn't deny to themselves that they had been in the presence of something electrifying.

In the Saturday morning *Abilene Reporter-News* was a team photo of the district champions, taken during the week to replace the pre-season team photo in which Bob Gay and Ronnie McDearman appeared. Saturday morning dawned cool but clear and bloomed into one of those special West Texas December days with no wind and a sky the color of faded denim. At around 8 a.m., residents for blocks around Fair Park Stadium cocked their ears toward what sounded like a bell ringing.

It was the Victory Bell, already stationed on the Eagle sideline at the stadium. The Bell Team would keep the bell ringing all the way to kickoff, the introduction of what turned out to be a tradition for Saturday afternoon games in Abilene.

Into this setting rolled the Panthers of El Paso Austin High School, champions of District 2-AAAA. Under any conditions, the Eagles would have been clear favorites to defeat the Panthers. As it was, the Abilene team was sky-high with inspiration after Friday afternoon's Victory Bell ceremony. And it was at a late hour Friday afternoon when the Panthers finally arrived in Abilene after the 445-mile bus trip from El Paso, via U.S. Highway 80. Now it is

Interstate 20, but in 1954 U.S. 80 was two-lane and only as fast as the slowest truck.

Not only Midland, but Pampa, had beaten EP Austin in the regular season, both by two or more touchdowns. Austin, meanwhile, had beaten Borger, 27-7. The Panthers had a good offense, sparked by 155-pound all-district fullback Bobby McCune, and had beaten all four of their district opponents by a combined total of 130 points to 24.

~

KICKOFF WAS AT 2 P.M. The Panthers made a game of it for six minutes. Then the Eagles drove 80 yards, including a 64-yard run by halfback Henry Colwell, who also got the touchdown on a one-yard dive. It was 13-0 by the end of the first quarter as the other starting halfback, Jim Millerman, scored on a four-yard run.

EP Austin ran three plays on its ensuing possession and then Millerman took the punt back 73 yards down the sidelines for Abilene's third TD.

The Eagles muffed the following kickoff, the ball being mis-hit and going only 15 yards. It didn't matter. Eagle sophomore guard Guy Wells recovered the ball at the El Paso 45 and a minute later Colwell circled around on a Statue of Liberty play and carried 22 yards into the end zone and it was a lightning-quick 27-0 with more than six minutes left in the half.

On came the Eagle second and third teams. The final score was 61-0. Millerman ran back another punt in the third quarter for his third touchdown of the afternoon. Colwell finished with two touchdowns and 148 yards on only nine carries. Sophomore fullback Glynn Gregory scored two touchdowns and in the second half took over point-after placement duties from quarterback H.P. Hawkins. Hawkins booted four PATs, Gregory three.

Junior quarterback David Bourland threw a 30-yard scoring pass to junior end Freddie Green, the only pass Abilene completed all day. They only tried four. El Paso attempted 14 and completed only one, for 14 yards. Abilene rushed for 450 yards, El Paso 69. Abilene's last score came on a 61-yard run by third-string fullback Jack Self.

The bell continued to ring into the sunset, long after the game was over. Moser and Abilene officials went up to the pressbox to meet with representatives from Fort Worth Poly, 25-7 victors over Dallas South Oak Cliff in another bi-district game. Abilene lost the coin flip and the game was set for Saturday afternoon, Dec. 11, at Farrington Field in Fort Worth. The El Paso Austin Panthers filed out of the field house and onto the bus and settled in as best they could for the 444-mile ride home.

Abilene 61, El Paso Austin 0
Dec. 4, 1954

Dec. 11, 1954

"HUNTER ENIS" WAS A NAME to be feared, even more than the name "Wahoo McDaniel," because Enis was a quarterback and a bona fide star.

Everybody in Texas who cared about high school football knew who Hunter Enis was. He was big and athletic and so good a passer that his school, the Fort Worth Poly Parrots, ran something called the "spread formation." Nobody in West Texas had ever heard of the "spread formation," in which ends and backs lined up from sideline to sideline and then ran downfield to catch passes from the strong, deadly arm of Hunter Enis.

All week, Abilenians read the newspaper and wondered: "We can stop Fort Worth Poly, but can we stop Hunter Enis?" They were the kinds of thoughts that could bedevil fans of upstart teams suddenly plunged into the rarified atmosphere of the state semifinals. Only three other teams left. And boy, they must have been awfully good to get here.

And Poly was there because of Hunter Enis, who was so skilled that in college, at Texas Christian, he would make all-Southwest Conference and eventually play quarterback in the National Football League. Enis had passed for 1,111 yards and it didn't matter that Poly had been beaten badly, 34-0, by San Angelo, or that the Parrots had lost three other games. Those were early in the season.

The game was in Fort Worth, at 20,000-seat Farrington Field, the biggest stadium in which any of the Abilene Eagles had ever played. Around 2,500 Eagle students and fans made the trip and of course the Victory Bell was there. Thousands more listened on the radio at home, anxious to see if the Eagles could survive Hunter Enis and get into a state championship game for the first time since 1931. At kickoff there was a low overcast and a constant threat of rain.

ABILENE TOOK THE KICKOFF and moved 20 yards to the Poly 40, where halfback Henry Colwell fumbled. The Parrots recovered. Poly on its first series set sail from its 40, moving scarily forward on Enis's completions of nine and 30 yards and the running of fullback Earl Brown and halfbacks I.B. Childs and Joe Del Selman. The Parrots reached the Eagle 15, but then Childs fumbled. Eagle tackle Glenn Woods recovered.

This time the Eagles went 85 yards. Highlights were a third-down 16-yard gain by Colwell on a reverse and a 28-yard completion from quarterback H.P. Hawkins to end Twyman Ash that put the ball at the Parrot 17. Four plays later Colwell scored from five yards out and the Eagles led, 7-0.

Then something happened. After their first look at Enis and the Poly offense, the Eagle defense, carefully prepared by defensive specialist coach Hank Watkins, appeared to know what was coming. They stopped the run, and all their stunts with the linemen and linebackers, designed to pressure Enis, worked so well that Enis lost almost as many yards trying to pass as the yards he gained with completions.

After its first drive, Poly never again got deeper into Abilene territory than the Eagle 47. At the half it was 20-0, after second-quarter touchdowns by Colwell (following David Bourland's long punt return) and Hawkins after the Eagles blocked a Parrot kick. It could have been worse. Abilene lost the ball on fumbles at the Poly 20 and the seven in the second period.

The Eagles scored again in the third period on sophomore Glynn Gregory's run. Then, against a demoralized defense, Eagle subs scored two more touchdowns in the last six minutes. Abilene's final score was an appropriate nail in the coffin of the Eagle fans' fears as defensive halfback Jim Busby intercepted a Hunter Enis pass and returned it 32 yards for a touchdown.

THE FINAL SCORE was 46-0. Enis finished with nine completions in 20 attempts for 99 yards and three interceptions, and the Parrots managed only 15 total yards rushing and 10 first downs. Eagle guard John Thomas led the way with six tackles, and Ash, sophomore end Stuart Peake and guard Hubert Jordan had five each.

It was a terrific defensive effort, but that's not what Poly Coach Dan Campbell talked about after the game.

"They've got the darndest downfield blocking I ever saw," Campbell said.

"Their blocking looked good, didn't it?" Chuck Moser agreed. Abilene collected 23 first downs and 398 yards in total offense, including 323 on the ground.

A "team victory," Moser called it, and if it was, it was a reflection of the Eagles' season. No dominant names, like Hunter Enis or Wahoo McDaniel, had emerged in the Eagle offense to make state headlines, because too many people played. Abilene's leading rusher in the semifinals was third-string fullback Jack Self, with 83 yards, and Self said it wasn't so much him as it was the downfield blocking. The starting halfbacks, Colwell and Millerman, had 65 and 51 yards respectively. The other 124 yards in the Eagles' rushing total were divided among eight other backs who got into the game.

In a tearful Poly locker room, Campbell told his players they were as good as any in the state. Of the Eagles, he said, "It's a great team."

However they got there, it was clear that the Eagles belonged in the state's elite. In two playoff games, the Eagles had outscored their opponents, 107 to nothing. On the blackboard in the Eagles' side of the Farrington Field locker room, someone had chalked: "Beat Houston!"

In the championship game, the Eagles would meet the Mustangs of Houston's Stephen F. Austin High School, 21-20 victors over Corpus Christi Miller in the state's other semifinals game.

The game for the championship of Class AAAA was set for 2 p.m. Saturday in Houston's Public Schools Stadium.

Abilene 46, Fort Worth Poly 0
Dec. 11, 1954

Dec. 18, 1954

THE JUGGERNAUT FROM ABILENE was favored to beat Stephen F. Austin by three touchdowns in the state championship game at Houston.

Instead, with 5:49 remaining in the game, the Mustangs on fourth down lined up at the Abilene six-yard line to kick a field goal that would put them ahead of the Eagles, 10-7.

No one in Houston was surprised. Maybe they were having heart attacks, but they weren't surprised.

While Abilene was pounding two playoff foes by a cumulative score of 107-0, Stephen F. Austin in bi-district barely squeaked past Galveston Ball, 21-20. In the semifinals, the Mustangs faced a Corpus Christi Miller team that had beaten them soundly, 25-6, in the third game of the season. The Mustangs won, again by 21-20.

It was the team that wouldn't quit. Just to get into the playoffs, in the last game of the regular season the Mustangs had to beat the defending Class AAAA champions, Houston Lamar. And they did, 16-14.

If these nail-biters were hard on the Mustangs' fans, it was hell on the 3,000 fans that had followed the Eagles to Houston's 20,000-seat Public Schools Stadium.

Abilene had begun the game routinely, taking an early 7-0 lead. After a fumble recovery at the Eagle 48, quarterback H.P. Hawkins hit left half Jim Millerman with a 22-yard pass to the Mustangs' 26. Millerman took a hit in the head on the play and was knocked silly. He was replaced by sophomore Jimmy Carpenter.

Two plays later, Hawkins scrambled 18 yards to the 10 and carries by right half Henry Colwell and Carpenter moved the ball to the four.

On the sideline, team physician Dr. Dub Sibley had been worried about Millerman, who appeared to be out cold when he was carried off the field. But Millerman came to, knew where he was, and was quickly back on his feet and back into the game. From the SFA four, he took a pitchout on a sweep right and scored. Hawkins kicked the PAT and with 4:47 left in the first quarter, the Eagles were up 7-0 and it looked like business as usual.

BUT IT DIDN'T WORK OUT that way. Even with a stiff wind at their backs in the second period, the Eagles couldn't add to their lead. Abilene threatened once, moving to the Austin six before being stopped by a hard-hitting, determined Mustang defense. "It was the roughest game of the season," Millerman said. "I think they're as good as anybody we played."

SFA, meanwhile, drove to the Eagle 30 before losing the ball on downs, then recovered a bad snap on an Eagle punt attempt and set up shop again at the Abilene 30. Quarterback Vince Matthews, thought by many to be even better than Hunter Enis, took the Mustangs to the Eagle 13, but there he fumbled and after a scramble the Eagles finally recovered on the 26.

The Eagles were having trouble moving the ball, partly because of the Mustang defense but partly, Moser said, because they were tense "and trying too hard."

"Everything we tried went wrong," he said. "Their defense was so good they made us throw the ball."

Austin got the wind again in the third quarter and a big assist from the Eagles, who received the second-half kickoff. End Freddie Green returned the kick 17 yards but then fumbled, and the Mustangs recovered at the Abilene 43. Seven plays later, Mustang fullback Bethea Brindley rambled seven yards through left tackle to score. Sophomore halfback Randy Sims, who had missed only five placement kicks all season, added the point after and it was 7-7.

Though Hawkins was playing brilliantly, the Eagles didn't threaten in the third period, running only 11 plays. Their only advantage came with the beginning of the fourth quarter, when they got the wind again.

But it was the Mustangs moving the ball in the fourth quarter. Showing the tenacity that their fans had come to expect, they put together their best overall drive of the day and eventually had a first down at the Eagle 11.

Three plays, though, gained only five yards. With fourth down and five to go at the Eagle six, Mustang coach Alvin (Bull) Kotrola called for a field goal. The reliable kicker, Randy Sims, lined up a kick that was into the wind, but only four yards longer than an extra point.

But he rushed it. "He didn't hit it square," Kotrola said. The kick sailed wide to the left. Abilene got the ball at the 20-yard line with 5:49 left in the game.

~

THE MUSTANGS HAD A KNACK for hanging in there, but the Eagles had developed a knack of their own. They had become good at beating the other team at its own game. When it was Midland fullback Wahoo McDaniel, the answer was Eagle fullback Jim Briggs. When it was Stephen F. Austin quarterback Vince Matthews, the answer was Eagle quarterback H.P. Hawkins. In the state championship game, it was the Mustangs' tenacity. In the last five minutes of the game, could the Eagles answer with a tenacity of their own?

"I didn't think we could score again," Moser said. "It seemed like everything was turning against us." Before the game, Moser and Mustangs coach Kotrola agreed in the event of a tie game, their two teams would be declared co-champions, as opposed to a winner being declared on penetrations (a team earned a penetration each time it moved inside the opponent's 20-yard line).

But suddenly the Eagle offense started to move at its old familiar clip. In two and a half minutes the team in the white jerseys roared 79 yards to the Mustang one.

"When we held them on the field goal, we began to catch fire," Moser said.

Third down at the one. Hawkins kept the ball and dived straight ahead on a quarterback sneak. He crossed the goal line. But now the ball was rolling free in the end zone, and the Mustangs' Randy Sims fell on it. The officials huddled as the crowd, on its feet, waited, and then decided Hawkins had fumbled before crossing the goal line. They ruled a touchback, awarding Stephen F. Austin the ball at the Mustang 20. The score was still 7-7.

All the air went out of the crowd and then rushed back into the lungs of the hometown fans. On the Abilene sideline, Moser wondered if he could rally his team. But then Hawkins came up to him.

"I expected him to come out of the game heartbroken, maybe even in tears," Moser said. "I was afraid he'd lose his confidence. But instead he came up to me, put his arm on my shoulder, and said, 'Don't worry, Coach. I'll get a touchdown for you.' "

The Eagle defense, playing ferociously, stopped the Mustangs on three downs and Matthews had to punt into the wind. On the crisscross return play, Colwell wound up with the ball at the Eagle 45 and found a lane down the sideline. He ran 55 yards and scored easily with 2:40 remaining in the game.

Eagle fans erupted as Colwell sprinted toward the end zone, but back upfield, there was a flag. Abilene was called for clipping. In barely a minute, the Eagles had had two touchdowns called back. The referee stepped off the penalty and placed the ball on the ground at the Abilene 31-yard line. If there was to be Eagle tenacity, this was the time for it. One more time, the Eagle offense came back onto the field. On the scoreboard behind the end zone, the clock showed 2:40. A state championship was 69 yards away. On the public address system, the score of the AAA championship game was announced: Breckenridge 20, Port Neches 7.

"Abilene fans cheered," said Abilenian George Minter, "because we knew Breckenridge had been yelling for us."

EAGLE LEFT END TWYMAN ASH, No. 81, during the season had earned a nickname, "Old Glue Fingers," because the tall blond senior who was also a starter on the Eagles' basketball team never dropped a pass. In the championship game, Hawkins had gone to him only once. But now, with the title on the line, Hawkins threw twice to Ash, once for 38 yards and again for 17. After five plays, the Eagles were poised at the Mustang 16, with a little over a minute left on the clock.

Hawkins called another pass. He took the snap and rolled right. Colwell, split to the right, went down and out. Millerman from his left halfback position went straight down the field between the safeties. Ash followed along behind and found himself open. But Mustang defenders had caught Hawkins. They threw him for a 13-yard loss back to the 29-yard line.

Now there were 56 seconds left. Ash trotted back to the huddle and told Hawkins he could get open again. "We were trying to split their safeties," Hawkins said. "We had a split to the right, Twyman on the left and Jim (Millerman) running a flag up the middle to split the safeties." Hawkins called the same play. On the sideline, sophomore Glynn Gregory was getting ready to try a field goal. It would be a long one, but Gregory would have the wind at his back and Moser said, "He's kicked them 40 yards before."

The Eagles came to the line. Hawkins took the snap and rolled right. Both Colwell and Millerman were covered. Mustang coach Kotrola had dropped one of his defensive ends into secondary coverage, giving him five defenders covering three receivers. "The first two guys weren't open," Hawkins said. Then he saw Ash at the five-yard line. He threw.

The ball was high, but Ash leaped, arched his back and snared the ball on his fingertips between two defenders. On the sideline *Reporter-News* photographer Don Hutcheson caught No. 81 in that fully extended instant that became probably the most reproduced photo in Abilene media history.

As he came down Ash had a step on the defenders and hustled five yards into the end zone. There were no flags. The Eagles led 13-7. On the sideline, the Eagles were jumping up and down. Someone in the excitement came back with an elbow that caught Moser squarely on the brow above his eye, splitting it open. Blood gushed, but Moser quickly found a towel and pressed on the gash as he watched Hawkins kick the extra point to make it 14-7.

THE VICTORY BELL RANG and rang. A drained crowd watched the Eagles kick off and bat away the Mustangs' last efforts and then it was over. The Abilene Eagles were the Class AAAA state champions.

"If that touchdown pass had carried six inches either way, one of my boys would have knocked it down," Kotrola said.

"How can you lose," Moser said, "when you've got kids who come through for you when you need them most?"

Kotrola said he couldn't single out any Abilene heroes.

"There were about 20 of them," he said. "We were out-manned and they had a fine team."

H.P. Hawkins had thoroughly outplayed the much-heralded Vince Matthews. Hawkins threw only 13 passes but completed eight of them for 173 yards, a season high for the Eagles, and of course one of those was the pass that won the championship. Matthews completed 12 of 26 for only 88 yards.

"Abilene had the best defensive team we've played all year," Kotrola said. "Nobody bottled up our passing like that." Of his own Mustangs, Kotrola said it was the "greatest battling team I ever coached." Eagle guard Sammy Caudle said, "They never quit trying. They hustled more than anybody we played."

The bloodied Moser came out of the locker room and thanked several hundred Abilene fans who had gathered around, then went back in where team doctor Dub Sibley closed the gash above his eye with three stitches.

Statistics were deceiving. The Eagles had 17 first downs, the Mustangs 11. Abilene amassed 334 total yards to 198 for SFA. But Abilene fumbled five times, and there was the Mustang tenacity that couldn't be measured in yards.

That morning, at 11 a.m. before the 2 p.m. kickoff, the Eagles had gathered in their hotel for their pre-game meal of dry roast beef, a dry baked potato and dry toast. Now, as state champions, they ate what they wanted in a private room in a restaurant.

"It was all our teammates and coaches alone in one room together," Hawkins said. "There was a feeling of happiness, of closeness, and of accomplishment that I will never forget."

Twyman Ash had in his possession the game ball. In the locker room he had approached Moser with it.

"Coach," Ash said, "you take it."

"No, sir," said Moser. "You boys earned it." So Ash, who had three catches in the winning drive, carried the ball home.

At 7:30, the Eagles boarded their chartered Martin 202 for the flight back to Abilene. Waiting for them at the airport that night was a crowd of 3,000 people.

Abilene 14, Houston Stephen F. Austin 7
Dec. 18, 1954

Celebration

SPREAD ACROSS ALL EIGHT columns at the top of Page One Sunday morning in Abilene was the headline: "Warbirds Soar to Title, 14-7."

Underneath the headline, across seven columns, consuming all the page above the fold, was a team photo of the state champion Abilene Eagles.

The game story started in column eight and jumped to an inside page of the A Section that ordinarily was reserved for so-called hard news. One such news story gave details of the throng of 3,000 at Municipal Airport that met the team on its return from Houston.

The crowd started building about 8 p.m. when radio stations said the team plane was due about 9:30 p.m. The crowd overflowed the airport lobby area onto the tarmac and grassy areas around the terminal building. It was cold, but nobody cared.

The crowd got to cheer twice. A shout went up as an airliner's lights appeared, on approach. The plane landed and taxied back to the terminal and the crowd roared. But it was a plane chartered by Eagle fans for the Houston trip who nevertheless hugely enjoyed their reception.

The team plane appeared several minutes later and the crowd roared again as the twin-engine aircraft parked and this time deplaned the players down stairs in the tail of the Martin 202. The players were reserved but all smiles as they waited to collect duffle bags containing their pads, helmets and cleats from the plane's baggage hold.

There were more photos and stories in the sports section, including stories from reporters on the Eagle sideline and in both locker rooms after the game. There was a photo of Moser with his gashed eye and a photo of No. 81, Twyman Ash, making the game-winning catch. On the front page was a small box proclaiming: "5 Shopping Days 'til Christmas." It was wrong.

NOT MUCH READING, WRITING OR ARITHMETIC got done Monday at Abilene High School. Instead the school day was more like a progressive pep rally. Members of the bell team starting ringing the Victory Bell at 8 a.m. and it didn't stop all day. Assistant principal J.H. Nail said the students "walked on air" all day Monday.

"We had to pick them off the ceiling every once in a while," Nail said. "They had something going all day long."

At 4 p.m., members of the Eagle Booster Club, mostly business and professional men in the community, arrived in convertibles to take the team on a parade through downtown. The parade crossed the T&P tracks to North First, then up Cypress and down Pine with the Eagle Booster Club banner and the Victory Bell leading the way.

In the lead convertible were Eagle tri-captains Twyman Ash, Jim Millerman and John Thomas. A reporter said the players looked uncomfortable with all the attention from the thousands of Abilenians lining the streets. Behind the string of cars came hundreds of AHS students and the Eagle band. Students carried a "State Champions" banner that stretched almost all the way across the street.

It was the Eagles' fourth state championship, to go with titles won in 1923, 1928 and 1931, but this was the first in the more formalized statewide classifications introduced by the University Interscholastic League for the 1951 season. It was different to be from a town whose high school team had emerged champions from a system that more or less insured that only the best teams from all corners of the state moved forward through the playoffs.

Seven Eagles made the All-District 1-AAAA first team. Named to the first-team offense were end Twyman Ash, tackle Cullen Hunt, guard John Thomas, center Elmo Cure, quarterback H.P. Hawkins, and halfback Jim Millerman. Ash, Thomas and Millerman were also first-team defensive selections, along with defensive back David Bourland.

Named to the second-team offense were guard Sam Caudle and halfback Henry Colwell. Caudle, Cullen Hunt and Bob Hubbard were second-team defense selections. Juniors in that group included Cure, Bourland, Colwell and Caudle.

Other lettermen returning for the 1955 season were guard Stuart Peake, end Freddie Green, tackle Rufus King, guard Hubert Jordan, halfback Jimmy Carpenter, fullback Glynn Gregory, tackle Homer Rosenbaum, center Joe Taylor, guard Guy Wells and backs John Barfoot, Jim Busby, Jerry Henderson and James Welch. There were 17 lettermen in all, but that was slightly misleading since Moser had lettered the entire squad that went to Houston for the championship game. Welch, for example, played on the B team most of the season before being brought up to the varsity for the playoffs.

Moser never shrugged, but a typical eyebrows-up quizzical look came to his face when there was a question he couldn't answer.

A newspaperman asked him if he thought the Eagles could win the District 1-AAAA championship and get into the playoffs again in 1955. Up went the eyebrows.

"It just depends on how the boys develop," he said.

The school, the Eagle Booster Club, and other sponsors hosted a football banquet for the team at the end of every season. For many adults, the banquet was just another obligatory event to attend. The 1954 banquet was different. Moser and the Eagles for a second time presented Abilene High principal Escoe Webb the District 1-AAAA championship trophy, and then the state Class AAAA championship trophy, Abilene High's first since 1931.

In turn, the Eagle Booster Club presented gifts to the coaches: checks, ranging from $1,500 for the varsity coaches to $400 for B Team assistants like Tommy Morris, who was only a couple of years out of Abilene Christian College. It didn't sound like much, but $400 put a big grin on the faces of assistants like Morris, whose annual salary was $3,500.

The Booster Club had a gift for the head coach as well. Moser was presented the keys to a new 1954 Buick.

Twyman Ash, No. 81, pulls in the winning touchdown pass against Houston Stephen F. Austin in the 1954 championship game, probably the most reproduced photo in Abilene media history.

Photos and documents courtesy of Abilene High School and Gerald Galbraith.

H.P. Hawkins

Twyman Ash

Henry Colwell

Sam Caudle

David Bourland

Glynn Gregory

Harold "Hayseed" Stephens

Jimmy Carpenter

July 22, 1955

Dear Eagle - ("A" Squad) Center

Football season is near. In order to win our first game in Dallas September 9 vs Highland Park, you must be in top shape when we start practice August 26. Here is a schedule that I hope you all will follow.

<u>August 1</u>: Start working out on the practice field each day. Please stay off the stadium field. You should push-up, work on the chute, take starts, do lots of running (the first week do mostly all easy running). Punt, pass, and play touch football. (40 to 60 minutes is plenty of work)

<u>August 9 (Tues)</u>: You should come by my house and pick up your plays. If you are out of town, let me know where you are and I will mail them to you. You must know all plays, rules, and material by the first day of practice.

<u>August 15</u>: Everybody should work out together and run plays, pass, and do hard running.

<u>August 16</u>: Starting on this date you must take your physical exam at the doctor's office. At the bottom of this page it will tell you when and where to take your physical exam. Please be there.

<u>August 26</u>: Start practice. Be on the field at 7:45 and 4:00 until school starts.

Enclosed are the training rules we should all know and abide by. Boys with the proper spirit will start abiding by these rules August 1.

I realise some of you will be out of town in August for a few days. You still should work out everyday and try if possible to work out together August 15 and thereafter.

Remember that spirit and desire to learn and excell is what makes great teams. I know that you will not let us down.

Coach

P. S. I will be at the stadium every morning from August 15-26. Come by the stadium if you have time, I would enjoy the visit. See me if you have questions or problems.

Dr Sibley's Office
Aug 17th 5 pm

This is the letter from Coach Moser that started it all for Eagle athletes each summer. Note the assignment for Aug. 9.

When Chuck Moser drew up downfield blocking, this is what he meant. Guy Wells, No. 60, and Clint Murphy, 75, at full speed toward a Sweetwater defensive back with ballcarrier Glynn Gregory close behind.

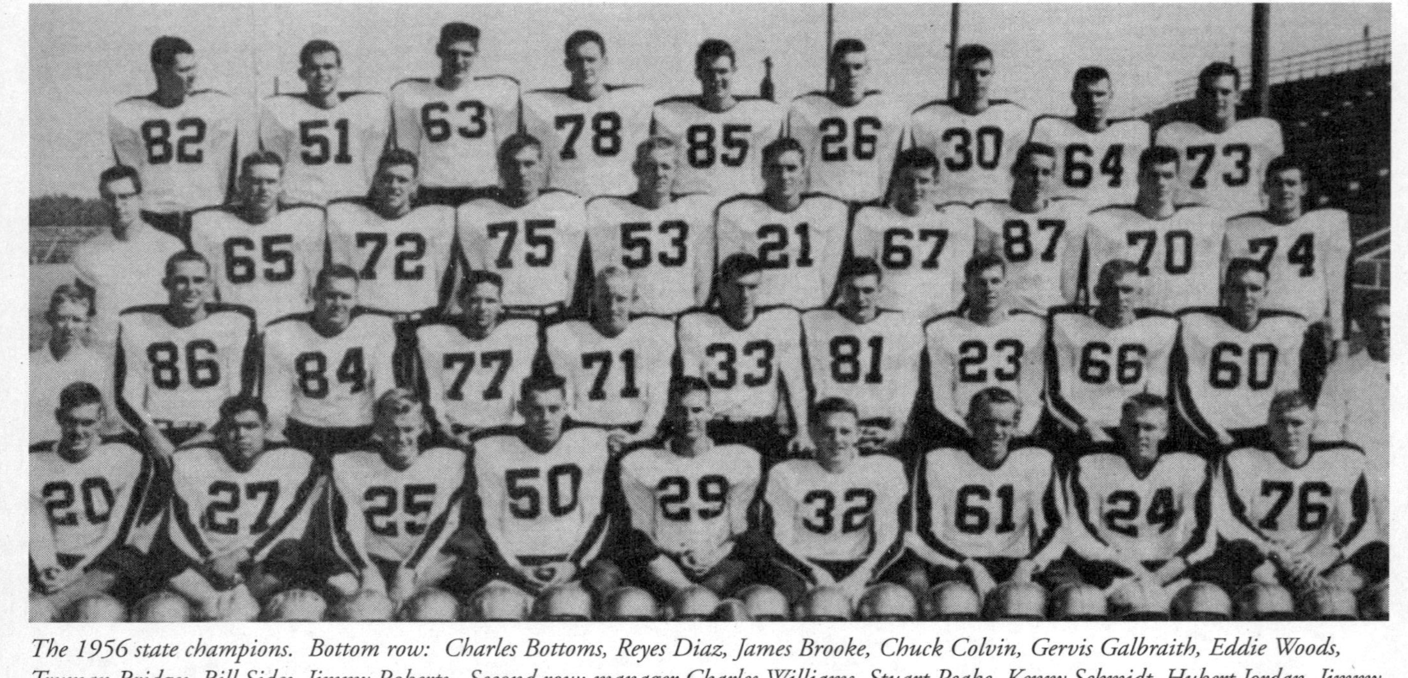

The 1956 state champions. Bottom row: Charles Bottoms, Reyes Diaz, James Brooke, Chuck Colvin, Gervis Galbraith, Eddie Woods, Truman Bridges, Bill Sides, Jimmy Roberts. Second row: manager Charles Williams, Stuart Peake, Kenny Schmidt, Hubert Jordan, Jimmy Carpenter, Harold Stephens, Butch Adams, Charles Bradshaw, Ervin Bishop, Guy Wells. Third row: manager Jimmy Johns, Mike Pelfry, Bufford Carr, Clint Murphy, Jim Rose, Glynn Gregory, Kim Winston, Ralph Bruton, Boyd King, Rufus King. Back row: Joe Ward, Gerald Galbraith, Jimmy Perry, Mike Bryant, Mike McKinnis, Bob Swafford, Alan Peake, John Young, Frank Aycock.

1955

THE RETURNING EAGLE PLAYERS who reported to Chuck Moser in August were the same young men who filed so self-consciously off the airplane in December that had brought them home from the 1954 state championship game.

The faces were the same. But the world had changed, was changing, under their feet. And their feet, feeling the change, had begun literally to move with it.

To people with only a general attentiveness to history, the 1950s have receded into memory as a quiet time, a period of Eisenhower-era tranquility. The tumultuous 1960s by contrast certainly did what they could to enhance that memory.

In fact, the 1950s were themselves tumultuous with change. The media and consumer driven world of the early 21st century could trace its roots directly to events of the 1950s. The Pulitzer Prize-winning reporter and author David Halberstam saw so much happening in the 1950s that he wrote a complete book, titled, simply, "The '50s."

It is true that at the time, in Abilene, much of that change occurred with the force of a pebble dropping unheard into a distant pond, such as the unanimous Supreme Court decision of May 17, 1954, that ended the "separate but equal" doctrine of educational facilities for whites and blacks. That ripple would not reach Abilene for another decade.

Other changes, like television, advertising, and longer, sleeker cars, were more apparent. But there was one change that more or less blew the others away. It occurred on a Friday night in April, at the Paramount Theater downtown. Friday night was the traditional movie night for high school and junior high students. Admission was a quarter, Milk Duds were a nickel, cokes and popcorn a dime. Each teen group had its chosen area, its turf, in which to sit in the large theater, built in the popular fashion that suggested an ornate outdoor playhouse under a dark blue sky. In the sky were "stars," and across it moved floodlight-generated "clouds." It could get noisy, and ushers with their flashlights were on constant patrol.

~

THE MOVIE THIS FRIDAY NIGHT was "Blackboard Jungle," starring Glenn Ford and Anne Francis. Also in the cast were two young actors, Vic Morrow and Sidney Poitier. None of the kids in the theater knew anything about the movie; they were there because it was Friday night. First there was the black-and-white newsreel, then the cartoon, then the curtain fell in preamble to the feature. The effect was to set up anticipation, and in fact the crowd became quiet. There were two or three moments of relative calm. Then:

"One two three o'clock four o'clock ROCK!

"Five six seven o'clock eight o'clock ROCK!

"Nine ten eleven o'clock twelve o'clock ROCK!

"We're gonna ROCK around the CLOCK tonight!"

It was music, very loud and urgent, and it thundered on into its first verse—"When the clock strikes one, join me hon"—but the kids in the Paramount Theater sat rock-still, stunned, staring at the rising curtain, transfixed by the energy blasting at them from Bill Haley and the Comets.

These young people knew there was something happening to music out there somewhere. They could catch snatches of it on local stations KRBC and KWKC, but they had better luck if they searched for stations in New Orleans, Oklahoma City and Nashville, that came in sometimes with remarkable clarity through a still-uncluttered sky. This was high-energy music that came from people with exotic names like Fats Domino, Chuck Berry and Elvis Presley, and it didn't sound at all like what they were accustomed to hearing from Gisele MacKenzie, Mitch Miller, Les Baxter, Perry Como, Bing Crosby and Rosemary Clooney.

They were intrigued by the new music, but it had come from somewhere else far away across the sky. Now they sat in their very own Paramount, with its big speakers and this high-speed music rocketing at them, and for several seconds they were frozen by it. Then they reacted. They jumped up and yelled and the cooler ones got into the aisles and danced in frenzy. It was a before-and-after moment that no one there would ever forget.

The title of the song was "Rock Around the Clock," and it came to Abilene and all the other cities as a nice example of cross-media marketing. The recording industry's principal marketing outlet was radio. Listeners who heard a song on the radio might then go buy it at a record store.

~

BUT THERE WERE ONLY 24 hours available in a day, and not many radio stations. In 1955, Abilene had only two, meaning there were only 48 music marketing hours available in any given day. Worse, the stations used much of their time to broadcast soap operas, news, and shows like "Farm Roundup," "Mixing Bowl," and "Arthur Godfrey." Their music playlists leaned to proven artists and songs like "Hard to Get," "The Yellow Rose of Texas," and "Love is a Many Splendored Thing." It would be years before enough radio stations existed to develop what came to be called "narrowcasting." In 1955, on KRBC and KWKC, you took what you got, in a very mixed bag.

So "Rock Around the Clock" rode a movie into town, and the results were instructive to future students of cross-media marketing. "Rock Around the Clock" became the first example of this new music to reach No. 1 on the Billboard Magazine rating charts, and it did so very quickly, reaching No. 1 in June.

The movie was electrifying, too, about gangs in schools not only challenging, but intimidating and literally attacking authority. The teacher, Richard Dadier, played by Glenn Ford, wins in the end, the punk Vic Morrow is hauled away, and Sidney Poitier (a black kid!) leaves the bad guys and becomes a good one. The movie was so controversial that many communities would not allow it to be shown, including, of all places, Memphis, Tennessee.

But Abilene did, and kids who came out of the Paramount that night weren't the same kids who went in. They came out in possession of a new kind of music, and they knew a new word: "daddio." It was the first night in Abilene of a new extension of culture that would become a culture unto itself. It can only be imagined what the parents thought on Saturday morning, encountering this change for the first time. Parents were one thing. Chuck Moser was something else. Daddio? Not in a hundred years would the Eagle players have uttered this word within earshot of their coach. But it was out there. Many new things were out there.

Sept. 9, 1955

ALWAYS AT 8:30 on the Friday morning before the game, the entire school went to Eagle Gym for a pep rally. The first pep rally of 1955 was especially poignant and exciting.

Days before, on the first day of school after Labor Day, Abilene High students attended their first classes at the sprawling new brick and glass high school at the corner of North 6th and Mockingbird. The old and storied high school on South 1st became the third of Abilene's junior high schools and was named Lincoln. Their colors were black and white, and the football team was called the Longhorns.

On Sept. 9, the student body filed into the new Eagle Gym for the first-ever pep rally at the new school. Compared to the old Eagles' Nest, the new Eagle Gym was cavernous, and the new dimensions seemed to make room for more noise, and there was an incredible amount of light. At the east end of the basketball floor sat the Eagle Band, and it was blaring as the students arrived. In the center of the floor was the Victory Bell, and it was ringing. Next to the Bell was a standing microphone. Between the Victory Bell and the Band were the cheerleaders, always five, always seniors, selected in spring elections. In 1955, the Eagle cheerleaders were Sharon Osburn, Ruth Ann Polk, Sylvia Hamilton, Judy Matejowsky and Sharon Hooks.

In the other half of the court were folding chairs and into these rows, once everyone was in place, filed the football team: varsity in the front rows, then the junior varsity, then the B team. The roar, welcoming the defending state Class AAAA champions, was deafening. The rally went forward on a traditional schedule. There was a prayer, fight songs played by the band, yells led by the cheerleaders, a few words said by one of the players, a skit, and then the traditional closing "Warbirds" yell, surprisingly deliberate, and then the stately old school song:

We love you,
Dear old Abilene High,
Grand old Abilene High,
Champion school of all the West
Loyal just to you,
We're faithful and true blue,
We always will uphold you as the best
School of Eagle fame,
Winners of the game,
Fight right on to victory,
Fight right to the end,
And when you've won it then,
Three cheers for grand old Abilene High.

On Sept. 9, the Eagle bus was parked right outside the gym. After the pep rally, the team filed out and went straight onto the bus and driver Bert Berry steered through the crowd out of the parking lot and turned east toward Dallas.

THE EAGLES OPENED THE 1955 season against the Highland Park Scotties again, this time in Dallas.

Moser had lost an all-state halfback and left end, his starting quarterback and three other seniors who had made the 1954 1-AAAA all-district first team. There were holes, but one of Moser's strategies was already starting to pay off.

At the quarterback position, he always wanted a senior, a junior and a sophomore on the team. In 1954, the junior, David Bourland, had taken a lot of snaps in relief of the starter, H.P. Hawkins. Bourland, a smooth ball-handler himself, had learned a lot of shifty moves from Hawkins.

There were 11 juniors and six sophomores returning now as seniors and juniors. Three of these, center Elmo Cure, halfback Henry Colwell, and guard Sam Caudle, were returning offensive starters, and Colwell, Caudle, Bourland and end Stuart Peake had started on defense. Several others, including halfbacks Jimmy Carpenter and Glynn Gregory, tackles Rufus King and Homer Rosenbaum, and end Freddie Green, had accumulated considerable playing experience as the '54 Eagles had developed their habit of making sure the game was over by the end of the first half.

Moser realized he had some talent, but he was still experimenting as the season opener against the Scotties arrived. Starting '54 halfback Henry Colwell was listed as the starter at fullback for the Highland Park game. Junior Glynn Gregory, a quarterback in junior high and a varsity fullback as a sophomore, was penciled in at right halfback. Junior Jimmy Carpenter, small but very quick, was at left half. Moser felt this backfield gave him the best combination of speed and power.

Maybe even more than talent, the 1955 Eagles had confidence. The seniors had been sophomores when Moser arrived, and in their two seasons with him the Eagles had lost only three of 23 games. They had won a district championship and then a state championship. They didn't need any convincing that their coach knew what he was doing. They may have won a state championship but in the August two-a-days if Moser drilled them on fundamentals until their tongues hung out, fine. There had to be a reason for it. If he ran them ragged in the heat, fine. If he told them they had only one goal, and that was to beat Highland Park, they believed him. They were a gang, whether they knew it or not. Moser certainly did. For him, "Blackboard Jungle" merely became another talking point.

AT HIGHLANDER STADIUM it didn't take long for that confidence to show up. At the half, it was 27-0. Another touchdown, an 80-yard punt return by Henry Colwell, had been called back for clipping. The Scotties' offensive output at the half totaled 19 yards. In the press box, Dallas sports writers told Jack Holden of the *Reporter-News*: "Looks like you've got another winner on your hands." The victory also kept intact Moser's string of victories in 11 opening games as a head coach.

Moser spoke frankly: "The game didn't help our first team much, but it did our second string. It helped our reserves a lot." All 32 Eagles on the traveling squad played in the game.

The coach said his offense appeared "more consistent" than at the same time a year before. The Eagles moved 45 yards to their first touchdown with three runs and a 27-yard pass from Bourland to Carpenter. Colwell, running from fullback, got the score on a seven-yard run.

Their second score came three minutes later, on Colwell's 29-yard burst behind a downfield block by end Freddie Green.

Touchdown No. 3, in the second quarter, featured Colwell's 32-yard run that ended when the ball came out of his hands, bounced, and came back to him. He was tackled at the five, and right half Gregory got the touchdown on the next play with 4:25 left in the half.

The Eagle defense sent Highland Park three-and-out and scored again just as the half ended on a 24-yard run by senior James Welch, in for Colwell at fullback. Welch had another long gain of 21 yards in the drive and he also was starting to run his way into Moser's thinking. He appeared to be an up-and-coming late bloomer. As a junior, Welch had nevertheless started the 1954 season on the B team, then made it onto the varsity late in the season. Now he was running with speed and authority against Highland Park, and Moser started thinking.

The Eagles scored again early in the third period on Carpenter's five-yard run. The touchdown was set up by a 32-yard pass from Bourland to Green. For the game, Bourland connected on six of 9 passes for 96 yards and Moser was pleased.

"We've worked a lot on passing," he said. "We know you can't win tough ball games without it."

Defensively, Moser named a lot of stars in the group that held the Scots to 116 yards total offense, including Stuart Peake, Elmo Cure, Sam Caudle, Freddie Green, Boyd King, Gregory and Carpenter.

If the Scotties hadn't given the Eagle first team much of a challenge, Moser knew that would be coming soon.

"I'm sure they'll learn more from the Sweetwater game," he said.

Abilene 34, Highland Park 0
Sept. 9, 1955

Sept. 16, 1955

THE EAGLES' 1955 HOME OPENER was against Sweetwater. Fair Park Stadium in ordinary light didn't look like much. It was bleachers on either side of a field. But on Friday nights in autumn, it looked different. And on Friday, Sept. 16, 1955, it looked like the home of the state champion Abilene Eagles, and there wasn't a finer stadium to be had.

The Victory Bell was in place and ringing before sundown. This was the first regular season home game for the Eagles to have the bell after winning the district championship in 1954, and the sound of it transformed the place. The bell sat on the sideline in front of the Abilene student section at the south end of the east side. When the Eagles came out of the field house, they entered the field at the corner in front of the Abilene student section, where sat students and the 100-plus-member Eagle Band. At the north end was the visiting student section and in the middle, between the 30s, was a buffer zone of adult reserved seating. Reserved seats were $1.50.

The strip between the east sideline and the fence separating the field from the bleachers was very narrow, not nearly wide enough to accommodate a team bench. So the two team benches were both on the west side, the Eagles at the south end and visitors at the north. The west side bleachers were all reserved seating. Views of the action from this side could be sliced by the middle two of four thick utility poles on which the light standards were mounted. Ordinary capacity at Fair Park Stadium was about 11,000, on wood plank seating affixed to a spidery steel substructure. If a cold north wind blew through Fair Park Stadium, there was no escape from it. The press-box was at the top of the west bleachers. Parking was in dirt lots behind either end zone and east of the stadium in the Fair Park area.

The field itself was beautiful and beautifully maintained. It was crowned in the middle, for drainage, just like the fields in the big cities. Every September before the beginning of the regular season, all the elementary school teams in the city came to the stadium and paired off in short scrimmages under the lights before a paying crowd. Proceeds from the event went to the West Texas Rehabilitation Center. Sixth-graders hunkered on the sidelines waiting to play were amazed by the depth of the thick green grass and by the fact that they couldn't see the opposite sideline. The field was higher in the middle, something they had never seen before.

~

SWEETWATER HAD NOT BEATEN Abilene in six years. The count was five losses and a tie.

It was a big deal, a big rivalry between two towns of similar size only 44 miles apart, a rivalry dating from 1911. It didn't matter that Abilene after the war had grown more than Sweetwater, and that the Eagles played in Class AAAA and the Mustangs in AAA. There was nobody the Mustangs wanted to beat in 1955 more than they wanted to beat Abilene.

In Sweetwater, Sept. 16 was declared officially, "Beat Abilene Day." On Thursday, there was a parade and a pep rally in downtown Sweetwater. On Friday there was another pep rally. More than 1,500 fans drove the 44 miles to the game at Fair Park Stadium. Many of them were still finding their seats when on the first play of the game Eagle fullback Henry Colwell took a handoff on a power play at left tackle, broke into the clear and ran 76 yards for a touchdown.

Four minutes later right half Glynn Gregory took the ball on the belly play at left tackle and went 36 yards to the end zone. The Eagles added 21 more points in the second quarter and at the half led, 33-0, after second-string quarterback Harold "Hayseed" Stephens scored on a three-yard keeper 1:10 before the half.

Abilene, wearing new gold jerseys for the first time, had gained 241 yards in the first half, running mainly at the right side of the Mustangs' defensive line. End Freddie Green, tackle Rufus King and guard Stuart Peake, the left side of the Eagles' offensive line, ripped open huge holes for Colwell, Gregory and left halfback Jimmy Carpenter, while the right side—Sam Caudle, Homer Rosenbaum and Jerry Avery—hustled downfield to cut down secondary defenders. It was a simple formula of speed and technique.

A FEW SWEETWATER FANS went to their cars, looked forlornly at the red and white crepe paper streaming from radio antennas, and made an early start home. Others stayed and saw the game Mustangs under new coach Elwood Turner (hired away from Class A Albany) crank up some offense in the second half against the Abilene substitutes. Sweetwater, led by halfback Harroll Hobbs, managed to put three touchdowns on the board, all scored by Hobbs, and the Mustangs actually gained more rushing yardage than Abilene in the second half, 109-89.

But the Eagles added two more scores of their own and the final score was 45-20. Moser had said his first team, hardly challenged by Highland Park, would "learn more from the Sweetwater game." Either the coach had been wrong, or the Eagles were so frighteningly good that they couldn't be challenged. Abilene had 23 first downs and 401 yards of total offense, including 330 on the ground. Sweetwater managed 223 total yards, most of that in the second half.

Maybe even a bigger story in Abilene High football on that Friday came out of Austin. Rhea H. Williams, director of the University Interscholastic League, announced new district lineups for the 1956-57 seasons. It placed Abilene in District 2-AAAA, with San Angelo, Odessa, Midland and Big Spring.

Going into District 3-AAAA were Amarillo, Borger, Lubbock High, Lubbock Monterey, Amarillo Palo Duro, Pampa and Plainview. After 1955, the long treks in the Eagle Bus to the Panhandle would be over.

Abilene 45, Sweetwater 20
Sept. 16, 1955

Sept. 30, 1955

EACH WEEK, ON THE FIRST PAGE of his scouting report, Chuck Moser wrote a short message to his team summarizing his thoughts about the upcoming game. On Monday, Sept. 26, the Eagles received their scouting reports and read Moser's message:

> *"Remember they beat us last year 35-14 and enjoyed rubbing it in the last quarter. They will tackle, block and be in perfect condition."*

The Eagles were coming off an open date. After Sweetwater, Moser would have preferred to play Port Arthur or somebody, some state power who could give him a better look at his team under real fire.

Instead, the Eagles scrimmaged each other and went to the movies on Friday night.

Then came Breckenridge.

It had been a year. The Buckaroos had come into Abilene and blown away the Eagles (actually the score had been 35-13), and in the process maybe had awakened a giant. The Eagles had not lost a game since that night, had won the state championship, and now carried a 12-game winning streak into the '55 game.

Breckenridge had won state also in 1954, in Class AAA, and the game between the two bitter rival state powerhouses was an 11,000-plus sellout at Fair Park Stadium. Because of a decline in enrollment, Breck had dropped from AAA to Class AA in the off-season, but that didn't matter much on the football field. The Buckies in any year never could put as many as 30 players on the field, but they were good players.

They included quarterback Bennett Watts, the dazzling architect of the Bucks' '54 triumph at Fair Park Stadium. Only one other Breckenridge starter returned, end Jerry Payne, but the presence of Watts alone was fearsome enough for Abilene fans who had seen that last game. Also missing from the Buckaroo sideline would be coach Joe Kerbel, who had left to become head coach at Amarillo High. Taking his place at Breckenridge was Emory Bellard.

Abilene returned only one starter, Henry Colwell, a halfback then and a fullback now. Other Eagles like Sam Caudle and Elmo Cure became starters later, but in the Breck game in '54, only Colwell was on the field for the first play of the game.

~

THE GAME WAS TANTALIZING. Breckenridge was Breckenridge, quick and hard-hitting and relentless, and the Eagles responded offensively with something less than aplomb. They lost five of seven fumbles.

Defensively, it appeared the Eagles couldn't do anything. On its opening drive, Breckenridge, running straight into the line, churned from its 21 into Eagle territory, and then Watts got loose on a 37-yard ramble for a touchdown. But the play was called back because Breckenridge was offsides.

"A mighty important penalty," said Eagle line coach Hank Watkins.

Finally the Eagle defense stiffened, but nobody in black and gold felt comfortable.

Abilene went up, 7-0, at the end of the first quarter when Colwell capped a 75-yard drive with a five-yard burst into the end zone. In the second quarter, right half Glynn Gregory got loose and ran 49 yards to the Breckenridge 10, where he was hit from behind and fumbled and the green shirts recovered. Once more before the half, Abilene was driving deep in Buckie territory when Colwell coughed it up at the six. At the half, it was still 7-0.

Abilene's defense, meanwhile, led by Caudle, Cure, end Stuart Peake, tackle Rufus King and guard Guy Wells, was coming together and gaining some revenge for the '54 embarrassment. In the second period, Breckenridge was poised at the Abilene 39. On third and 10, Eagle end Freddie Green, who had been ill during the week, caught fullback Bill Taylor for a four-yard loss. On fourth down, Watts hit Payne for a 13-yard gain to the 30, but a yard short of the first down as the Eagle secondary closed quickly.

The Buckies got the ball back and moved to the Abilene 21, but there time ran out in the first half. In the third period the Bucks moved once to the Eagle 21 and another time to the 28, but a fumble stopped one drive and the other ended on downs.

MIDWAY IN THE third period, the Eagles cranked up a drive from their 25 that ended when Colwell bolted 37 yards on a counter play into the end zone behind devastating blocking. Glynn Gregory missed the PAT and it was 13-0 with 2:49 remaining in the third period.

Breckenridge kept coming. In the fourth period, the Buckies drove from their 41 to Abilene's five, but there on fourth and three, the Eagles stopped them after a yard as the 11,000 fans screamed.

Abilene was driving at the Breckenridge 18 when the game ended. The circle begun on Oct. 1, 1954, had ended with the Eagles' 13th straight victory. Abilene had rushed for 304 yards, more than 50 yards better than the Buckies' total offense, but it was the defense that really won this game.

"That's what we needed," Moser said. "It'll help us."

Why so many fumbles?

"This was the first team we've played this year that hit so hard," Moser said. "Our kids just weren't used to it." The coach was grateful. Big, hard-hitting Odessa was only two weeks away.

"I think Odessa has the best chance of going undefeated," Moser said.

On their radios, driving home after the game, Abilenians learned that actor James Dean, star of the edgy new movie, "Rebel Without a Cause," had been killed in a car collision in California.

Abilene 13, Breckenridge 0
Sept. 30, 1955

Oct. 7, 1955

THE "BEAT ABILENE" THING was becoming something of a cause as District 1-AAAA play began against the Borger Bulldogs. It was not entirely because Abilene was a district opponent. It was a reaction, an awareness of the streak.

The Eagles left on Thursday and stopped for a practice in Childress. When they rolled into Borger, all of downtown was draped in red and white. On the marquee of the Borger Theater was the movie now playing: "One Night of Terror." Above that, the words, "Beat Abilene."

The team checked in at the Borger Hotel and saw in a display case a red-and-white Borger High School uniform. The desk clerk answered the phone: "Borger Hotel, beat Abilene." That night, traffic stretched a mile working its way toward a sold-out 5,000-seat stadium.

It helped that the Bulldogs were undefeated after three games, outscoring their opponents 85-20. Those were Abilene High-like numbers. The Bulldogs' strong ground game, led by halfbacks Eldon Wetsel and Gary Braden, had 1,111 yards in three games compared to 955 for the Eagles.

But then the game started and all the hopes and statistics disappeared into the autumn Panhandle breeze. Five different Eagle backs scored touchdowns. The Eagle defense surrendered a grand total of

88 yards to the Bulldog rushing attack. The Bulldogs did score in the second period after recovering an Abilene fumble at the Eagle 26.

AND THAT WAS a problem. After losing five fumbles to Breckenridge, the Eagles lost four more to the Bulldogs. Like the Buckies, the Bulldogs were game and hard-hitting. Apparently the Eagles still weren't used to getting hit hard. And Odessa was next over the horizon.

Moser used the same backfield that had senior Henry Colwell at fullback and juniors Jimmy Carpenter and Glynn Gregory at left and right halfs respectively. But during the game Moser continued to fool around with a lineup that put hard-running senior James Welch at fullback, Gregory at left half, and Colwell at right half. That combination provided more size and seniority without giving up much in speed.

Gregory got the Eagles' first touchdown on a 17-yard run in the first period. Quarterback David Bourland snuck a yard later in the first quarter and Colwell tallied on a nine-yard score in the second period. Borger quarterback Bob Page got the TD following the Abilene fumble in the second quarter.

Borger returned the fumble favor, Eagle guard Guy Wells recovering at the Bulldog 13 in the third quarter. Carpenter quickly scored and it was 28-6. Abilene's final score came on a 32-yard pass from second-string quarterback Harold "Hayseed" Stephens to 149-pound sub fullback Charles Bradshaw.

The final was 35-6, and the streak stood at 14. Abilene had 246 yards rushing and 83 passing. Borger's total offense was 194 yards. But Moser was looking mainly at one number: four fumbles lost.

"We can't make any mistakes and beat Odessa," he said.

Abilene 35, Borger 6
Oct. 7, 1955

Oct. 14, 1955

ON MONDAY CHUCK MOSER handed out the Odessa scouting report with stars all over it connoting Bronchos who were outstanding at their positions.

Then he told the Eagles that against Borger, and Breckenridge, they had looked sloppy. When he was unhappy, a look came onto Moser's face that was not anger or disappointment, but sort of a facial shrug, an ultimatum. It said: "If you don't do this thing, then that thing will happen."

The Eagles knew what it meant. Moser was going to make sure they did "this," so "that" didn't happen. And "this" always meant fundamentals. To Chuck Moser, football was a simple game. Hustling, blocking, tackling, hitting, precision. On the practice field, as Moser was making sure they did "this," other specific problems like fumbling and sloppiness just sort of went away.

"We worked hard on fundamentals this week," Moser told the *Reporter-News* in what the players would call classic understatement.

The Abilene-Odessa game was the highlighted game statewide, featured even over the Tyler-Corpus Christi Ray battle of unbeatens because it was a district contest. Abilene was top-ranked in the state, followed by Tyler and Wichita Falls, and Odessa was No. 4. The Eagle-Broncho winner was in the driver's seat to win the District 1-AAAA championship and advance to the playoffs.

Odessa was unbeaten but had been tied, 7-7, by mighty Port Arthur in the season's first game. Odessa would easily be the biggest, most physical team that Abilene had faced.

"The Odessa boys look like giants," said Eagle assistant coach and scout Wally Bullington.

In practice, Moser made the change he had been thinking about. He put 164-pound James Welch in as the starting fullback, moved Glynn Gregory from right half to left, and made Henry Colwell the starting right halfback.

⁂

AT 4:30 ON FRIDAY afternoon, a special train, 22 cars long, pulled into the T&P Depot from Odessa. Fans, band and students in red and white poured out of the train and streamed northward, across North First Street into downtown Abilene.

"Beat Abilene!" they yelled, so loud that it was hard to hear. They blew horns and waved red and white banners. At North Third and Cypress, pep squad leaders gathered about 1,000 Broncho boosters together for a spontaneous pep rally. Abilene police re-routed traffic and even escorted the throng as it moved up Cypress and across North Fourth to Pine Street where another rally broke out in front of the Hotel Windsor, Odessa team headquarters.

At one point an Odessa student looked around and said, "I don't see anybody from Abilene." Eventually the crowd broke into smaller groups that packed every café, cafeteria and drug store soda fountain, and the cheering went on until it was time to head for the stadium. Authorities said more than 12,000 tickets were sold for the game.

At the stadium, something happened that was almost impossible to believe. Abilene beat the Bronchos, 47-0. Everyone from Port Arthur to Amarillo knew that Odessa High School, state finalists in 1953, had a very good football team, fourth-ranked in the state, with a decades-long tradition of pride and competitiveness. Now hearing the score, people looked at each other and wondered: if Odessa is all that, what is Abilene? Across Texas that night and the next morning, the Eagles earned something that not even a state championship and a winning streak could provide. When they beat Odessa, 47-0, the Eagles acquired an aura.

⁂

THE EAGLES' FIRST PLAY of the game made perfect sense, as if the whole week had been scripted toward it. The Bronchos had roared into town, roared onto the field, roared downfield on the kickoff and lined up ready to roar into the Eagle backfield. Quarterback David

Bourland took the snap, dropped back three steps, and on came the Odessa giants, eyes as red as their jerseys.

Bourland slipped the ball into the grasp of the new starting fullback, Welch, on the draw play. Welch burst immediately into the clear between the charging linemen and went 75 yards behind numerous downfield blocks thrown smartly and fundamentally. He outran the last defender, speedy Odessa halfback Leroy Scott, and Abilene was up, 7-0, with less than a minute gone in the game.

It was the only score of the first quarter and Odessa might have found its wind. But Abilene scored 20 points in the second quarter and 20 more in the third. The Eagles made 27 first downs and rushed for 483 yards. Welch alone, in his first start, accounted for 233 yards and scored twice more on runs of six and 37 yards. The new backfield lineup of Welch, Gregory and Colwell accounted for almost 400 yards and five touchdowns. Bourland got a long score in the third period with a 75-yard punt return. And the Eagles only lost one fumble.

Odessa finished with 29 yards rushing and 148 passing, but 66 of those passing yards came on the last play of the game and carried to the Abilene five. Until that last pass, Odessa's deepest second-half penetration into Eagle territory was the 43.

Now it was the Eagles' turn to release emotion. They were relatively quiet, normally, after a game, but now they were bouncing off the ceiling of their locker room in the stone field house.

"It's the first time this year they've really been elated," Moser said. "They played one of the most nearly perfect games I've ever seen. Never in my coaching career have I had a team that made so few mistakes."

Moser said the draw play to Welch on the game's opening play was in fact chosen to take advantage of Odessa's eagerness. And it stung the Bronchos, he thought, to the extent that they never recovered.

In the press box, scouts for the Pampa Harvesters gathered up their papers and headed down the stadium steps to the parking lot. Nobody interviewed them; it would have been interesting to hear what they had to say.

The 22-car train departed the T&P Depot for Odessa at 11 p.m., its low rumble the only noise of any kind downtown at that hour.

Abilene 47, Odessa 0
Oct. 14, 1955

Oct. 21, 1955

SUCH WAS THE SHOCK in Odessa—the Bronchos had been fourth-ranked!—that on Monday night the Broncho Booster Club at its regular meeting gave the Odessa coaches a "vote of confidence" and a standing ovation.

That, wrote Spec Gammon of the *Odessa American*, "should squelch out-of-town rumors that Odessans are ready to fire Cooper Robbins. When a ball club loses one like Odessa did to Abilene, the rumors start circulating, but fast.

"A father of one of the players," Gammon wrote, "got up at the meeting and said that his son had told him in effect: 'It wasn't the coaches' fault; we boys just didn't have the ability to play a team as good as Abilene.' "

In Pampa, the coaches and players had a week to think about the information the Harvester scouts brought back from the Abilene-Odessa game.

It took only four plays to convince them the scouts hadn't made any of it up.

Of the Eagles' first four plays from scrimmage, three went for touchdowns.

Pampa took the opening kickoff and punted to the Eagle 44. Quarterback David Bourland on the Eagles' first play hit right half Henry Colwell for 28 yards to the Harvester 28. On the next play Bourland dropped back again but this time handed the ball to left half Glynn Gregory, circling around on the Statue of Liberty play. Gregory went untouched to the right corner of the end zone. Abilene 7, Pampa 0.

Pampa took the kickoff, couldn't move, and punted to the Abilene 22. Again Bourland faded to pass. This time he hit end Butch Adams running free at the Pampa 45. Adams, behind a clearing block from Colwell, went the rest of the way to complete the 78-yard scoring play. Abilene 14, Pampa 0.

~

PAMPA PUNTED AGAIN AFTER the kickoff and Abilene set up at its own 40. Gregory took a pitchout on a sweep around right end, guard Sammy Caudle and fullback James Welch threw key blocks, and Gregory went 60 yards for the touchdown. Abilene 21, Pampa 0. People were starting to calculate: If the Eagles got the ball back every three minutes, and took one or maybe two plays to score, what would the final score be?

The final score was a very respectable 40-12. It could have been worse, but an apparent 37-yard TD pass from Bourland to Colwell on the Eagles' fourth series was called back for clipping. The Eagles did get a fourth touchdown in the first quarter, when Bourland scrambled 23 yards to the end zone when he couldn't find a receiver. It was starting to look as if Moser had decided to use the game as a passing scrimmage.

At the half it was 34-0 (Gregory kicking all but one extra point) after Colwell's six-yard burst in the second quarter.

The Eagles threw one more chill into the calculators' hearts when on the second play of the second half, fullback Welch went straight up the middle, 76 yards to score. That made it 40-0, and the Eagles' first team and most of the second team was finished for the night.

If the intent was to work on the passing game, Moser must have felt satisfied. Bourland and his backup, Hayseed Stephens, completed six of 11 passes for 168 yards, an average of 28 yards per completion. The new starting backfield, with Gregory and Colwell the halfbacks and Welch the fullback, in its second game collected an aggregate of 294 rushing yards. Gregory by himself rushed for 129 yards on only three carries, an average of 43 yards per carry.

IT WAS GAUDY. And it was the last time the Eagles and Pampa would ever meet. With the 1956 season, Abilene would belong to the new District 2-AAAA, while Pampa, Borger, Amarillo, Lubbock, Plainview and the new Amarillo and Lubbock high schools would comprise new District 3-AAAA.

To Abilene coaches and, to some extent the players, it meant the end of what was essentially a three-day road trip to play one game of 48 minutes. The players, all ages 16 and 17, thought travel something of an adventure: two nights in a hotel and a day and a half out of school. The coaches saw it in terms of time. That's why many an assistant coach spent many pre-dawn hours on the winding, two-lane highways between the Panhandle and West Central Texas. They left in cars right after the game, to get back to Abilene and get started on the preparations for the coming week.

Pampa won the five-game series between the two schools. In 1951, the Harvesters massacred the Eagles, 46-7, and held Abilene to 37 yards rushing. In 1952, Pampa scored on a four-yard pass with 15 seconds left in the game to win, 13-7. In 1953, Chuck Moser's first year in Abilene, Pampa won, 7-6, on a cold, rainy Panhandle night.

In 1954, the Eagles finally broke through, pounding the Harvesters, 41-7, in Abilene, a game that would become No. 3 in the Eagle winning streak.

And now, in Harvester Stadium in 1955, it was Abilene 40, Pampa 12. With its two victories in this new Chuck Moser era, Abilene had seized the scoring edge, 101-85. After the evening of Oct. 21, 1955, Harvester fans were grateful it was no worse than that, and they were happy to see the Eagles go. Better to take your chances with Amarillo.

Abilene 40, Pampa 12
Oct. 21, 1955

Oct. 28, 1955

AFTER A SEASON like 1954, which included losses like 47-0 to Abilene, the Amarillo Sandies went looking for a new coach.

They got Joe Kerbel.

Kerbel, whose Breckenridge Buckaroos had beaten Abilene, 35-13, in that same 1954 season.

Kerbel was a great coach and Chuck Moser knew it. Kerbel always gave Moser trouble. That's the way it was among coaches. Moser could have a six-and-oh powerhouse with talent at every position, and Kerbel could have a three-and-three team heavy with sophomores and juniors, and Moser knew Kerbel would give him trouble. In the life of any coach, there were always one or two other coaches who somehow leeched away that coach's confidence.

And the players knew it. It created a tension during practices that was not quite fear but more of a nagging sense of doubt, that things could go wrong, contrary to their best preparations and their faith in their coach. If anybody could beat Chuck Moser, it was Joe Kerbel. He had, after all, been the last to do it.

So when it was 7-7 at the end of the first quarter in Abilene, people on the Abilene side had reason to wonder if the hex was in. Abilene had scored on its opening drive, but here were the young Sandies, playing with the quickness and tenacity that were trademarks of Kerbel teams. It was the first time in 1955 that any team had been in a tie score with Abilene after the first touchdown of the game. Their first score followed an interception of a David Bourland pass at the Eagle 43.

Kerbel's game plan was to be aggressive. After their tying TD with three minutes left in the first quarter, the Sandies tried an on-sides kick. It worked, when Eagle end Freddie Green fumbled his attempt to field the ball and the Sandies' Lynn Lafon recovered at the Eagle 34. As fans tried not to think about Breckenridge, Amarillo moved smartly to the Eagle four.

There the Eagles held. Staying on the ground, Abilene moved to the Amarillo 35, then stalled. The Sandies likewise couldn't move, and Gene Cox punted to Bourland at the Eagle 16. Bourland made it to the right sideline, turned upfield, and behind blocks by the King boys, Rufus and Boyd, and Guy Wells, Bourland sprinted 84 yards to score.

AT THE HALF, it was 14-7. Midway in the third quarter it was 14-13, after another Eagle mistake. Green was involved again, this time as the punter. The Sandies blocked the kick, the first block against an Eagle team since Moser had become coach. End Tommy Pace broke through and reached the kick, and then Travis Columbus scooped up the ball at the Abilene 34 and carried it to the Eagle one.

Halfback Keith Lafon scored on the next play and the PAT was no good. The Kerbel aggressiveness had created three Abilene mistakes and the young Sandies were very much in the game against a superior team.

But here the superiority could be suppressed no longer. The Eagles set up at their 25 after the kickoff and started ripping off chunks of yardage. Glynn Gregory collected 15, then fullback James Welch 22, then Gregory for 16, and very quickly Gregory was going the final 10 for the touchdown that made it 21-13 at the end of the third quarter.

Early in the fourth, right half Henry Colwell bolted 46 yards to the goal line but fumbled there when he was hit and Amarillo recovered in the end zone. No matter. Abilene quickly got the ball back and Gregory took off over right tackle on the belly play, 69 yards for his third touchdown of the night to make it 28-13 with 9:55 remaining.

Amarillo, with a 35-yard burst from fullback Roy Northrup, drove to the Eagle 28 before giving up the ball on downs. A series later, Abilene drove 66 yards as Bourland collected the last yard and Gregory kicked his fifth extra point. The final score was 35-13, same as Kerbel had done to Moser and the Eagles the year before.

IT WAS A JITTERY GAME despite the statistics. The Eagles finished with 20 first downs and 444 yards rushing to totals of eight and 92 for Amarillo. Gregory scored three touchdowns, kicked five extra points and ran for 220 yards on 14 carries. Colwell had 114 yards rushing and Bourland, atoning for his early interception, scored twice, on the long punt return and the fourth-quarter sneak. Moser of course was pleased.

"I don't believe we've had a better running game all year," he said. "I was real proud of the kids. I think we expect too much of them sometimes, but they did a fine job in the second half when the pressure was on."

For a change, many of the Eagle starters played most of the game, on offense and defense. They included guard and linebacker Sammy Caudle, center and linebacker Elmo Cure, guard and end Stuart Peake, end Freddie Green, who was the leading tackler, the King boys, and Colwell, Gregory and Bourland.

Moser also pointed out something else, and that was the Eagles' own tenacity.

"They're dangerous," he said. "We lost yards on two straight plays against Amarillo and then scored from 53 yards out on the third one."

Moser said that after seven games the Eagles were a stronger offensive team than the '54 state champions but a little weaker defensively.

"We made fewer mistakes last year," he said.

Like Pampa, this was the Eagles' last district game against Amarillo. This time it was the Abilene fans who were glad to see Joe Kerbel out of their lives. But the Eagles would meet the Sandies and Kerbel again, in a storied game a little farther down the line.

Abilene 35, Amarillo 13
Oct. 28, 1955

Nov. 12, 1955

PIETY WAS A STRONG FEATURE in West Texas thinking, and it had found a particular focus in Abilene, where there was a church for every 100 people, and three denominational colleges: Hardin-Simmons, operated by the Baptists; McMurry, operated by the Methodists; and Abilene Christian, operated by the Church of Christ. The "Western Parson," who hosted an after-school show for kids, was a local TV celebrity.

Much of this attitude had been imported with the early Texas settlers from the South, who brought along their Christian fundamentalism, and it was reinforced by living in a region where God's stern hand was so evident in the lay of the land and the extremes of the heavens.

It was not an environment in which to gloat or to tease fate. Safer all around to be tough as a boot but meek as a lamb, and on this principle was the culture grounded. That his own thinking passed through this cultural filter is the only way to explain the first paragraph of *Reporter-News* sport editor Jack Holden's column of Oct. 30, 1955:

"Things began to tighten up in Abilene's conquest of a second straight District 1-AAAA title here Friday night, and the Eagle coaches say it's a foretaste of more bad medicine."

He was writing about an Abilene Eagle team that in four District 1-AAAA games had scored 157 points while allowing 31; and had amassed 1,815 yards of total offense and 71 first downs, while giving up 623 total yards and 29 first downs.

And it wasn't just the sportswriter. Holden quoted Chuck Moser, who taught Sunday school at St. Paul Methodist Church, as saying the Eagles hadn't met a tough test yet.

"Our three toughest games are yet to come," he said.

The first, after an open date, was in Lubbock, against the 5-2 Westerners, on Saturday, Nov. 12.

"In the Westerners," Holden wrote, "Abilene may find another tough cookie."

The score in Lubbock on Saturday was 62-7.

LUBBOCK WAS A VERY GOOD team, anchored by the best player on the field that day, 205-pound tackle E.J. Holub, who later would be All-American with Texas Tech and All-Pro with the Kansas City Chiefs.

Holub was so tough that Eagle left guard Sammy Caudle broke his helmet blocking him.

But it wasn't the first helmet that Caudle, who played like a missile, had broken. In fact broken helmets was an ongoing problem for the Abilene team managers. Moser taught his players who to block and how to block them, and if the helmets couldn't hold up, the Eagles didn't use it as an excuse not to knock people down.

In the *Reporter-News* Sunday sports section was a panoramic photo of the Lubbock game, taken from the press box, with a dotted line showing the route of the runner, in the style of the day. The photo shows fullback James Welch loose in the Lubbock secondary, having run through a hole that was, as they say, the size of a Mack truck, with E.J. Holub nowhere to be seen. Downfield are three Lubbock defenders and zeroing in on each one is a gold helmeted Eagle blocker. It is an exact living re-creation of the play as it was drawn on the blackboard.

Covering the game that afternoon for the *Reporter-News* was news editor Dick Tarpley. His stature didn't necessarily mean it was the day's top game. The *Reporter-News* was a true regional newspaper, with a circulation area of about 100 miles in all directions from Abilene. Within that area were dozens of high schools, from Class B to Class AAA, and almost all of their games received at least two or three paragraphs in the Saturday or Sunday morning paper. The *Reporter-News* sports department on a Friday night particularly was a busy place to be. News reporters earned overtime taking calls from stringers or coaches from Ranger to Big Spring, from Brady to Seymour.

And of course the paper staffed the big games of the week. Additionally, all three colleges—the Hardin-Simmons Cowboys, the Abilene Christian Wildcats, and the McMurry Indians—had Saturday games, usually in the afternoon. A six-man sports staff became stretched thin.

SO TARPLEY FILLED THE HOLE at Lubbock, and he was good. He loved sports, particularly football, and wrote the occasional locker room story after an Eagles' game. But he was a newsman first and more objective in organizing his material than a pure sports writer might have been. When a story contains more information than will organize itself into an easy narrative (you never want to make the reader work too hard), the reporter will simply offer a list, called "bullets," of all the things that happened.

Faced with the gluttony at Lubbock, Tarpley wrote several summarizing paragraphs ("Abilene's merciless Eagles ground out a lusterless 62-7 rout"), then with the simple declaration, "Here's how the scoring went," he bulleted the game quarter by quarter.

Senior halfback Henry Colwell scored four touchdowns, junior halfback Jimmy Carpenter scored twice, and quarterback David Bourland threw for two scores. It was 35-0 at the half and when the Eagles scored on their first possession of the second half, Moser cleared the bench.

It set up Abilene's annual battle with the Midland Bulldogs with the winner being the favorite to ring up the District 1-AAAA championship and advance to the playoffs. It also seemed that every year God arranged it so that Abilene played a Saturday game before the Midland game, so Bulldog coach Tugboat Jones became committed to scout the Eagles personally. He was in fact on hand at Lubbock and was "non-committal," Tarpley reported, about Midland's chances against Abilene. Much of Jones' thinking, watching the game, must have been about his team's only loss, three weeks earlier, in district play. That was to Lubbock, 19-14.

Abilene 62, Lubbock 7
Nov. 12, 1955

Nov. 18, 1955

"This is a great ball club. They can throw, run wide, and run inside. They have lots of experience, size and speed. We must beat them to win the 'championship.' Their coach will moan all week about his little boys, all hurt, etc. He does it every week. Some teams have believed him and got beat."

IT WOULD HAVE BEEN INTERESTING after the Lubbock game to ask Midland coach Tugboat Jones which he thought would be the tougher job: stopping the Abilene offense, or moving against the Abilene defense.

Chuck Moser knew. The offensive numbers were gaudy and attracted most of the attention, but Moser knew and said as much that the Eagles were truly a defensive ballclub. Ends Stuart Peake and Freddie Green, guard Rufus King, tackles Homer Rosenbaum and Bufford Carr, linebackers Elmo Cure and Sam Caudle, and backs Glynn Gregory, Jimmy Carpenter and David Bourland were superior defensive football players who just happened to also play offense when Abilene had the ball.

Peake (who some would argue was the team's best player) and Caudle in particular were ferocious in their intent to get to the ballcarrier, and Gregory, Carpenter and Bourland were marvelous athletes with instincts and reflexes not often seen in a single player, much less three of them, in a high school secondary.

On Monday, Moser gave these athletes a scouting report developed from information brought back by assistant coaches B.L. "Blacky" Blackburn and Wally Bullington that showed all the opposition's offensive formations and plays run from those formations, along with tendencies based on down and distance. During the week these athletes watched at least one game film of the opposition. The coaches prepared a defensive game plan and in practice the defense put the plan into action against plays run by the scout team. There were two reasons why Abilene subs tended to play well in a game. One, they accumulated a lot of game experience in the second half. Two, they had to run plays full speed against this Eagle defense in practice. It was a hardening experience.

By Thursday these Eagle defenders knew the Midland offense almost as well as the Bulldogs did. Then on Friday night they ran onto the field with one of Moser's favorite commandments foremost in their minds: If you hit the other player really hard the first couple of plays, they won't play as hard for the rest of the game.

THIS WAS WHAT TUGBOAT JONES and the Bulldogs spent the week getting ready for and Friday night they came to Abilene followed by 1,000 fans wondering if this might be the year.

It wasn't.

Jones had the great fullback Wahoo McDaniel and a key to the game might be to keep the Abilene offense off the field. If the Bulldogs could stay close, they might have a chance at the end of the game.

It looked like it could work. Abilene always scored on its first drive and the Midland game was no exception. The Eagles went 55 yards. Gregory and fullback Jim Welch gouged out yardage and Bourland threw a pair of nine-yard passes, one to Welch and the other to halfback Henry Colwell. From the 20, Gregory took a handoff from Colwell on a reverse and scored easily. Gregory kicked the extra point.

Moser acknowledged that the reverse was a tribute to Midland's own strong defense. "We ran five reverses, scored on two of them, and had one called back," he said. "But they stopped a lot of our basic plays."

There was no Lubbock avalanche this time. Deep into the second quarter it was still 7-0. Midland in fact moved the ball, mostly on McDaniel's back, and was successful in keeping the Eagle offense off the field. Early in the second quarter Midland moved to the Abilene 24 where McDaniel lost a fumble. Then late in the second quarter, Abilene scored again, set up by Caudle's pass interception at the Bulldog 32. Gregory actually scored on a 13-yard run but it was called back by a penalty. Pretty soon the Eagles were at the Midland four, Gregory got the call again, but fumbled. The ball bounced across the goal line and was recovered by Eagle center Elmo Cure with an assist from tackle Homer Rosenbaum. Now it was 14-0 with 1:05 remaining in the first half.

THEN CAME THE KEY PLAY in the game and it involved McDaniel. He couldn't pick up the kickoff and Abilene's Welch recovered at the Midland 35. Gregory carried 29 yards to the six and a play later scored from the two with 10 seconds left in the half.

Abilene 21, Midland 0. Out the window went Jones' hopes for ball control. In the second half the Bulldogs and their left-handed quarterback Larry Cooper went to the pass. The Eagles intercepted four of them, two by Bourland, one by Caudle (giving him two for the night) and one by Carpenter. Bourland's first interception, in the third quarter at the Eagle 32, set in motion the Eagles' final touchdown. Gregory ran for 10 and Bourland hit Freddie Green with a 41-yard pass to the Bulldog four. From there Bourland scored on a quarterback keeper.

Midland got a touchdown in the fourth quarter on a four-yard pass from Cooper to end A.W. Hammock and was driving at the Abilene 10 as the game ended but by then the subs were in.

Game statistics showed that Jones at least had the right idea. The Eagles gained only 195 yards rushing, by far their lowest total of the season. First downs were even at 16 each. The difference was defense, of course, with the Eagles granting McDaniel his 105 yards on 22 carries, none of which originated anywhere near the goal line.

"We knew we couldn't stop them cold," Moser said. "We didn't try to. Midland made most of its yardage in the second half anyway."

Moser said linebacker Elmo Cure was assigned to go with McDaniel wherever he went. McDaniel's longest gain was 16 yards and he had another for 12 but most were the three or four-yard variety.

Midland tried 11 passes and the Eagles picked off five, four in the second half. The Bulldogs also lost two fumbles, both ironically by McDaniel. A greater team than Midland couldn't turn the ball over seven times against Abilene and expect to win.

Gregory was the game's leading rusher with 106 yards in only 12 carries, an 8.8 yards per carry average. McDaniel's average on 22 carries was less than five. All that work, and then the Eagles made it look so easy.

Next was San Angelo, six days away in the traditional Thanksgiving Day regular season finale. As the Eagles were beating Midland, the Bobcats beat Odessa, 27-26. San Angelo had only one district loss, to Midland, so it meant the Eagles were in a district championship game for the second week in a row.

Abilene 28, Midland 7
Nov. 18, 1955

Nov. 24, 1955

SAN ANGELO COACH BOB HARRELL wanted to beat Abilene in the worst way.

It wasn't Abilene that bothered him; it was his own pride, and Abilene's coach, Chuck Moser, his old rival from the Rio Grande Valley. Both coaches had come north in 1953 to revitalize programs. Moser obviously had done more than revitalize the Eagles. His teams had lost only three games in three years, had won a state championship, and brought a 19-game winning streak into the game with San Angelo.

Harrell had done well, too. Before his arrival in 1953, the orange and blue Bobcats had lost 18 straight games. In his first year the

Bobcats went 3-5-1; in his second they were 6-2-2; and the '55 Bobcats brought a 7-2 record into the Abilene game at Fair Park Stadium.

San Angelo had lost but once in District 1-AAAA, 35-27 to Midland six weeks earlier. Moser said if the Bobcats and Midland played again, San Angelo would probably win by a touchdown. If they could beat Abilene, the Bobcats would tie for the district championship and advance into the state playoffs. More than 2,000 San Angelo fans followed the team up U.S. 277 to Abilene, hoping for the best.

For the Abilene defense, it was going from thunder to lightning. Wahoo McDaniel had been the thunder; Marvin Lasater was the lightning. Lasater, a senior, was the district's total offense leader with 1,112 yards, almost twice that of McDaniel, who was second with 691 yards. The difference was Lasater's versatility. In six district games he had run for 663 yards and passed for 449 more. Lasater was also the district's leading scorer with 76 points: 12 touchdowns and four extra points.

Harrell had designed his offense around Lasater. In the starting lineups he was listed as a halfback. But when the Bobcats went into the spread formation, which was often, Lasater took the deep snap with the option to either run or throw. The Bobcats would also run unbalanced lines, a double wing and even the old single wing.

Lasater had great speed, as did his running mate, halfback Norman Marshall. Both could turn a 10.1 in the 100-yard dash. Moser said the Bobcats had "the fastest all-around squad in the district."

THANKSGIVING MORNING IN ABILENE was cool and sunny and almost tragic. Glynn Gregory's father, who operated a gasoline station, had gone to work early as usual, even on Thanksgiving Day. Later he called the house to wake Glynn up. His son answered the phone, but then his father heard nothing further. Mr. Gregory dialed again until the phone rang. Glynn answered.

"What happened to you?" said his father.

"I fainted," Glynn said. Then apparently he fainted again. His father heard a "plop" as he hit the floor. Mr. Gregory raced home and found his son's room filled with gas. A gas heater had gone out. He flung open windows and got his son outside and Glynn after a little while appeared okay. In the distance in the still morning the Victory Bell was already ringing at Fair Park Stadium.

The story got around the pressbox and by the middle of the second quarter the sports writers were joking that Gregory should get a jolt of gas before every game. By that point, three passes had been thrown in the game, one by Abilene and two by San Angelo. Gregory caught all three. Gregory intercepted Lasater's first pass of the game, in San Angelo's opening offensive series, and returned it from the Abilene 45 to the Bobcat 42. Three plays later, on fourth down from the San Angelo 36, Bourland sent Gregory on a play-action route through the line and deep and hit him for the Eagles' first touchdown.

Gregory also figured in the Eagles' second touchdown, taking a handoff, getting in trouble, and pitching out to the trailing fullback, James Welch, who went 24 yards for the score seconds into the second quarter.

After the kickoff, Lasater threw again and Gregory intercepted again, this time at the Bobcat 20. He returned it to the five, and on fourth down Bourland dived six inches for the touchdown to make it 21-0.

The good field position was significant because San Angelo came out with seven defenders stacked inside the Eagle ends. "Five men just can't block seven very well," Moser said.

YOU COULD LOOK AT the district statistics another way. At the top was Lasater with all those yards. But his was the only name from San Angelo among either the rushing or passing leaders.

Directly below him in the rushing statistics, meanwhile, were not one, not two, but three names from Abilene: Gregory, with 588 yards (on only 41 carries, a gaudy 14.3 average); Welch, also with

588 yards; and halfback Henry Colwell, with 442 yards. That was a rushing total of 1,618 yards. Among passing leaders, Lasater was No. 2 with 449 yards. Abilene's David Bourland was fifth with 345 yards but his completion percentage of .517 was 100 points better than Lasater's .414.

While Lasater dominated the individual statistics, Abilene's starting backfield had run and passed for 1,963 yards. It made a point about versatility. San Angelo had a lot of formations and one good player; Abilene had a few formations and a lot of good players.

The point was made again with bookend touchdowns on Abilene's first two plays in the second half. If San Angelo was going to stack the middle, then the Eagles would run wide. On Abilene's first play from scrimmage in the second half, Gregory took off on a sweep right behind blocks by Bourland and end Freddie Green and ran 56 yards to score. After the kickoff the Eagles recovered a San Angelo fumble at the Abilene 44. On the first play Colwell ran wide left on a reverse and followed blocks by tackle Homer Rosenbaum and ends Jerry Avery and Green 56 yards to score. Midway through the third quarter the Abilene subs came in and added to their experience.

"They're a great ballclub," said Harrell after the game. "They just had too many horses for us. They're all good." None of the San Angelo players could single out any one Eagle standout either. "They're all great," Lasater said.

Harrell said Lasater played a great game, "even with Eagles hanging on to him wherever he went." Lasater finished with 48 yards rushing and 136 yards passing, including an 11-yard pass to halfback Rudy Powell for the Bobcats' only score.

On the Eagles' side of the stone field house, Moser said to his team, "We've done what we started out to do, win 10 games. Do you want to quit now?" The Eagles' "NO!" could be heard outside above the ringing of the bell. Moser told his players to go home and enjoy the whole rest of the Thanksgiving holiday weekend. "You've earned it," he said.

In the pressbox, Abilene and El Paso representatives met for a coin toss. Abilene lost. The Eagles would travel the 444 miles to El Paso to meet El Paso High in the first round of the state playoffs.

Abilene 35, San Angelo 6
Nov. 24, 1955

Dec. 3, 1955

ON MONDAY AT THE BEGINNING of his chalktalk, Chuck Moser told his team that any player who so much as cracked a smile during practice that week would not make the trip to El Paso.

"We're dead serious about this game," he said. He said it without breaking into a grin of his own, and it was that kind of commitment that set him apart as a coach.

No one smiled that day, or for the rest of the week when Moser was around, but everyone in the community knew what the score was. Even Moser told the Eagle Booster Club that Abilene should beat the El Paso High Tigers, "if we take the game seriously." In a non-district game early in the season San Angelo had seriously beaten the Tigers, 59-0. Just looking at comparative scores, it meant Abilene was 88 points better than El Paso.

A year earlier, the 1954 Eagles had beaten Austin High, the El Paso bi-district representative, 61-0. The sports writers called District 1-AAAA the "Little Southwest Conference." They called El Paso's District 2-AAAA the district that had to play the Little Southwest Conference in the bi-district round of the state playoffs. El Paso officials had become so weary of the annual maulings that after Abilene's 61-0 triumph in 1954, the school board fired every head coach at every high school in the district.

The Associated Press reported: "The changes followed comment in El Paso newspapers concerning the need of measures to strengthen schoolboy football in the city. The district has been traditionally weak in football for years. The last El Paso school to win a bi-district football clash was El Paso, which upset Lubbock in 1949."

Named new head coach at El Paso High was former assistant Jack Marcello. In a nine-game 1955 season, the Tigers had gone 6-3. They seemed to catch fire after beating archrival EP Austin, the defending district champion, 14-13, in October. They walloped their last three opponents by a combined score of 139-21, including a 73-0 thrashing of El Paso Burges (a brand new high school playing its first season of football) in the regular-season finale.

The Tigers had size going for them with three defensive linemen of 200 pounds or more. They would line up, Marcello said, against an Eagle offensive front that was "only mediocre" from tackle to tackle.

THE EAGLES MISSED SOME VALUABLE practice time because of icy rains at midweek.

The team departed the Abilene airport at noon Friday in two chartered DC-3s for the long flight to El Paso. At Midland they hit turbulence, blowing dust and 80-mph headwinds. One plane managed to fly above it, but the other, with the starting team aboard, had a rough ride. *Reporter-News* photographer Don Hutcheson, a veteran of the Army Air Corps in World War II, called it one of the toughest trips he could remember since the war.

Several Eagles became airsick. Guard Sam Caudle became sick so fast that he didn't have time to remove his partial dentures before throwing up into the airsickness bag. Somewhere in there was Caudle's bridgework and he had no choice but to fish it out.

(Oddly, another Eagle flight to El Paso three years later made front-page news. The 1958 team flew, again in two chartered DC-3s, to meet Ysleta High in bi-district. Over Big Spring, the second of the Eagle planes, carrying the subs, was in a near-miss with an Air Force fighter jet taking off from Webb Air Force Base. The Eagles' pilot saw the jet, cut all the power in both engines, rolled left and dropped about 1,000 feet to avoid the collision. The pilot estimated the two planes missed each other by 25 feet. The worst injury on the Eagle plane was a sprained ankle.)

The weather in El Paso was cool and sunny on Saturday for the 14,000 who jammed R.R. Jones Stadium for the 2 p.m. kickoff. It got cooler for Tiger fans in a hurry. The Tigers won the toss, couldn't move after the kickoff and punted to the Abilene 49. On the Eagles' first play, halfback Henry Colwell took a belly handoff through left tackle between blocks by end Freddie Green and tackle Rufus King. Colwell cut back and ran 51 yards to score. Hutcheson took a photo of Colwell breaking clear behind tackle Homer Rosenbaum's downfield block, and Colwell was not smiling. He looked very serious. El Paso punted again after the kickoff, this time to the Abilene 43. On the first play Gregory took the belly handoff through right tackle between blocks by end Jerry Avery and tackle Homer Rosenbaum and ran 57 yards to score.

THE RACE WAS ON. At the end of the first quarter the score was 34-0. Abilene had run eight offensive plays. At the half it was 48-0 and it was okay for the Eagles to smile.

Gregory and Colwell scored two touchdowns apiece, one of Colwell's on a 60-yard punt return in the first quarter. Sophomore fullback Bill Sides also scored twice, halfback Jimmy Carpenter got one score and subs Butch Adams and Charles Bradshaw got TDs in the second half, Bradshaw's on an intercepted pass. The Eagles' starting quarterback, David Bourland, didn't throw a pass. His substitute, junior Harold "Hayseed" Stephens, threw three, completing two, one for the touchdown to Adams.

The Tigers managed 149 yards rushing, most of it in the second half, but had three of 12 passes intercepted and completed only three for 38 yards. El Paso's deepest penetration was the Abilene 26 in the fourth quarter.

In the second half, third-string fullback Reyes Diaz, a favorite with his fellow players, had a chance to shine. Diaz, short and stocky, was fun to watch because he knew only one direction: straight ahead. He bulled for 40 yards on five carries as the sideline cheered him on.

After the game, Moser won a coin toss with Dallas Sunset coach Byron Rhome, whose Bison had defeated Ft. Worth Paschal, 16-7, in a Friday night bi-district game. Abilene and Sunset would meet in Abilene on Saturday at 2 p.m. in the state semifinals. The Eagles bussed to the airport, got back on the two DC-3s, and had a smooth flight home.

Abilene 61, El Paso High 0
Dec. 3, 1955

Dec. 10, 1955

IN DECEMBER OF 1955, THE game was still bigger news than the streak. The Eagle faithful in Abilene were more concerned about beating Dallas Sunset in the state semifinals than in the team winning its 22nd game in a row.

The playoffs had a different feeling in 1955. In 1954, being in the playoffs had been a novelty, and even if the Eagles had lost, it would hardly be the end of the world after such a fine season.

But then the Eagles won the state championship. They were the big-city high school football champions of Texas! In a culture where state regulations had been created to stop illegal recruiting of high school football players, this was a very important achievement in the community. It put Abilene on the map the same way Dwight Eisenhower put Denison on the map. The community wanted to enjoy that feeling again. Knowing the feeling, knowing it was there, was what put the pressure on in 1955. The possibility of losing to Dallas Sunset, and thus losing a shot at a second state championship, was far worse than the possibility of the streak being stopped at 21.

In fact in his Saturday morning advance story for the game, Jack Holden of the *Reporter-News* wrote 15 inches about the Sunset game's significance before mentioning the streak. And then he got confused. "The Eagles are after victory No. 21," he wrote.

In the game story itself on Sunday, Holden never mentioned the streak. Of course he had more important stuff to write about. Abilene's 33-6 victory put the Eagles into the state championship game again, against the powerful, undefeated Tyler Lions.

SUNSET WAS A STRONG team, with an 11-1 record, and an unusual one because it ran the antiquated single wing offense. By the 1950s, so few teams ran the single wing that defensing it was difficult to teach in one week. It turns out the Bison could have beaten Abilene, so long as Abilene played its second string throughout. Early in the third quarter at Fair Park Stadium, on a chilly but clear Saturday afternoon, Sunset smartly drove 73 yards against the Eagles' second-string defense for a touchdown to cut Abilene's lead to 27-6. Moser sent his first string defense back in after that, a team that Sunset couldn't beat.

It was an interesting turn of events. With the exception of the Amarillo and Midland games, no one ever saw the Abilene first string offense or defense playing in the second half. There is no answer to the question, "How good were the 1955 Abilene Eagles?" Almost half of their potential performance was missing. Like Holden said about El Paso, the score could have been 80-0 if Moser had let the first string play the entire game. Actually, potentially, it could have been 96-0, if the Eagles in the second half maintained the pace that had brought them a 48-0 halftime lead. Likewise the potential Sunset score would have been 54-0. After 12 games, the Eagles would have outscored their opposition, 630 points to 38, and in rushing alone the Eagle starting backfield would have had nearly 6,000 yards.

But then they would have been despised. As it was, they were simply awesome. In the second quarter at Fair Park Stadium, with the score already 14-0, Sunset had to punt from its own 45. In the pressbox, a Dallas sportswriter wondered why the Bison bothered to punt at all. "They (the Eagles) can score as easy from the 5 as they can from the 50," he said.

The Sunset punt went out of bounds at the Eagle 5. The Eagles then drove 95 yards to their third touchdown. Fullback James Welch did most of the damage with 53 yards in the drive.

WELCH WAS THE GAME'S leading rusher with 101 yards on 19 carries and he scored four touchdowns, once again demonstrating the Eagles' offensive versatility. Welch had hardly been unproductive, but he hadn't made headlines since the 47-0 thrashing of Odessa on Oct. 14. Now here he was again, his fullback position singled out by Moser and his scouts as the key to the winning strategy against Sunset. Sunset ace Robert Robinson, meanwhile, the tailback in the single wing, came into the game with 1,207 yards in 11 games. Against the Eagles, Robinson gained 72 yards before leaving the game with broken ribs in the third period.

The game's longest and prettiest play was an 83-yard touchdown pass from quarterback David Bourland to halfback Glynn Gregory in the first quarter. Gregory caught the ball at the 50 and outran three defenders to the goalline.

In the game, both Gregory, with 59 yards rushing and Henry Colwell, with 70, went over the 1,000-yard mark for the season. Welch's 101 yards brought his season total to 911.

The game's turning point?

"When we walked on the field, I guess," said Sunset coach Byron Rhome.

In the other state semifinal, the Tyler Lions shut out Baytown, 20-0, to remain undefeated. The Lions had three players of all-state quality, led by quarterback Charles Milstead. A Tyler-Abilene clash, long anticipated in statewide media, was now a reality.

In the stone field house after the Sunset game, Moser told his players how tough Tyler would be. "We'll be lucky to beat them," he said. He asked his players where they wanted to play. There would be a coin toss, but not for home-and-home, where stadiums couldn't handle a crowd expected to be 20,000 or more. Their choices were Fort Worth or Dallas. They said Fort Worth, the city "Where the West Begins." Both cities had more than one large stadium, but it was foregone that the game would be played either in the 73,000-seat Cotton Bowl in Dallas or Amon Carter Stadium, Texas Christian University's home field, in Fort Worth, that would seat 37,000.

On Sunday morning, Moser, Abilene Superintendent A.E. Wells, Abilene High assistant principal Alex Edwards, and school board trustee Morgan Jones Jr., flew to Love Field in Dallas in a West Texas Utilities Co. plane. There they met Tyler coach Buck Prejean and Tyler Superintendent Hollis Moore. Abilene won the coin toss. Moser selected Amon Carter Stadium as the site of the 1955 Class AAAA state championship game between the Abilene Eagles and the Tyler Lions.

Abilene 33, Dallas Sunset 6
Dec. 10, 1955

Dec. 17, 1955

"We are playing a great ball club. Let's make History—win two state championships for ABILENE in A ROW. Everyone do his part this week."

DURING THE WEEK IN THE statewide media, Abilene was established as a one-touchdown favorite over Tyler, and the feeling was that it would be something like 21-14, based on the Eagles' power to score. Moser himself felt that way. For several weeks he had been telling his coaches (but no one else) that the 1955 Eagles were the best offensive team he ever saw.

"If we can hold them to two touchdowns," Moser told the Eagle Booster Club, "we'll win, I believe."

Abilene, in West Central Texas, and Tyler, way over in East Texas, had never met on a football field. They had some mutual adversaries in Waco, Wichita Falls and Dallas Highland Park, but their meeting at Amon Carter Stadium for the 1955 state championship would be their first.

Having won the Love Field coin toss, Abilene, as the home team, got to pick its jerseys. Moser told his team leader, quarterback David Bourland, that new white jerseys had arrived. Bourland quickly voted in favor of the old gold jerseys. The belly series depended on deception, particularly on the part of the quarterback, and Bourland had become very good at it. He always liked to wear the gold jerseys, because the ball was too easy to see against the white.

Moser had taught his quarterback a trick that made the belly option even more effective. Bourland walked into Moser's office before the Lubbock game and the coach tossed him a deflated football from off his desk. "Pass it behind your back," he said, and Bourland did, first right to left and then left to right. "Can you do that with a real ball?" Moser asked. "Sure," Bourland said. In the game, when Bourland faked to the fullback, he then passed the ball behind his back, from right hand into left or vice-versa depending on the direction of the play, making the ball actually disappear for an instant. It was a very deceptive move. The Eagles' dark gold jerseys with black numbers helped the illusion. So the Eagles would wear gold and Tyler would wear its white jerseys with shiny blue numbers.

ABILENE AND TYLER BOTH HAD 12 straight victories against no defeats. In the playoffs, Tyler first defeated Corpus Christi Miller, 22-7, then Baytown, 20-0. Abilene had averaged 39 points a game, Tyler 29. The Eagles had surrendered 10 fewer points than the Lions, 77 to 87. Against their lone common opponent in 1955, Abilene had beaten Highland Park, 34-0, in the season opener; Tyler beat the Scotties, 33-13, in their next-to-last district game. Abilene's scouts, Blacky Blackburn and Wally Bullington, told Moser the Lions were a great team. Moser told the Eagles they would have to do "everything right" to win.

The Lions were big and fast. Center Jim Davis and tackle Billy Sims both weighed 200 pounds and both were all-state candidates, as was 186-pound halfback Joe Leggette, who had 980 yards rushing. But the star of the team, and probably the best all-around high school football player of the 1955 season, was 6-2, 190-pound quarterback Charles Milstead.

"Another Walt Fondren," Jack Holden wrote, "a Doyle Traylor," comparing Milstead to star Southwest Conference quarterbacks of the era. Tyler ran the same belly option offense as Abilene, and Milstead's ability to run or pass gave the Tyler system a dangerous extra option.

Members of Abilene's state championship teams of 1923, 1928, 1931 and 1954 were special guests at the Friday pep rally. The team left for Fort Worth on the Eagle Bus right after the pep rally and headquartered at the Texas Hotel. More than 5,000 Abilenians made the 140-mile trip the next day, including almost 1,000 on a special Texas & Pacific train. The Victory Bell went in a truck and the 100-plus members of the Eagle Marching Band went in buses. After about 8 a.m., two-lane U.S. 80 was lined up with cars going east, through Baird, Cisco, Eastland and Ranger, streaming black and gold crepe decorations, headed for Fort Worth. About the same number of fans came from Tyler. Crowd estimates at kickoff went as high as 30,000 in the 37,000-seat stadium, meaning as many as 20,000 people from Fort Worth and other parts of the state came to the game. It promised to be a big game between two powerhouse teams, maybe even a classic. It turned out to be a classic, all right, one that had fans shaking their heads that afternoon and 45 years later.

IN FORT WORTH IT WAS a beautiful Texas December afternoon for football, but windy. During warm-ups, the teams had trouble making the football stay on the kicking tee. Moser argued for taking the wind if Abilene won the coin toss.

"I was afraid we might bog down and have to kick into that wind," he said.

But his assistants talked him out of it. When they won the toss, Eagle co-captains Sam Caudle and Henry Colwell chose to receive. Then, disaster. Glynn Gregory had trouble fielding the opening kickoff and slipped on the badly worn turf and went down at the Abilene 5. Immediately five white shirts were around him. Tyler had come to play.

"I really thought we were in trouble," Moser said.

So did everyone else. Tyler fans roared, Eagle fans caught their breath. This was a game in which breaks could make the difference.

The Eagles lined up at the 5 in the straight-T. On Moser teams, the quarterback called almost all of the plays. But to start the game, Moser sent the quarterback in with the first three or four plays. Abilene's first play was a straight-ahead handoff to right halfback Henry Colwell. The line's rule blocking for the play was also straight ahead. Colwell picked up five yards behind blocks by guard Sam Caudle, tackle Homer Rosenbaum and end Jerry Avery.

The second play had been created for this game. The Eagles never went into a game without some special play or strategy based on scouting reports. This play was designed to exploit the Tyler defensive line's quickness and ability to penetrate. It also addressed the scouts' assessment that most of Abilene's plays should be run to the right side. In the Eagle playbook it was named "Tyler 4 Trap." It began as the same straight-ahead dive, only to the left side, to Gregory. Bourland took the snap, pivoted left, and handed to Gregory, moving forward. The other backs, Colwell and fullback James Welch, sprinted to the left and the Tyler line and linebackers leaned toward that flow.

~

BUT AS HE TOOK THE handoff, Gregory cut sharply to the right. In front of him, left guard Stuart Peake had "pulled." He had taken one step back and was now streaking across to block Lions' left defensive tackle Tracy Webb who had in fact been allowed by Rosenbaum to penetrate across the line of scrimmage. Caudle and center Elmo Cure sealed off the inside, Peake hit the tackle square—in the next three minutes, Webb would see enough of Stuart Peake to last him several lifetimes—and the hole at right tackle was wide open. Leggette, rushing up from his defensive back position, almost got to Gregory but Avery cut him off.

Gregory veered outside, got two more blocks, and was off, up the sideline, for 48 yards. He was caught, amazingly, by a linebacker, attesting to Tyler's team speed, but the Eagles were out of the hole. It was the biggest play of the game. "I know that stunned Tyler," said Abilene assistant Bob Groseclose. "Those Tyler boys didn't believe their big linemen could be moved that easily."

First and 10 on the Tyler 42. Gregory went straight ahead for six yards. On second down, fullback James Welch ripped through the middle, a standard fullback trap play just off the center's right hip, for 13 yards. Bourland ran the same play again and Welch got 15 more. Eagle blockers Cure, Caudle, Rosenbaum and Peake were chewing up the left side of Tyler's defensive line and Peake, pulling on every play, was more or less dismembering Tracy Webb.

From the Tyler 8, Bourland faked the trap to Welch and handed to Gregory coming across, who followed yet another Peake block to the 3. Gregory carried again on the straightaway play to the 1, then Welch burst through cleanly on the trap play again for the touchdown.

ON EITHER SIDE OF THE field, people didn't quite know what to think. After a nerve-rattling start, the Eagles had moved 95 yards in eight plays, all of them rushes inside the tackles, and they did it in three minutes and seven seconds against the unbeaten Tyler Lions, who had allowed only one touchdown in the playoffs and only 87 points all season. On the field, the Lion players were shocked.

"They were twice as good as we thought they were," said Milstead, a safety on defense. "We had no idea they were so terrific," said all-state end Mickey Trimble. "They played like they knew they were going to win from the start."

After a wind-blown kickoff, Tyler had the wind at its back and excellent field position at its 38. Two belly options and a fullback dive netted eight yards. Moser said line coach Hank Watkins "did a tremendous job with our line in setting the strategy to stop Tyler's option stuff." Defensive ends Peake and Guy Wells were coached to turn all of Tyler's option plays inside. "Hank worked with those ends all week and really did a tremendous job," Moser said.

Milstead punted and Gregory let the ball roll dead at the Eagle 10. Fifteen rushing plays later, the Eagles scored their second touchdown on a four-yard sweep right by the fullback Welch. Milstead had a shot at him at the 2, but Welch muscled underneath the Tyler star and dived across the goal line just inside the corner flag with 43 seconds left in the first quarter. The key play in the drive came on third and six at the Eagle 14, after Abilene was penalized five yards for moving before the snap. Bourland faked to Welch up the middle, then waited for Gregory, who was circling around to the left, and thrust the ball into his belly. But then the quarterback pulled the ball out again and as defenders veered left toward Gregory Bourland took off around right end. He got a clearing block from Colwell and broke up the sideline for 18 yards and a drive-saving first down.

~

TYLER ALL-STATE CENTER and linebacker Jim Davis thought that second drive broke Tyler's back.

"When they stopped us on our first drive and then they drove 90 yards for their second TD, we never could get going," Davis said. The first quarter ended. Abilene was leading, 13-0, and Tyler had run five offensive plays for a net of 11 yards.

In the second quarter Colwell made a leaping interception of a Milstead pass at the Tyler 48 and returned it to the 25. Three plays and a penalty later, Abilene faced fourth and 25 from the Tyler 40, out of field goal range. The way his defense was playing, Moser didn't mind running a play on fourth down from the opponent's 40. He sent in a play to Bourland.

The Eagles came to the line in a flanker left, with Colwell lined up far outside left end Freddie Green. Bourland took the snap and dropped back. Welch moved to the right to pass block. Three white shirts surprisingly broke through and rushed toward Bourland. The first one reached him and hit him, but at that instant Bourland handed the ball to Gregory who had taken a couple of stutter steps to the left, then circled back and with perfect timing crossed behind Bourland for the handoff.

It was the Statue of Liberty play. Gregory took off to the right, his cleats kicking up chalk dust at the 50 as he turned upfield. The right side of the Eagle line sealed off Tyler defenders, while the left side had brush-blocked their defenders and then sprinted downfield. In front of Gregory was left tackle Rufus King. Gregory galloped across the 40, then the 30, with King five yards in front. At the 20, running at full speed, the 185-pound King hit Milstead with a block that knocked the 6-2, 190-pound Milstead five yards backward and to the ground at the 15. Behind King's block, Gregory cut back across the field. Of the nine players near him, six wore gold jerseys. Green, racing across in front of Gregory, knocked down one defender who in turn rolled into a second Tyler back. Near the goal line, Colwell set up to screen off the last defender, who wasn't going to catch Gregory anyway as he strode into the end zone.

THE EAGLE LINE OF 1955 got downfield to block with a speed and intensity rarely seen at any level of competition on a football field, then or since.

"They had terrific blocking," said Tyler coach Buck Prejean, "by far better than we've faced this year."

"They had lots of speed," said defensive back Joe Leggette, "but their blocking was the difference."

Gregory missed his second PAT in the strong wind and the Eagles took a 19-0 lead to halftime. They hadn't thrown a pass.

"I told David to lay off throwing," Moser said. "Heck, we could make five yards running our handoffs, so why risk passing? I've never seen as fine a blocking line in my life. We'd run a handoff on first down, and then we'd have second down and five to go, or three, or one. That kept the pressure on Tyler the entire game."

Colwell, who was born in Tyler, scored the Eagles' fourth touchdown on a one-yard run to climax a 45-yard drive late in the third quarter. Gregory closed out Abilene scoring with a four-yard run two minutes deep into the fourth quarter, and Abilene led, 33-0. In three quarters against Abilene's first-team defense, Tyler had managed a total of two first downs. And Milstead looked nothing like the Charles Milstead that had led the Lions to 12 straight wins. Moser thought it was because of the pounding Milstead took while he was playing defense.

"We were sticking a helmet in his stomach on those blocks every play," Moser said, "and that took a lot out of him. I know he didn't look at all like he did in earlier games." Specifically, Moser cited Rufus King's block on Milstead during Gregory's 40-yard scoring run in the second quarter.

IN FACT IT WAS Ken Talkington, Tyler's backup quarterback, who led the Lions to their first touchdown in the fourth quarter. Talkington threw a 33-yard scoring pass to Newell McCallum with 4:32 left in the game, and then Milstead came back to lead a short drive after a fumble recovery that ended with Leggette's 10-yard TD run with 2:26 remaining. For the game, the Lions finished with 52 yards rushing and 80 passing, on five completions. Gregory had 171 of Abilene's rushing total of 351. The Eagles tried only two passes, completing neither.

"Abilene was brutal," summarized the Associated Press.

Milstead, approached after the game by a young Tyler fan wanting an autograph, told the boy he should go get Abilene players to sign instead. "Everybody on that team was great," Milstead said, "simply great." He said the Lions "could play Abilene every day in the week and never beat 'em."

"They hit hard and never let up," said Trimble, the Tyler end. "They'd knock you down, and when you got back up, knock you down again. It was tough."

In the Eagle locker room, senior co-captains Caudle and Colwell were blubbering into their coach's shoulder. They and the other seniors were the first class to play all three years under Moser.

"Coach, I can't play any more," said Caudle, a starter on both offense and defense for both the 1954 and '55 champions, and a two-way all-district selection as a senior.

"Sure you can, son," Moser said. "You've got college games ahead."

But that's not what Caudle had meant. He couldn't be an Eagle any more, part of a team that had won 23 straight games and a second state championship. It was a feeling of achievement and of belonging that might be part of this black and gold gang for a long while, with junior players like Gregory, Jimmy Carpenter, Stuart Peake and Rufus King in the room. It was not an easy thing for an 18-year-old to leave behind.

Abilene 33, Tyler 13
Dec. 17, 1955

Culmination

IN THE DAYS AFTER THE Tyler game, Jack Holden of the *Reporter-News* tried to get a handle on the Eagles' greatness.

> "The Eagles' ultimate success can be traced to several things," he wrote, "and whether we have them in the right order or not we don't know:
>
> "1. Superior coaching (and we definitely think this comes first). Moser and his staff had every detail organized to perfection. There was little lost motion. The assistants did a

terrific job. Moser gives them credit for doing most of the actual coaching, but it was his organization that made it possible.

"2. An unbeatable attitude by the boys themselves. Almost all the coaches have remarked repeatedly: 'These kids want to be coached. We've never seen any boys as eager to learn.' The boys studied hard and worked hard. They kept themselves in top condition.

"3. A good foundation in football. Abilene's junior high coaches and even those in elementary school instilled in the Eagles a love of the game, a desire to learn and taught them good fundamentals. They just needed to be polished in high school.

"4. Teamwork. On this team there was no star. All 11 were stars, and they worked as nearly like a unit as possible.

"5. Fine support from the city, the Eagle Booster Club and the students. All these groups went all out for their boys."

HOLDEN MIGHT HAVE ADDED a sixth element: time.

Witnesses, coaches and media have routinely used the word "perfect" in describing the Abilene Eagles' performance in the first half of the 1955 state championship game against Tyler.

Even Chuck Moser said it.

"That game was something a coach lives for," he said the day after the game. "Our first team played a perfect game all the way."

It was the 23rd victory in the streak, but in history the Tyler game stands out from all the others. It was a culmination of all that had happened since the Friday the 13th meeting at which the Abilene School Board voted to offer Moser the job, and Moser accepted it, and the news was published on Valentine's Day, 1953. All the mimeographed policies, all the coordination, all the teaching, all the drills, all the decisions, all the chalk talks, all the practices, all the eligibility slips, all the plays in practice, all the plays in the 35 previous games that Moser had coached the Eagles, all of it was practicing to be perfect, and it all came to 24 minutes of fruition in the first half of the 1955 state championship game.

From his first day in his 10-by-10 office in the old Eagles' Nest on Peach St., Moser taught perfection. All that attention to detail was motivated by Moser's desire to give his team its best chance to be perfect. That was always the goal, though Moser realized that some percentage of perfection, 75 or 80 percent, would provide his team a great advantage against its opposition. That advantage was obvious in the Tyler game. In the films, there is a glaring difference between the two teams. The Tyler players carried out their assignments, then stopped. The Abilene players carried out their assignments and kept running to the play and then ran back to the huddle.

~

WATCHING FILMS OF THE 1955 Eagles, a person can start to wonder if the Eagles didn't have 17 or 18 players on the field; 11 at the line of scrimmage, then after the play starts, another seven or eight down field. A team could not be perfect unless it hustled until the whistle blew. You couldn't be perfect if you didn't play perfectly for every second of the game. Moser taught that from the first day of spring training in 1953, and people who were watching understood it immediately.

"We know one thing for sure," Don Oliver of the *Reporter-News* wrote during those first spring training days, "win, lose, or draw, they'll be the hustlingest ball club that has represented Abilene in a long time. Those that don't hustle won't play for Chuck Moser very long."

But it took time to reach even a percentage of perfection, and three years to approach the sort of potential that the Eagles realized at Fort Worth. Expert witnesses to the Tyler game knew they had seen something climactic. Said Waco High School coach Carl Price: "Abilene's state champions of this year are 30 points better than the 1954 champions. If they improve another 30 points next year, they might as well get in the Southwest Conference."

"Abilene's triumph was the most complete victory scored in championship play in 21 years," wrote Dave Campbell of the *Waco News-Tribune*.

The *Fort Worth Star-Telegram* was even more definitive: "There was general agreement among the long-time observers that Moser's 1955 champions were the most powerful in the 35-year history of the Texas Interscholastic League. What made it a great team was the coiled-spring swiftness and the lightning reactions of the linemen, the versatility of the backfield which made every ball carrier a threat, and the tremendous defensive efforts in the clutches."

Jack Stovall, an Abilenian living in Dallas, sent a telegram to the *Reporter-News*: "Have started rumor that Abilene High used star players from Hardin-Simmons, McMurry and ACC against Tyler." He had the right idea, but a weak concept: Abilene might in fact have beaten the collegians he mentioned. Nearer the mark was Hunter Schmidt, who covered the game for the *Tyler Telegraph*: "I'd give anyone Notre Dame and 14 points against Abilene."

In Midland, Tugboat Jones had seen enough of Abilene. He resigned as coach of the Midland Bulldogs and moved to Dallas to become head coach of the Highland Park High School Scotties.

1956

AFTER SPRING TRAINING in 1956, Chuck Moser and his staff developed their varsity roster for the coming fall.

"We'll have a better squad than last year because we'll have better reserves," he said. "But our first team—I don't see how it could possibly be as good." What else could he say, after the Eagles' performance in the first half of the Tyler game?

Only three players—halfback Glynn Gregory, guard Stuart Peake and tackle Rufus King—returned from the offensive lineup that started against Tyler. But these three were dazzling, all-state players, and there were six defensive starters returning, and the new starters and those "reserves" had accumulated almost as much playing time in 1955 as the starters. It was significant that Moser had so many good interior linemen that he moved Rufus King to left end. Taking over at tackle was Boyd King, Rufus's brother.

And the new starting right halfback, replacing Henry Colwell, was a player who had already developed a reputation of his own. In football or baseball, when the chips were down, Jimmy Carpenter delivered. To his teammates and coaches, Carpenter was "the money player."

It was a stunning senior nucleus and the first Eagle team to represent its coach's complete design for a winning program. When Moser came to Abilene in 1953, these players were ninth graders, in junior high, where Moser's program really began.

By fall of 1956, 750 Abilene boys were playing football after school. There were 14 sixth-grade teams, three seventh-grade teams, three eighth-grade teams and three ninth-grade teams, all playing to city championships; and at Abilene High there was a sophomore team, a B team, and the varsity.

AT THE END OF THE school year, as he did every year, Chuck Moser sent the following letter to the parents of each player on the roster:

"Parents of 1956 Eagles:

"Your boy will probably be on the Eagle football squad next fall. As you know, all of our coaches have two aims: one, to help your son be a better boy and a better athlete, and secondly, to have a successful season this fall.

"Since the coaches will have less contact with your son this summer, we would like for you as parents to know what we expect of our boys during the summer, and encourage your son in trying to abide by our policies. Enclosed are a few policies that we like for our boys to abide by during June and July. We will write your son later, telling him the conditioning program we feel he needs in August.

"We enjoy working with your son, and we hope that he is receiving a great deal of benefit from it.

"Sincerely,
"Coach Moser"

Parents of Eagle varsity players were arrayed across the usual demographic range. Most were husband and wife, but there were also single parents. Practically all were in the middle class, a few were professional, others salaried, some owned or ran businesses. Most moms were homemakers unless they were single and had to go to work. And their degree of interest in high school football might have been genuine—many parents of players were graduates of Abilene High—or created simply by their son's presence on the team.

BUT IF THERE WAS ONE thing they might all agree on, it was the nice feeling of being part of something as successful as the Abilene High School football team. Most of the people in town knew the players by sight, and a few, like Glynn Gregory, who had made the all-state team as a junior, were real celebrities. It made the parents feel special, and there was only one place that feeling could have started. Not very long ago, the Eagles had been just another football team. Then in 1953, Chuck Moser came to town. Three years later, the Eagles had won two straight state championships. Now here the parents were, getting a letter from the man himself. If he wanted their help, they were inclined to give it. Thus the coach acquired lieutenants to do work he couldn't possibly do alone. He could count on parents to read the enclosed page of summer policies.

I. General

a. Show all adults and especially parents the highest type of respect.
b. Go to Sunday School and Church each Sunday.
c. Run around with other athletes or boys who abide by our Training Rules.
d. Work outdoors in the summer and save your money.
e. If you take a vacation, do so before August 15.

II. Exercise

a. Work with the weights two times a week.
b. Do some running two times a week.
c. Do 50 sit-ups and 20 push-ups each day.

III. Training

a. No smoking or drinking.
b. Be home at 10:30 (or earlier) except Friday and Saturday (12:00 Fri. and Sat.). Sleep is important.
c. Do not eat between meals.
d. Do not drink much water until after eating.
e. Do not drink milk until after the meal.
f. Eat foods that give you energy as: eggs, meat, breakfast food, fruit, vegetables, potatoes (not fried), graham crackers and honey. Malts, candy and ice cream is O.K. right after a meal. Stay away from pastries, doughnuts, popcorn, nuts, fried foods and cokes. These foods are not rules but only suggestions.

At the same time, even as they were Scotch-taping the policies to their refrigerator doors, some of the parents realized they had acquired a powerful third parent in the family, who wanted the same things they did.

It wasn't just the parents. One of the attractions of sport is its power to let people share success without doing any work. People participate vicariously, both in the feats of the athletes (and any performer or artist for that matter) and in the results. It is in their best interest to keep the success going. If Moser wanted his Eagles to work outdoors in the summer, there were plenty of construction and roofing contractors, petroleum companies, lumberyard owners, homebuilders and landscapers eager to hold or even create jobs for these boys. The city itself provided jobs in maintenance and sanitation. Humping garbage cans into a truck in the heat of July was a great way to stay in shape for football.

A community proud of "its" success could also be counted on to become an effective intelligence network. Eagle players, being part of such a wonderful gang, weren't inclined to break rules anyway, and they remembered what had happened to Bob Gay and Ronnie McDearman. But it didn't hurt when people all over the community, people they might not even know, came up to ask them how the team was going to do this fall. These people wouldn't know the rule about drinking cokes. Or would they? The simple thought that word would get back to Moser was an effective deterrent.

Moser reinforced this sense of community involvement with the team by becoming involved in the community. He taught a junior high Sunday school class at St. Paul Methodist Church and never missed a class, even after Saturday games in the Panhandle. The year he led St. Paul's fundraising drive, the drive set records. He was active in the Kiwanis Club, flipped pancakes at the annual Pancake Breakfast at Rose Field House, and eventually became club president. He was a division leader in the annual United Way drives, and he was president of the Boy Scout Council. He might have done these things anyway, even if his teams had been 5-and-5 every season. But nobody would have noticed.

Sept. 14, 1956

THE 1956 EAGLES reported in late August for the pre-season two-a-day workouts, but they already had undertaken considerable preparation, as outlined by Moser to each player in a letter mailed in late July.

> "Football season is near," the letter began. "In order to win our first game with Edison of San Antonio, you must be in top shape when we start practice August 31st. Here is a schedule I hope you will follow."
>
> The schedule called for the players to begin working out on their own on Aug. 1, 40 to 60 minutes each day at the high school, including running and playing touch football. At mid-August, the players were to go by Moser's house and pick up playbooks. "You must know all plays, rules and material by the first day of practice," Moser wrote. "Study this written material each day." He gave them the date for the team physicals at the office of team physician Dr. W.R. "Dub" Sibley, and he said workouts would begin twice daily on Aug. 31, at 7:45 a.m. and 4 p.m.
>
> "Enclosed are the training rules we should all know and abide by," he wrote. "Boys with the proper spirit will start abiding by these rules August 1.
>
> "I realize some of you will be out of town in August for a few days. You still should work out every day and try if possible to work out together August 14 and thereafter. Remember that spirit and desire to learn and excel is what makes great teams. I know that you will not let us down. This year's team can be as good as you want to make it. By example show your teammate how to get in tip top condition.

"P.S.: I will be at the gym every morning from August 14-29. Come by the gym if you have time; I would enjoy the visit."

SAN ANTONIO EDISON WAS a Class AAA school with a place in Moser's history. In 1952, his last season at McAllen, the Bulldogs defeated Edison, 28-6, in the first round of the state playoffs. Abilene had become an attractive early-season game for teams like Edison, who could do nothing but learn by playing a team like the Eagles.

Of course the Eagles were heavily favored. A pre-season poll of 16 high school coaches from around the state (Moser was one) picked the Eagles to repeat as state champions. Abilene received a total of 140 points in the poll. Second was Corpus Christi Ray, with 100. Waco and San Angelo, both on the Eagles' schedule, were in the top five.

There were an estimated 10,500 fans at Fair Park Stadium for the 1956 opener. Reserved seats were on the west side, student sections and bands on the east side. Coming out for the kickoff, the Eagles exited the stone field house in gold jerseys and black pants, walked across the track, gathered at the fence gate, then started through the corridor across the field made by 100-odd members of the Eagle Booster Club. As they came, the entire west stands rose and cheered for the two-time state champions.

Abilene's offensive starters against Edison were ends Kenny Schmidt and Rufus King, tackles Bufford Carr and Boyd King, guards Stuart Peake and Guy Wells, center Jim Rose, halfbacks Glynn Gregory and Jimmy Carpenter, 149-pound fullback Charles Bradshaw, and quarterback Harold "Hayseed" Stephens.

MOST OF THEM PLAYED less than a half. At that point the score was 28-0, Abilene had 207 yards rushing, and Edison had two first downs. The final score was 41-6, the Eagles had 428 yards of total offense to 153 for the Bears, and the Eagle with the most playing time was second-string quarterback and starting cornerback Gervis

Galbraith. Junior halfback Chuck Colvin was the game's leading scorer with three touchdowns. Gregory, playing only 21 minutes, carried nine times for 66 yards and caught three passes for 63 more.

"I believe we were in a lot better physical condition," Moser said. "They were a pretty good club there for awhile, but they seemed to get tired a lot quicker than our kids."

Later, when the stadium was dark and the town was quiet, a caravan of Sweetwater fans and band members arrived downtown, on their way home from Breckenridge, where the Mustangs had shut out the Buckies, 14-0, a real reason to celebrate. About 200 strong, they took over Cypress Street near the Greyhound station and staged a noisy pep rally that woke up many residents on the north side.

"We want the whole town to know we're going to beat you next week," one of the fans told the *Reporter-News.*

Abilene 41, San Antonio Edison 6
Sept. 14, 1956

Sept. 21, 1956

CHUCK MOSER SAID HE was pleased with the way the Eagles' second team moved the ball against San Antonio Edison. The second team, he said, was "a lot" stronger than the 1955 second string.

"You know," he said, "last year there wasn't anybody our second string kids could move against."

So it had come to this. Talking about Abilene's first team offense had essentially become pointless. In comparing the Eagles with their opposition, it was more relevant to talk about the second team. Moser would never say it, but it was reasonable to suppose that the Eagles' second team might finish third in the district, behind San Angelo and, of course, the Eagles' first team. The second team had "won" its first game, 13-6, over Edison after the first team had retired with its 28-0 halftime lead.

Sweetwater was no Edison. Both clubs competed in Class AAA, but Sweetwater's potential was such that the Associated Press made the Abilene-Sweetwater game one of the state's top matchups. Part of the media's motivation was also based on an emerging reality: at 24, the winning streak had become The Streak. In 1956, it started to make every Abilene game significant and provide every opponent with incentive.

The Sweetwater Mustangs needed no such motivation; any season was a good one in which the Mustangs beat Abilene. But the new motivation was there nonetheless. It was "Beat Abilene Week" in Sweetwater, same as it was every year, but this year was different. Beating Abilene would make statewide headlines.

THE MUSTANGS WEREN'T GIVEN much chance. Abilene was made a two- or three-touchdown favorite. But the game was being played in Sweetwater, in the noisy Mustang Bowl, amid a red-and-white sea of 9,000 fans. In 1953, the last time the Eagles played there, they were lucky to tie Sweetwater, 13-13, with an 80-yard march and a TD run in the last minute by Jim Millerman. Moser remembered Millerman broke into the clear, then stumbled, but recovered. "If he had stumbled and fell, we would have lost it, that's all there is to it," Moser said.

Moser designed practices to correct the early-season mistakes typical of a first game. He was also troubled by the way Sweetwater shut out Breckenridge at Breckenridge. Then at midweek his quarterback, Harold "Hayseed" Stephens, was hit by a virus that kept him home on Wednesday. Stephens was at practice Thursday but still queasy and very weak. Gervis Galbraith's playing time against Edison was looking fortuitious. The Eagle bus left Abilene at 3:30 Friday for the short 44-mile ride down U.S. 80 to Sweetwater and a 5:30 pre-game meal. "We're as ready as we'll ever be for Sweetwater," Moser said.

Sweetwater was as ready for Abilene as it would ever be. Maybe too ready. The crowd roared as the Mustangs won the toss, took the opening kickoff, and ran a play. They ran so hard that they forgot the football. Abilene recovered the fumble and in two plays had its first touchdown on a seven-yard run by 149-pound fullback Charles Bradshaw. There were less than two minutes gone in the game. Sweetwater fumbled on its next possession, and a botched punt on its third possession gave Abilene the ball at the Mustang 36. The Eagles quickly scored, again on a Bradshaw run, this one of 11 yards.

On the second play after the kickoff, the Mustangs fumbled a third time, the Eagles recovering at the Sweetwater 36. Glynn Gregory gained nine, then sub halfback Chuck Colvin broke for 20 yards to the Mustang 7. Gregory scored on the next play, it was 19-0 midway in the second period, and the Mustangs were helping themselves get beaten by a favored team. The crowd had fallen quiet.

THE FINAL SCORE WAS 39-7. Bradshaw scored three times. The Eagles piled up 334 yards rushing and completed five of nine passes for 107 more yards. Moser praised quarterback Stephens for his good play after his midweek illness. "He hit every one of his eight passes right on the nose," Moser said. "Jimmy Carpenter dropped one, Glynn Gregory dropped one and on the other he threw a perfect pass about 40 yards in the air to Glynn and the Sweetwater boy played it perfectly and broke it up."

Two other touchdowns, including a long punt return by Gregory, were nullified by penalties.

"We got penalized 70 yards," Moser said. "Those hurt us a lot, and could really hurt us in a tight ball game."

The coach was pleased with his defense, that limited Sweetwater's fast but light backfield to 100 total yards rushing, 50 of that on one play, a third-quarter reverse against the second-team defense that went for a touchdown.

After two games, Moser said he thought the 1956 offensive line was "more powerful" than the 1955 team but not as quick.

"We're not as fast, and aren't opening up the holes like the line did last year," he said. "We're pushing the defense straight back instead of opening up those big holes. You haven't seen very many plays this year in which the backs have had a big, gaping hole to run through like they did in 1955."

Abilene 39, Sweetwater 7
Sept. 21, 1956

Sept. 28, 1956

HIGH SCHOOL TEAMS WITH long winning streaks weren't necessarily a big draw beyond their own communities. About 3,000 showed up to watch Abilene play the Lubbock Monterey Plainsmen, a decidedly small knot of people in spacious Jones Stadium, home of the Texas Tech Red Raiders.

Very few Abilenians came, obviously, not caring to make the 170-mile trip to watch a slaughter. It took only a few city blocks and a couple of traffic lights to convince Lubbock citizens not to go, for the same reason.

Those who did come knew what was going to happen, but they were there because they were students and adults building loyalty for their school. Monterey was the new high school in Lubbock, opening in the fall of 1955. A community whose sons had won state championships for Lubbock High in 1951 and 1952 had seen its talent pool divided by the new high school, with inevitable results for both teams.

It was the creeping football fate of cities like Lubbock and Amarillo, medium-large cities with one high school but growing populations. The smaller Class AAAA cities like Abilene, Midland and Odessa were safe for awhile in their obvious advantage. But it was just a matter of time. By the 1960s, those cities, too, would have second high schools and diluted talent pools. Abilene, new home of Dyess

Air Force Base, was pointing toward 1960 for completion of its second high school, far out on the south side.

So to watch Monterey play Abilene seemed pointless to many. And there was a second reason to stay home. When they beat Monterey, the Eagles' winning streak would stand at 26, only three short of the Class AAAA state record of 29. That record was held by Lubbock High School. If anyone thought Monterey had the slightest chance to stop Abilene's streak, Jones Stadium would have been half-full.

AS IT WAS, THE SCORE was 41-0, but as Jimmy Browder of the *Reporter-News* pointed out, it could have been 100-0, or whatever total Chuck Moser chose. On their first possession of the game, the Eagles lost a fumble at the Plainsmen 9-yard line. The next five times they got the ball, they scored. It was 35-0 at the half on two touchdowns by right half Jimmy Carpenter, one by Glynn Gregory, one by sub halfback Chuck Colvin, and one by fullback Bill Sides. Eagle subs played the second half and beneath the stands, concessionaires leaned on their elbows and waited for the final gun.

Abilene finished with 435 yards rushing, and quarterback Harold "Hayseed" Stephens attempted four passes and completed four, for 117 yards. Abilene's two top rushers were both subs. Colvin carried 13 times for 95 yards and halfback Charles Bottoms gained 76 yards on 11 carries. Monterey managed 99 yards rushing, 64 passing and only five first downs. The Plainsmen's deepest penetration was to the Abilene 27 in the fourth period. Abilene had a first down on the Monterey 8 as the game ended.

The loss dropped Monterey to 0-3. The Eagles stayed overnight at the Caprock Hotel and headed home early Saturday with No. 26 in the bag. The Abilene and state media started reminding readers that the state record was 29. That game would be against Waco, in Waco, on Oct. 19.

Abilene 41, Lubbock Monterey 0
Sept. 28, 1956

Oct. 5, 1956

FOR THREE YEARS, ABILENE had begun district play with the fourth game of the season. But after the 1955 season, the governing University Interscholastic League revised district lineups to account for schools either growing into or shrinking out of the various classifications.

Big Spring, for example, after 1955 moved up from Class AAA to Class AAAA. Geographically it made sense to put the Steers in a district with nearby Midland and San Angelo. But if that were the only change, it would place nine teams in District 1-AAAA, which would mean an eight-game district schedule. That was too many.

So the old District 1-AAAA was broken up. The Panhandle teams, Amarillo, Pampa, Borger, etc., formed a new district with the Lubbock teams. The southern teams, Abilene, San Angelo, Midland and Odessa, went into new District 2-AAAA, with the new initiate, Big Spring.

The changes meant several things to the Abilene Eagles.

No more 300-mile trips to the Panhandle. Abilene's longest district road trip in 1956 would be to Midland, a mere 160 miles west on U.S. 80.

Less margin for error in district play. With only four games on the district schedule, it magnified the meaning of a single loss.

Better scouting reports. Assistant coaches no longer had to drive 600 miles round-trip, leaving on Friday and returning through the night toward Saturday dawn. They had more time and energy to analyze and assemble the information they had gathered.

An enhanced atmosphere for error in non-district play. In 1956, Abilene would play twice as many non-district games, six instead of three. Coaches like Chuck Moser might have preferred to play games with more on the table. A team could lose its "edge." But in Abilene at least, the Eagles had their streak to protect. And to fill those three extra dates, quality teams sought Abilene as an opponent. Against Abilene, teams could always learn something. Former district foe

Lubbock High stayed on the Abilene schedule in 1956, and powerful Waco was added.

More "practice" games would provide the team greater opportunity to prepare for play in a tough district that had gotten tougher. After three games, Abilene was ranked No. 1 in the state in Class AAAA, Wichita Falls was No. 2, and San Angelo was No. 3. The state rankings appeared in the *Reporter-News* each Tuesday morning. Unbeaten Midland was in the top 10, and Odessa had suffered only a single loss, to powerful and state-ranked Port Arthur. Big Spring was the only weak team in the district.

IN THIS CONTEXT, ABILENE'S traditional third-game foe, Breckenridge, was bumped back to No. 4. The Buckies, state Class AAA champions in 1954, had fallen into decline, failing to score in two losses to open the season. But that didn't matter in Abilene, where the 1954 game had already started to acquire the patina of history.

Moser was steamed on Monday, in fact, when his team practiced poorly. Perhaps it was a function of "losing the edge," but the scout team had too much success running Breckenridge plays against the first-team defense. "Blue Monday," Moser called it, lifting a line from new music the radio people were calling "rock and roll." He promised to get the mistakes worked out on Tuesday. Moser also learned the team would lose starting guard Guy Wells for the week with a knee injury. The Eagles had been lucky, avoiding any major injuries in the victory run. But luck could always turn.

In the Friday morning newspaper, sports writer Fred Sanner began his game advance with a reminder of the 1954 Breckenridge victory. A near-capacity crowd of 10,000 was expected. The Eagles couldn't beat the Buckaroos badly enough.

It looked like the Eagles might try, though. Jimmy Carpenter scored on a 13-yard run with barely two minutes gone in the game. Five plays later it was 14-0 after Glynn Gregory's 29-yard touchdown run. It was Gregory's first touchdown against Breckenridge in his three years as an Eagle. He got his second one a couple of minutes later, this time on a run of 47 yards. After nine minutes of play, Abilene led Breckenridge, 20-0.

~

IN THE SECOND PERIOD, Carpenter ran 18 and 33 yards for touchdowns. Eagle subs played their usual game in the second half, beating the Buckies, 7-0, on a two-yard plunge by fullback Reyes Diaz late in the fourth quarter. The final score was 41-0. After four games, the 1956 Eagles had scored 162 points and allowed 13.

Gregory was a one-man highlight film. He ran for 146 yards on six carries, almost 25 yards every time he touched the ball. Jack Holden had said the Eagles had no stars, but Gregory couldn't help it. He was fast, he was an accomplished athlete (he was an all-state catcher on two Eagle state championship baseball teams), and as a senior he had filled out to almost 190 pounds. Coaches knew he was the first player they had to stop.

But if they did, what about Carpenter, on the other side? The program listed Carpenter at 157 pounds. But he was fast and a tough runner and another multi-sport athlete and an all-stater on the baseball team. He and Gregory were the starting safeties on defense, and Moser thought they might be better on defense than on offense.

Carpenter, whose trademarks were his No. 71 jersey number and his shock of blond hair, gained 91 yards on nine carries against Breckenridge. By the end of the first half, with Gregory and Carpenter leading the way, the Eagles had 310 yards rushing. The Eagles tried only five passes, completing two, both by starter Hayseed Stephens, for 37 yards.

Abilene 41, Breckenridge 0
Oct. 5, 1956

Oct. 12, 1956

PLAYING THE LUBBOCK WESTERNERS one week later could have been perfect. It could have been the game in which Abilene, seeking to tie the state record for consecutive victories, played the team that held it.

But Oct. 12 was close enough. It meant Lubbock was the team with the last chance to defend its record before Abilene could go for the tie.

The Westerners had won 29 straight, from 1951 into 1953, a run under legendary coach Pat Pattison that included state championships in '51 and '52 and incidentally included annual floggings of Abilene, its old District 1-AAAA opponent.

Abilene's run going into the Oct. 12 game at Fair Park Stadium stood at 27. The Eagles, having won four games by an average score (rounded off) of 41-3, were heavily favored. But Lubbock, after a slow start, had won its last two games by an average of 43-14. And stranger things had happened in athletics, when this kind of pride was at stake.

Lubbock coach Wilford Moore was no stranger in Abilene. He was the former head coach at McMurry College. Two of his assistants had also played their college football in Abilene, at McMurry and Abilene Christian College. Moore had succeeded Pattison at Lubbock and had his hands full rebuilding the Westerners after the opening of the second Lubbock high school, Monterey. Moore only brought 28 players to Abilene. After opening losses to Dallas Adamson and Odessa (by one point, 35-34), Moore saw his team shrink by a third from injuries and players quitting for "lack of desire."

~

IT WAS QUITE A CONTRAST to the Abilene situation, where a secondary player was among the team leaders statistically. Junior halfback Chuck Colvin led the Eagles in rushing, with 308 yards, and he had scored five touchdowns. It was a matter of playing time.

In the Eagles' four games, they had outscored the opposition 131-0 in the first half. Regulars like Glynn Gregory, Jimmy Carpenter and Hayseed Stephens were retiring to the sideline before the first 24 minutes of play had been completed.

In the four games, Gregory had only carried the ball 28 times, but he was averaging better than a first down (10.7 yards) with each carry. Carpenter was averaging 7.4 yards and he had carried the ball only 31 times in the four games. Colvin on the other hand had 50 carries to lead the club.

Moser made one change in his starting lineup. Charles Bradshaw, the incumbent at fullback, was a fierce competitor and a terrific defensive player. But he only weighed 149 pounds. The fullback in the belly series took a hit on essentially every play, whether he carried the ball, faked into the line, or blocked for the other backs. Junior Bill Sides, in the substantial playing time that he, like all the subs got, showed he was a strong runner, had some speed, and was a good blocker. And he weighed 165 pounds. Sides got the starting call for the first time in the Lubbock game.

On Wednesday, at the club's regular luncheon at the Wooten Hotel downtown, Moser was elected president of the Abilene Kiwanis Club. Moser won in a runoff over Elmo Cure, father of the starting center on the Eagles' 1955 state champions.

MOORE SENT THE WESTERNERS into the game with a plan to hold onto the ball offensively and, defensively, to stack the line against Glynn Gregory.

Both strategies worked, sort of. Lubbock did manage to control the ball for a good part of the game and accumulated 202 yards rushing and 15 first downs, three more than Abilene. And placing an extra defender in the hole at right tackle, where Gregory would run on the belly series, was effective. Gregory only carried the ball four times in the game.

And he only caught two passes, the only two that quarterback Hayseed Stephens threw. The first one went for 47 yards and a touchdown on the first play of the game.

Lubbock actually won the toss and took the kickoff. Westerner star Charley Moore had a nice runback to the Lubbock 47, but he fumbled, and Charles Bradshaw recovered. With a strong wind at his back, Stephens brought the Eagles quickly to the line after the fumble and sent Gregory and two other receivers down the field and deep. The pass was perfect, Gregory caught it all alone at the 15, and coasted into the end zone.

Two series later, after a 13-yard Lubbock punt into the wind, Abilene moved 57 yards in three plays. Right half Jimmy Carpenter got the last 48 on a sweep left, away from Lubbock's overstacked defense, and it was 14-0 at the end of the first period.

On the first play of the second quarter Lubbock had to punt again, but this time, with the wind, Eugene Holt's punt carried 42 yards. Carpenter caught it at the 10, turned toward Gregory, and the two crisscrossed at the Eagle 6. Carpenter faked the handoff, tucked the ball in, and sprinted toward the Eagle blockers setting up their wall up the sideline.

BUT WILFORD MOORE HAD TOLD his players about the Eagle crisscross punt returns, and the wall. He told two of his defenders to fan out wide, outside the wall, where the blockers couldn't turn them in. The Eagles' Stuart Peake, seeing this, simply turned back toward Carpenter, reached the first Lubbock defender, and drove him to the outside. Carpenter cut upfield behind the block, reversed his field, faked a couple of defenders, and ran 94 yards to the end zone.

"Peake has everything a lineman needs," said Moser. "He's got speed, he's strong, and he's a very smart ball player."

Gregory scored his second touchdown a few minutes later, and on his way ran right through the defensive stack at right tackle, "shoving aside one of his own men," reported sports writer Don

Oliver, "and getting past two Lubbock defenders to highstep over the goal line." The 27-yard run climaxed a seven-play, 74-yard drive.

Abilene recovered another Westerner fumble, this one at the Lubbock 42, and Stephens sent Gregory downfield again. Scouts had seen that the Westerner secondary had trouble with multiple-receiver routes, so Moser, with the play, sent three receivers deep. This time, as with the first touchdown pass, Lubbock safety Holt had to choose who to cover, Gregory or end Kenny Schmidt. He chose Schmidt, Stephens threw to Gregory, and the play went for 42 yards and Abilene's fifth touchdown of the first half. On the sideline, Stephens said to Moser that all three receivers were so open that he didn't know which to throw to.

There was 2:50 left in the half, and the Westerners gamely played on. They mounted a good drive, but Eagle linebacker Guy Wells intercepted Holt's pass at the Eagle 19 with two seconds left in the half. Lubbock anticipated a pass, and Stephens in fact took the snap and dropped back. But then he slipped the ball into the grasp of the new fullback, Bill Sides, on the old "draw" play, so named because the play, looking like a pass, draws the defensive linemen toward the quarterback. It was the same play on which the Eagles scored on the first play of the game against over-eager Odessa in 1955. Sides popped through the advancing white shirts and was long gone, 81 yards, for the touchdown that made it 42-0 at the half.

Through five games, in the first half, the Eagle first team had outscored the opposition, 165-0. Lubbock actually scored in the third quarter, and Charles Bradshaw got Abilene's last touchdown on a three-yard run, but some number of Abilenians in the announced attendance of 7,500 didn't see this. Friday night games at Fair Park had an 8 p.m. kickoff. Some senior Abilenians knew they could go to the game and still be in bed before 9:30, and fall asleep knowing the Eagles' streak was still intact.

Abilene 49, Lubbock 7
Oct. 12, 1956

Oct. 19, 1956

"They have pointed for us for a year. They will be harder to beat because they lost last week. I know each of you will be physically and mentally ready."

WHILE ABILENE WAS POUNDING Lubbock, the Waco Tigers were being surprised by Arlington Heights, 40-23.

It was the Tigers' first loss of the season, and Abilene coaches thought they might have been looking ahead to the Eagles.

"Waco had allowed only two touchdowns to be scored against them in their first four games," Chuck Moser said, "so you know something was wrong against Arlington Heights. I would have liked to have played them when they were undefeated. A ball club as good as theirs on the rebound can be twice as rough."

Arlington Heights had beaten Waco with speed. Single-wing tailback Harry Moreland, "one of the fastest men in the state," Moser said, ran for 310 yards and five touchdowns. None of the Eagle backs had Moreland's speed, though Moser thought Glynn Gregory et al were quick enough to run outside against Waco. What worried Moser was the Tigers' size, and their preparation. Their coach, veteran Carl Price, was one of the best.

Waco assistant and scout E.B. Jones, meanwhile, made no attempt to mask his respect for the Eagles. Jones watched the Abilene-Lubbock game and after the game told sports writers he thought he had figured out a good defense against Abilene.

"A 30-30 rifle," Jones said.

Abilene and Waco didn't meet that often, but they had strong football history together. Though the modern classifications weren't introduced until 1951, Texas high schools had been playing to sanctioned state championships for decades. Waco in 1922 beat Abilene, 13-10, for the title, then in 1923 the Eagles won their first state championship, 3-0, over the Tigers. In 1927 the two met in the state finals again and Waco won, 21-14.

WACO WAS ONE OF TWO Texas high schools—Amarillo High was the other—to win three straight state championships, in 1925-26-27. Now Abilene was gunning for its third in a row. Waco had won more state championships than any other school, 5 ½ (a tie game produced co-champions). Abilene had five and looked like a reasonable bet to eclipse Waco's record with another championship in 1956. And of course Abilene needed only the one more win to match Lubbock's record winning streak at 29. A Waco victory at Municipal Stadium would make news in more ways than one.

After the previous week's embarrassment, and with all those records to protect or prevent, the Tigers were indeed fired up for Abilene and they played what their coach, Carl Price, called their best game of the season. "I just wish they had played that way last week," he said. Price asked his team to play ball control against the Eagles, and the Tigers responded by running 77 plays to only 38 for Abilene. Abilene ran only 17 plays in the entire first half.

But at the end of the half, having run only 17 plays, the Eagles led, 39-7. The final score was 45-14, the worst-ever margin of defeat for a Waco Tiger football team. But it was like Price had said after watching Abilene demolish Tyler in the 1955 championship game. He said the 1955 champions were 30 points better than Abilene's 1954 champions. "If they improve another 30 points next year, they might as well get in the Southwest Conference."

Here they were in Waco, in 1956, and veteran Waco sports writer George Raborn was similarly impressed. "Abilene's first team played three full quarters," he reported in *The Waco Times-Herald*, "and looked strong enough to beat either of the freshman teams that had played the night before at Baylor Stadium. In fact it wouldn't be too far-fetched to say Abilene could beat the Texas Longhorns."

The game bore an eerie resemblance to the Lubbock romp. If you switched game films, you might not know which you were watching. Waco played ball control and stacked its defenses against

Glynn Gregory. Both strategies worked, sort of. Gregory only touched the ball seven times. He carried five times for 72 yards and a touchdown. He caught two passes, the only two that Hayseed Stephens threw, for 122 yards and two more touchdowns.

Jimmy Carpenter, meanwhile, sped for three touchdowns in the first eight minutes of the game, including an 84-yard punt return (his return against Lubbock was 94) for the third TD. After that, wrote Don Oliver of the *Reporter-News*, "the fine crowd of 10,000 sat the rest of the way wondering just how bad it would be."

~

WACO RECEIVED THE OPENING kickoff and then fumbled, just as Lubbock had. Stuart Peake recovered and Abilene went 32 yards in five plays, Carpenter getting the last three yards on the dive play. The Tigers got a nice runback on the kickoff but then couldn't make a first down and punted to the Eagles at the Abilene 17. On first down, Gregory went straight ahead on the left-side dive play for 38 yards. On the next play, Carpenter carried on the same play to the right side and scored his second touchdown, from 45 yards out. Just like that, it was 13-0 with less than six minutes gone in the game.

Waco had to punt again, and this time Gregory fielded the ball at the 20. On the crisscross, he handed to Carpenter, who ran 84 yards up a clean blocking corridor along the left sideline to the Eagles' third score.

The Tigers then realized a measure of triumph. They took the kickoff and marched 77 yards to the first touchdown scored all season against the Eagles' first-team defense. The longest play in the drive covered 12 yards, and fullback Freddie Lamb, who bulled for 71 yards on the night, got the touchdown from the two-yard line. The PAT made it 19-7, and Waco was in the ballgame.

But on the second play after the kickoff, Stephens found Gregory running free in the Tiger secondary and hit him for 54 yards and a touchdown. A minute later, Carpenter intercepted a Waco pass. Two plays later, Stephens found Gregory again, this time for 68 yards, and Abilene's lead had exploded to 33-7. In the blink of an eye, Waco's success was a distant memory. The Eagles ripped off one more scoring drive, this one 78 yards in five plays, to make it 39-7 at the half.

In the second half, something happened that tickled the Eagles more than their first-half performance, or even tying the state winning streak. Stuart Peake scored a touchdown. It was the first of his storied Eagle career. An ongoing public argument said that Peake was the most valuable player on the team, for his play, but also for the intensity of his play, and for the way that intensity inspired his teammates. Early in the third period, Eagle junior linebacker Gerald Galbraith blocked a Waco punt. Peake picked it up and ran 33 yards to score, only he ran 43 yards and out the back of the end zone, just to make sure.

"I couldn't find the goal line," he protested as his teammates kidded him unmercifully in the locker room.

Price thought the two scoring passes to Gregory, so quickly after Waco's touchdown, were the difference in the game. "And that long punt return, and, well, everything hurt," he added. "It's a great ball club." Price identified "that No. 53," linebacker Jim Rose, as the Eagles' best defender, but in the same breath also identified Peake, Rufus King, Guy Wells and Charles Bradshaw, and he paused, trying to think of more names. "They were all great," he said.

Moser promised that back home the Eagles would work hard on defense, after Waco ground out more than 250 yards with a stubborn running game and short passes in the flat.

"The short passes outside hurt us the most," Moser said. "For seven yards at a time."

"They didn't look good on defense," said line coach Hank Watkins.

That was a coach talking, always thinking about the next game. It was great that the Eagles had won 29 straight, tying the record. But what really mattered was how would they play against Big Spring.

Abilene 45, Waco 14
Oct. 19, 1956

Oct. 26, 1956

SOME THINGS NEVER CHANGE. Sooner or later, the media always become part of a big story.

And so on Tuesday after the Waco game, Don Oliver of the *Reporter-News* presented himself at the Eagle field house and said he wanted to weigh the entire team. Oliver had read stories in Lubbock and Waco newspapers claiming the Abilene players were bigger than their listed weights in the game programs.

The weigh-in didn't take long. Apparently the coaches didn't mind. If any of them laughed, Oliver didn't record it. Nor did he get any quotes from the players about this process, and it's too bad. For many of them, it might have been their first exposure to the sort of attention that goes with fame. It would have been the perfect angle: getting weighed to see if they were bigger than they were for that phase of reporting that always follows fame seeking ways to make the story bigger than it is.

But, the media in the 1950s still didn't understand much about itself. And the public certainly didn't know. Oliver's results, published in his regular column titled "Oliver's Twist," seemed collected in all earnestness to answer a serious challenge, and everyone participated without comment. If there was no opportunity seen to educate the young players about their fame, it's likely they would not have understood it anyway.

"Of the 32 boys on the varsity squad who were on the main squad for the Breckenridge game, 18 boys have put on pounds, 13 have lost weight and one remains the same since weighed by Dr. Dub Sibley at the start of the season," Oliver reported. "There have been 81 pounds added to the team and 50 lost for a net gain of 31 pounds. This, divided among 32 boys, isn't enough to quibble about. We've put on about five pounds since August ourselves."

FOR THE RECORD, GLYNN GREGORY had lost four pounds, Jimmy Carpenter gained one, Stuart Peake gained two, Jim Rose gained four, Rufus King lost four, and Hayseed Stephens lost seven. Chuck Colvin, a junior in an apparent growth spurt, put on the most weight, gaining 12 pounds. The heaviest player at Oliver's weigh-in was third-string center Kim Winston, at 186.

The offensive line, according to these weights, averaged 181 pounds. The starting backfield averaged 161.

At the end of the column, Oliver couldn't contain himself. "Note to Waco and Lubbock scribes," he wrote, "them Eagles ain't big, they just look that way."

Never were they bigger than they must have appeared to the Big Spring Steers. In the course of breaking the old state consecutive victories record, the Eagles achieved a first in the streak: they scored 35 points in the first quarter.

For the Steers, it was a rough but appropriate introduction to life in District 2-AAAA. Only three years earlier, Big Spring had been in the state championship game of Class AAA (the Steers lost, 24-13, to Port Neches in 1953). On this night at home in Memorial Stadium, however, in their Class AAAA debut, they fumbled three times in the first quarter. Eagle cornerback Gervis Galbraith recovered the first one at the Big Spring 20 and Hayseed Stephens scored on a quarterback sneak three plays later.

Big Spring took the kickoff, had to punt, and Gregory returned it 61 yards for 14-0. The Steers' Ronnie Phillips took the next kickoff, fumbled, and Stuart Peake recovered. Three plays later Jimmy Carpenter scored from four yards out. Seconds later, after the kickoff, Steer quarterback Billy Johnson ran for good yardage on a keeper but tried to pitch to a trailing back as he was tackled. The ball went on the ground and Gregory recovered at the Steer 41. Three plays later Gregory ran 25 yards on a reverse and it was 28-0.

Stephens got the fifth touchdown of the quarter on another quarterback sneak as the period ended and the first team retired, penalized by excellence to the bench for the remaining 36 minutes of the game that made them the new keepers of the state's longest winning streak. Three-quarters of this historic game was essentially a game-condition scrimmage for the 1957 Abilene Eagles, and it was not at all exciting. But sometimes that is how history is made. And there wasn't anything the media could do about it. The final score, for the record, was 42-6.

Abilene 42, Big Spring 6
Oct. 26, 1956

Nov. 9, 1956

THE WEEK BEFORE THEIR GAME, teams exchanged game films, usually three games' worth. The film cans were brought back by the team scouts.

Over the weekend, the coaches would watch the films of the other team, comparing what they saw with the information brought back and assembled by the scouts. Football coaches watched game films the way actors watched movies, professionally, and critically, but always subject to the lure of the art's impact. It is not difficult to imagine coaches watching Abilene game films, their pencils at some point coming to rest, and silent, subjective minutes passing while they simply sat and watched how the Eagles played the game.

The films gave the Eagles a decided advantage over the next opponent before practice even began. They were intimidating, for one thing. What was a coach to make of a team that routinely had a 35-0 lead at the half, or on one occasion at the end of the first quarter? And Abilene films didn't provide much information about formations, plays and trends. It wasn't unusual for coaches watching the films to see Abilene's first team offense run five or six basic plays from one or two formations and then retire before the half with one of those big leads. They would see Abilene's first team defense run basic 5-2 and 4-3 defenses for as long as it took the opposition to run three plays and punt. The Lubbock and Waco films became highly prized because the Westerners and Tigers actually made first downs against the Abilene first team.

The films also showed the ferocity with which the Eagles hit early in the game, as Moser had coached them to do. If you hit a player hard on the first play of the game, he said, that player would remember it. That ferocity showed up in the Lubbock and Waco films as fumbles, on the kickoff by the Westerners and on the first play by the Tigers. Having watched this on film, should a coach tell his players how hard they were going to get hit? If he did, wouldn't the players think about it? And isn't that exactly what Moser wanted them to do?

Hayden Fry, seeing what he was up against, became determined to make the game interesting. Cooper Robbins, recipient of the Odessa Booster Club's "vote of confidence" after the 47-0 loss in 1955, was nevertheless gone after the '55 season, replaced by Fry, who had quarterbacked the Bronchos to the 1946 state championship. Fry was young, innovative and fearless. His team couldn't match up with the Eagles according to traditional criteria, but he could show the Eagles some things they hadn't seen.

WHAT HE MIGHT HAVE TOLD the Bronchos about the early hitting isn't known, but it happened again. Odessa halfback Dick Stice fumbled on the first play of the game at Fair Park Stadium and Abilene's Ervin Bishop recovered at the Broncho 12. Two plays later right half Jimmy Carpenter scored Abilene's first touchdown on the belly handoff at left tackle.

Abilene scored twice more in the first quarter, on runs of 55 and 31 yards by Carpenter and Glynn Gregory, whom the media had started to call Abilene's "touchdown twins" and "jet-propelled halfbacks."

The rout was on, but Fry kept it interesting. His offense ran an end-around off a fake pass. They ran pass plays off a deep-snap formation that would later be known as the "shotgun." They ran the bizarre University of Oklahoma "swinging gate" play. Breaking the huddle, the center, two guards and quarterback came up to the ball as the rest of the line and the backs sprinted into formation on the other side of the field. If it worked, the quarterback was supposed to take the snap and pass across to a receiver before the defense realized what was happening. Odessa didn't score with the play, but it entertained the crowd of 7,000.

Odessa did score, however, in the first half, only the second team in 1956 to score against Abilene's first-team defense. It came after the recovery of a Hayseed Stephens fumble at the Abilene 32. Using the shotgun, the Bronchos moved the ball to the one, where sub quarterback Dick Murphy scored on a sneak to narrow the margin to 19-6.

LESS THAN A MINUTE LATER, the Eagles responded to the affront by sending Gregory on a 66-yard touchdown run, the longest play of the night, that made it 26-6 at the half. Abilene received the second-half kickoff and went 57 yards, short gains, all on the ground, until fullback Bill Sides crashed across from inside the one to make it 33-6. It was 40-6 at the end of the third period after Carpenter ripped off a 40-yard scoring run.

In the fourth quarter, substitute safety Chuck Colvin intercepted a pass and carried it 45 yards for the last Eagle score. It gave the Eagle subs another "victory" in what had become their game within a game. They protected the victory with a goal-line stand late in the fourth period. After an interception, Odessa moved to the Abilene one-foot line, but there a handoff misfired. The ball shot straight into the air and when officials cleared the pile, there were three Abilene jerseys on the ball at the one-yard line.

Odessa actually marked up one more first down than the Eagles, but Abilene had 375 yards rushing to the Bronchos' 173. The Eagles only tried two passes, completing neither. Little did people realize that was a hint of big things to come.

It was the first time the Eagles had played at home as the new holders of the state Class AAAA record for consecutive victories. It was also the first game in which the Eagles added to their own record. From this night forward, every game they won would add to the streak.

Abilene 47, Odessa 6
Nov. 9, 1956

Nov. 16, 1956

BASED ON THEIR PERFORMANCE, it became legitimate to wonder if the 1956 Eagles weren't fulfilling the prophecy of Waco coach Carl Price, who had said if the Eagles continued to improve, the 1956 team might be 60 points better than the 1954 state champions.

In eight games, the '56 Eagles had scored less than 40 points only once, and that was 39, against Sweetwater. Through eight games, Abilene had outscored the opposition, 345-46. As with the 1955 Eagles, those totals were misleading, because they included all those second-half scrimmages between the Eagle substitutes and the opposing varsity. An imperfect but reasonable measure of the 1956 Eagles' true strength as Carl Price surmised it was to look at the totals for the first half of the eight games, periods in which predominantly the first team was on the field offensively and defensively.

In the first half of the eight games, the Eagles had outscored the opposition, 274-19. Based on those figures, if the first team had played the entire game each week, the totals would be 548-38. Apparently the first-team Eagles had the potential to out-score any opponent, 69-4.

Granted, there was a pointlessness to this kind of doodling that seems always to take place on the periphery of the extraordinary, like wondering how many 1956 Cadillacs Elvis Presley could buy. But Carl Price had been wondering about potential. Obviously the 1956

Eagles were potential being realized, and if that were so, was it potential that Chuck Moser had recognized?

In the 1953 city championship game between North and South Junior Highs, 12 boys played who would become starters on the 1956 team. They included Glynn Gregory, Jimmy Carpenter, Stuart Peake, Hayseed Stephens, Kenny Schmidt, the King boys, Jim Rose, Guy Wells, Ervin Bishop, Bufford Carr and Hubert Jordan. At the time of Chuck Moser's first visit to Abilene in February, 1953, these boys would have been in spring semester of the eighth grade. It is possible that Neal McLeskey, head coach at South in 1953, said to the young candidate from McAllen, "Coach, we are going to have some hosses." Moser acknowledged in his earliest mimeographed material that "the junior high program is about the most important part of our football program." In his February, 1953, visit, he would have scrutinized the junior high program and asked questions of McLeskey and others.

~

THERE IS ALSO EVIDENCE THAT those coaches and Moser could evaluate athleticism in boys as young as 12 or 13 simply by watching them in other school and summer sports. Comparing team speed before the San Angelo game in 1956, Moser said one of the San Angelo backs "used to outrun both Gregory and Carpenter in junior high track meets." Seasons in junior high were short enough to let eighth and ninth graders play all four major sports, and a good coach could always spot athleticism on a basketball court or a baseball diamond. Moser made it a point to encourage all boys in the Abilene school system to play sports other than football. High school players who didn't come out for the spring sports were enrolled in a special P.E. class called "Tumbling," overseen by Moser and his assistants, that stressed developing agility, speed and strength. An oil exploration company was happy to provide the class with barbells fashioned from lengths of steel pipe with used drillbits welded to either end.

If anyone ever directly asked Moser if he came to Abilene because he knew what was going to happen, it isn't on record. Later he would say of the '56 team that it had "tremendous personnel." On offense, only fullback Bill Sides, a junior, wasn't part of that 1953 junior high class. Now that team had stomped through eight opponents finally to arrive at what Moser called the tough and crucial part of the schedule: Midland and San Angelo.

The Eagles traveled to Midland on Nov. 16. They had a scare at midweek when Stuart Peake missed school with a virus but by Friday appeared okay. It was the Bulldogs' homecoming. Midland had won 6 and lost 2, including a 21-6 battle to San Angelo, that was ranked second in Class AAAA behind Abilene. The Bulldog defense, led by 201-pound linebacker Johnny Branson, was surrendering an average of just one touchdown per game. "This is the first team we've faced with any defense at all," Moser said.

The Bulldogs, pumped up by a sellout Memorial Stadium crowd and pre-game homecoming ceremonies, actually stopped the Eagles on their first drive, a crowd-pleasing rarity, and then settled into a ball-control offense that permitted Abilene only 13 offensive plays in the first half. With 43 seconds left in the half, the score was only 7-0, Abilene, with the Eagles backed up to their 10-yard line. This was something different.

"They three and four-yarded us to death," Moser said. "They wouldn't punt, and it's tough to hold a ball club to 10 yards when they run the ball four times. I wasn't surprised, but I expect a lot of our fans were," Moser said. He might have included the Midland fans, too. "A lot of scouts had thought the way to beat us was to keep the ball," he said, "figuring that if we didn't score early we might get rattled and make a lot of mistakes."

THEN CAME THE TURNING POINT. Abilene traversed the 90 yards in 43 seconds, despite drawing a 15-yard penalty. Moser helped the team manage the clock by instructing his runners to be sure they got out of bounds at the end of the play. The Eagles were at their 40 when Gregory broke free for 60 yards and the touchdown that made it 14-0 at the half.

It was a big score, because Midland attempted and recovered an onsides kickoff to begin the second half. From there the Bulldogs drove to the Abilene 7, where the Eagles held.

"If the score had been only 7-0 at the half, there's no telling what might have happened," Moser said.

Abilene punched the ball out to the 27, then Hayseed Stephens hit end Kenny Schmidt with a pass that carried 43 yards to the Midland 29. On the next play Jimmy Carpenter carried on a trap play, spun away from two defenders, and scored.

Two minutes later, Abilene had the ball back and Stephens threw again, this time to Gregory, who ran into the end zone from 57 yards out. Suddenly it was 28-0 and looking like old times again.

"I was real proud of Hayseed and the kids," Moser said. "Our kids never did lose their poise." Two series later, Carpenter scored again, on a 23-yard run, his third touchdown of the night. Sub halfback Chuck Colvin added one more touchdown. Midland, on the passing of quarterback Larry Cooper, managed a scoring drive against the reserves, and the final score was in the usual range, 41-6. But Moser was glad for the first-half tension.

"The fans should have really enjoyed a game like that," he said. "They really gave us a ball game." In the end, Moser said the Eagles played "the best game of the year. I sure didn't think we could beat Midland like that. As it was, when we got those three touchdowns, Midland had to do like everybody else we've played this year—gamble. And when they started doing that, we started increasing our margin."

At San Angelo, the Bobcats raced to a 29-0 lead to remain unbeaten with a 43-13 trouncing of Big Spring. The Eagles and Bobcats would meet at Abilene on Thanksgiving Day for the District 2-AAAA championship.

Abilene 41, Midland 6
Nov. 16, 1956

Nov. 22, 1956

"WE HAD TO CALL A HALT to the defensive scrimmage today because the boys were smashing each other too hard."

This was San Angelo coach Bob Harrell, addressing the Bobcat Booster Club on Tuesday evening.

"The team is ready," he said, "and I look for the boys to be hitting Abilene even harder than they hit each other."

San Angelo obviously was sky-high. The Bobcats were unbeaten and ranked either No. 2 or No. 3 in the state. Now they had a golden opportunity to beat the defending state champions and top-ranked team that was also their natural enemy. During the season there had been injuries to key players, but all were pronounced "in top shape." The team was fast and experienced. Nine seniors started on offense. Moser thought Phil Lane, the tailback in San Angelo's spread offense, was better than Marvin Lasater, now a freshman at TCU on full scholarship. "He throws a lot better and he is a more elusive runner," Moser said. Like Abilene, San Angelo could put quality high school athletes at every position.

The Bobcats were anywhere from a two to three-touchdown underdog. But they were 9-0, they had averaged 31 points a game and in nine games had allowed only three more touchdowns than Abilene's vaunted defense. Most of all, San Angelo simply wanted to beat Abilene. In San Angelo and Midland, players, coaches and fans viewed Abilene with a grudging respect. Each high school had great teams but couldn't even win the district championship.

The Thanksgiving Day date compressed the practice schedules in Abilene and San Angelo for the biggest game of the year. Both teams stressed defense. Abilene's B team ran San Angelo's multiple offense against the first-team defense, and Moser worried about speed.

"I scouted them against Midland, and overall they're a lot faster than we are," Moser said. "We've got one faster guard, Stuart Peake, and our two halfbacks, Glynn Gregory and Jimmy Carpenter, can outrun their halfbacks, but we're slower in the other eight positions." Moser said Bobcat junior fullback Jack Thompson would be the fastest player on the field, faster even than Gregory and Carpenter.

Bob Harrell and Moser both had come into the district in 1953 and both had succeeded in rejuvenating programs. But in their three meetings, Abilene had beaten San Angelo by 61-0, 27-0 and 35-6. Twice Abilene had won state championships. Every year, the Abilene game had ended San Angelo's season. A victory for San Angeloans at Fair Park Stadium in 1956 would mean even more than the district championship, a state championship, and the end of Abilene's winning streak. Abilene ticket managers sent 3,000 tickets to San Angelo, and they were gone in hours. It was the hottest ticket anyone could remember, in San Angelo or Abilene. A set of bleachers was trucked in from Waco and installed behind the north end zone. Those 284 seats went on sale for $1.50 each, limit four to a person, at Eagle Gym Wednesday morning. *Reporter-News* columnist Don Oliver used the occasion to call for a new Abilene stadium seating as many as 20,000.

~

THE VICTORY BELL, GUARDED BY two members of the bell team, started ringing early Thanksgiving morning at Fair Park Stadium. There were four students on the bell team. One of these was student leader Charles Craig, who used crutches because of polio. Summers in Abilene in the 1950s were dreaded by parents because of the polio threat. It was front-page news in September of 1956 when University of Pittsburgh physician/scientist Dr. Jonas Salk announced that "man eventually may gain long-term immunity against polio from as little as two injections." For Craig, a good athlete in junior high, the news came too late.

It had been cold during the week, but game day was cool and clear under a high blue sky, a typically beautiful Thanksgiving Day in West Texas. Kickoff was at 2 p.m. but by late morning there was activity in the stadium by students and other crews readying the field and stands for the game. Abilene High junior Will Cannon was among a group of students decorating goalposts when he heard a commotion. He looked toward the bell and saw scuffling. He raced over and dived into a group of young men who apparently were trying to upend the bell.

Police arrived, and when it was over the bell was upright, Cannon was en route to the hospital with a split lip, one of Craig's crutches was broken, and six San Angelo residents were in custody. Arrested on charges including disturbance, assault, battery, and carrying a prohibited weapon, were Jimmy Manitzas, Danny Joe Yancay, Donald W. Brown, Lank Powell, Edgar Ronald Lemon, and Lowell Hollway. All but Powell, who was 38, were teenagers, and one of the teens was carrying a switchblade knife. All were later released on bail totaling $95. It took four stitches to close Cannon's cut lip and he had to stay at home and listen to the game on the radio.

Abilene police were also patrolling that morning for possible trouble downtown. By 10:30 a.m. a crowd of 500 people, most of them youngsters, was milling in front of the Paramount Theater on Cypress Street. Most of them formed a loosely defined line that reached from the Paramount ticket booth all the way around the corner to the Wooten Hotel entrance on North 3rd Street. First in line was Wanda Barnes, from the Tye community west of town. She said she had been in line since 8:30 a.m.

She was waiting to see Elvis Presley. The first Elvis movie, "Love Me Tender," opened at the Paramount on Thanksgiving Day, 1956. This was the very first screening, at 11 a.m., and some of the kids in the crowd—which included kids from San Angelo—no doubt were going to the game later. Others could not have cared less about football on this day.

The crowd was typically juvenile, *Reporter-News* Amusements Editor Warren Burkett reported.

> "A group of boys, showing off, attempted to jam into the head of the line," Burkett wrote, "and milled around in front of the theater for awhile before going farther down. The rest of the youngsters waited calmly, bought popcorn, drinks and $1 'Elvis Presley' booklets, took their seats, and screamed at the proper places." One such place, Burkett observed, was "where Elvis twitches his hips and right leg much the same as a cotton-picker trying to shake a burr out of his overalls."

Burkett described the movie's plot and then summed up the experience: "End of the first show came with the passing out of Presley pictures to everyone. One of the 'show-offs' grabbed a stack of pictures from a theater worker and ran off up Cypress St. Another theater man recovered the pictures, however. And without riot or rampage, Elvis came to Abilene."

THE GAME COULD EASILY HAVE become another matter. The hitting was in fact fierce. Glynn Gregory got hit so hard on the second play of the game that he "saw little black spots in front of my eyes until the half." Even so, he scored the game's first touchdown on the 12th play of a 71-yard drive in the first quarter. When playing San Angelo, Gregory apparently thrived on adversity. In 1955 he passed out in the morning when natural gas leaking from a stove filled his bedroom, then in the afternoon scored twice and intercepted three passes.

In 1956, he had been knocked silly but seemed to be everywhere. The Eagles' first scoring drive began at the end of a strong San Angelo march to the Abilene 29, where halfback Norman Marshall fumbled and Gregory recovered. Then on third and two at the Abilene 37, Gregory picked up 12 yards on a sweep. Later Hayseed Stephens threw twice to Gregory, for 12 and 19 yards, the second completion putting the ball at the Bobcat 7. Gregory got two more, fullback Bill Sides was held to no gain, and then Gregory swept right, faked a pass, and ducked just inside the flag at the goalline. Maybe because of the spots, Gregory's point-after attempt was wide right and Abilene led, 6-0.

The teams exchanged punts as the second quarter began, and on the second one Abilene was penalized 15 yards when Marshall, signaling for a fair catch, was swarmed under by black and gold jerseys.

The penalty put the ball at the San Angelo 47, and the Eagles then were penalized five more yards for delay of game. Two Thompson carries totaling 18 yards put the ball at the Eagle 30. Tailback Lane passed to end Brian Barber for nine yards and a first down at the Abilene 21. The Bobcats were on the move.

Halfback Jerry Martin carried for two to the 19, then Thompson took a pitchout to the Eagle 12 and San Angelo had a third and two in the shadow of the Eagles' goalpost. Thompson carried and was stopped for no gain. Fourth and two. San Angelo sent Marshall off-tackle. Eagle end Ervin Bishop met Marshall in the hole, and other Eagles arrived quickly. No gain, and Abilene took over on downs.

"OUR KIDS DID JUST WHAT we told them to, keep San Angelo from scoring," Moser said. "The kids had the best defense of any team I've coached since I've been here."

San Angelo's Lane said it might have been a different game if the Bobcats had scored, and Fred Sanner, covering the game for the *Reporter-News*, said the play "broke the backs of the Bobcats."

It was 6-0 at the half, an unaccustomed tooth-and-nail situation for Abilene. "It was good for the team," reasoned Eagle end Rufus King. "It showed what we were made of."

The game was Abilene's homecoming, and at the half Abilene High junior Christie Smith was crowned Homecoming Queen. She was escorted to the center of the field by Charles Craig, on a new pair of crutches.

San Angelo, led by linebacker Ken Milliken, tackle David Ward and guard Kenneth English, was playing ferocious defense and stacking an extra defender to the wide side of the field to contain Eagle sweeps. The Eagles started running more inside and to the short side of the field, into the sideline. They drove deep into Bobcat territory to open the second half, but Gregory lost a fumble at the San Angelo 20. The Bobcats punted on fourth and six and Jimmy Carpenter returned the punt to the San Angelo 39. In eight plays, the Eagles scored again, on a 12-yard run by Gregory.

"They were really pursuing down the line fast," Hayseed Stephens said. "So I called 'Tyler Special,' the play that Coach Moser put in for the state finals last year. I knew Peake could trap that old boy and he really did and Greg went 12 yards for the touchdown that really made us feel better."

San Angelo came back, driving to the Eagle 32, but then tackle Rufus King and guard John Young drove Lane back four yards on third down. Lane threw on fourth down but the pass fell incomplete.

Abilene went 64 yards in only four plays. Stephens hit end Kenny Schmidt for 27 yards but then lost two trying to pass. Halfback Chuck Colvin broke loose for 11 yards and it was third and one at the Bobcat 28.

"They were in a short yardage defense," Stephens said. "It was third and about half a foot and they stacked up there in the gaps. So we knew we had them where we wanted them."

Stephens sent Bill Sides straight ahead on the fullback trap, center Jim Rose and guards Peake and Guy Wells popped open a huge hole, and Sides ran 28 yards untouched. "There was daylight all the way," Sides said. "Did you see that blocking?" Gregory's kick made it 20-0 with 9:19 remaining in the game.

~

THE BOBCATS HAD TO PASS. Abilene was laying for it and cornerback Gervis Galbraith intercepted Lane's pass at the Abilene 40. The Eagles were at the Bobcat 43 when Stephens took off on a keeper around the left side. Two Bobcats converged on him at the sideline, hit him hard just at the chalk and the pile tumbled out of bounds. The blue-shirted tacklers popped up. Stephens didn't. He stayed on the ground. Twelve thousand people fell silent as Abilene trainers and then Dr. Dub Sibley arrived to work on him. Then a stretcher was brought and Stephens, No. 33, was carried off the field with a broken bone in his leg.

Tumult followed. Now the 12,000 roared as a game already being played with such intensity threatened to become vicious. The Eagles and Bobcats flew at each other and the officials wisely clamped down. San Angelo halfback Jerry Martin and Eagle guard Stuart Peake both were ejected from the game in its final minutes, Peake later insisting he had done nothing wrong. San Angelo was on the Abilene 12 as the last seconds ticked away, and officials and stadium policemen were watchful. The Bobcats' last play of the game was a sweep that ended in a hard tackle and a pileup right at the end of the Bobcat bench. Several players moved toward the pile, but two officials were immediately on top of the play. At the sound of the gun, the players simply stood up, faced each other and started to shake hands. The tension resolved itself in two spent squads milling quietly toward the field house. Coaches, writers and fans all gratefully praised the teams for their sportsmanship.

"They're a great ball team but my 1942 Odessa team was better," San Angelo coach Harrell said of the Eagles. "I'd liked to have had that '42 team out there today."

It was not a particularly gracious thing to say in the presence of his exhausted, grimy, tearful players in the Bobcat locker room. *Reporter-News* news editor Dick Tarpley made it the lead in his post-game locker room story and let it stand without comment.

"But his players," Tarpley wrote, "were virtually unanimous in appraising the Abilene team as the greatest they had ever seen or played."

Beyond the wall on the Abilene side, talk was as much about the future as the immediate past.

"Get 'em, Gerv, you can take us all the way, too," Stuart Peake shouted at junior quarterback Gervis Galbraith, and the other players joined in. "I'll do my best," Galbraith said with tears in his eyes.

"Losing Hayseed was a tough break," Moser told his players, "but we can still go all the way and he'll be hollering for us."

~

MOSER WAS ALREADY THINKING about Monday's practice. Galbraith, a junior, had been a defensive starter at cornerback all year, and he had ample playing time at quarterback in the second half. But he had taken very few snaps with the first team, and now the Eagles were in the state playoffs. Moser said he would "experiment" with Glynn Gregory at quarterback. Gregory had the athleticism and he had played quarterback in junior high. "I've got to have two quarterbacks anyway," Moser said.

Jimmy Carpenter would move from right halfback to left, and senior fullback Charles Bradshaw and junior Chuck Colvin would work at right half. "I really don't know just exactly what we'll do," Moser said. "I just haven't had time to think it out, but I know we'll try it this way." Moser said he had "never seen two better teams against each other, nor have I ever seen a harder fought game." Eventually Moser made his way to the pressbox, where Abilene officials won a coin toss with representatives from Ysleta High School, near El Paso. The bi-district game was set for Fair Park Stadium, on Friday, Nov. 30, at 2 p.m.

The Saturday papers in Abilene and San Angelo were still buzzing with comment and news about the Thanksgiving Day game. Eagle guard Guy Wells fell ill and had to be hospitalized Friday with a kidney contusion suffered in the game, and there was a photo of a smiling Hayseed Stephens in his hospital bed, reading the Friday *Reporter-News* stories about the game. Bob Harrell complained that Abilene fans behind the Bobcat bench had given his team "an unmerciful riding. They are plain sorry." Don Oliver of the *Reporter-News* countered by questioning some of Harrell's "gestures" to the crowd.

It had been a busy news week in the sports pages and it wasn't over yet. Sunday morning, San Angelo subscribers opened up their *Standard-Times* to learn that Bobby Morrow of Abilene Christian College had won both the 100 and 200 meters in the Olympic Games at Melbourne. His :20.6 in the 200 was an Olympic record. Later Morrow won a third gold medal as a member of the 4x400 sprint relay team. In the Cold War climate, it was very pleasant news. Some San Angeloans might have caught themselves thinking it would have been even better if Morrow were from anywhere but Abilene.

Abilene 20, San Angelo 0
Nov. 22, 1956

Nov. 30, 1956

"I DON'T BELIEVE WE CAN beat San Angelo this week, but Ysleta can sure beat us if we don't start thinking about them."

This was Chuck Moser addressing the regular Tuesday night meeting of the Eagle Booster Club. The controversy over Hayseed Stephens' season-ending injury had been slow to abate, in large part because the Abilene School Board Monday night issued a statement protesting the "commando tactics" used by San Angelo in the game.

After that story in the paper Tuesday morning, the Eagle Booster Club meeting that night was standing room only. Moser's first order of business in his remarks to the crowd was to get a page turned.

"Hayseed was hurt on as clean a play as I've seen in football," Moser declared to the crowd. "I've seen the film 30 times, and there was nothing wrong with the play. The kid just fell on the leg the wrong way, that's all."

That was a view shared by the San Angelo School Board, which in its Tuesday night meeting issued a withering response which was phoned to the *Reporter-News* for Wednesday morning publication.

"Hurling charges through the newspaper is a poor way to attempt to settle a controversy," the San Angelo statement began, then summed up the board's own review of 1,400 feet of game film, stated its respect for and confidence in the sportsmanship of the Bobcat coaches and players, and said if the Abilene authorities wanted to pursue the matter, the board would happily dispatch the San Angelo game film to University Interscholastic League officials in Austin for their study.

"We do not believe the statements appearing in the press reflect the thinking of either Coach Chuck Moser or members of his football team," the statement concluded. "We congratulate them for their fine record and we are pulling for them to carry on to another state championship."

Moser was all for that.

"I've been coaching 12 years and I've learned two things," he said. "Never criticize the officials and never criticize your opponents. I don't want my kids thinking about San Angelo this week, we're playing a team called Ysleta."

THE EL PASO ENTRY IN the playoffs historically had not excited great concern among the Abilene coaches. The scores had been 61-0 in 1954 and 61-0 again in 1955. Assistant coach Bob Groseclose tried to tell the Booster Club what a good team Ysleta had, but Ysleta was not Moser's main headache. His team had lost its starting quarterback and its starting right guard. Moser knew the Eagles could probably beat Ysleta with the president of the Eagle Booster Club at quarterback, but what about the week after that? The Eagles were basically a running team, but Moser believed very much in the passing attack and always devoted significant practice time to it. "We know you can't win tough football games without it," he said. Stephens in 10 games had completed 30 of 48 passes (a 63 percent completion percentage) for 742 yards and six touchdowns. Galbraith had thrown 13 passes, completing three for a total of 36 yards. Moser knew another chilling statistic that described Stephens' loss. During the season he had quarterbacked 64 offensive drives. The Eagles had scored on 53 of these.

The newspaper called it "Operation Quarterback." Glynn Gregory and Gervis Galbraith shared time at quarterback, running the first-team offense in practice. Galbraith had the advantage of knowing and having run the plays from quarterback. Gregory had the advantage of athleticism. He had played quarterback in junior high, but there was a technique and a rhythm to quarterbacking a belly-series offense that required constant practice.

"Glynn still doesn't know all the plays," Moser said. "We're having to do three years' work in two days."

When Gregory was at quarterback, Jimmy Carpenter ran at left halfback, Bill Sides was the fullback, and junior Chuck Colvin moved in for Carpenter at right half. With Galbraith at the controls, he had the usual backfield of Gregory, Sides and Carpenter behind him. Moser said Galbraith "looked better than I thought he would. He sure has come along on his throwing and his ball handling is good. I will play both this week at quarterback unless one really comes through a little better than the other." When the playoffs began, Moser always promoted several players from the B team to the varsity. For the Ysleta game he brought up five such players. One of these was strong-armed sophomore quarterback Freddie Martinez.

THERE WAS ONE OTHER effect, and it was serious. As Don Oliver pointed out, "Gregory can't throw the ball and catch it, too." He was the Eagles' leading receiver with 19 catches for 553 yards. Closest to him was end Kenny Schmidt, with six receptions for 107 yards.

Progress reports from Hendrick Memorial Hospital indicated that Guy Wells probably wouldn't be able to practice for at least 10 days. Senior Hubert Jordan moved into Wells' starting spot at right guard, and junior John Young moved in for Wells on defense at end. In all, the Eagles were entering the 1956 playoffs without four of their first or second team players: Stephens, Wells, end Butch Adams, advised by doctors to drop football because of a rheumatic condition, and junior tackle Mike Bryant, who broke his leg in the Midland game.

Also injured and unable to practice was starting tackle Clint Murphy, who was one of three suffering sprained ankles in the San Angelo game.

During the week, Abilenians were more interested in what the "new" Eagle offense would look like than in what sort of threat the Ysleta Indians might represent. The Indians were 8-2 but had won eight straight and in those eight victories had not allowed more than a touchdown to the opposition. In fact the Indians and Eagles had allowed exactly the same number of points—39—in those last eight games. The two teams had no common opponents in 1956.

Nine Ysleta players had been named to the all-District 1-AAAA team, six offensively and three on defense. The Indians' offensive star was 165-pound quarterback Glen Adams, with 672 yards of total offense and 49 points scored. Ysleta was coming off a 47-0 thrashing of El Paso Burges. Going into the game, Abilene was made a two-touchdown favorite. Abilene chose its white jerseys for the game. Ysleta wore maroon. On Thursday, Moser named Gregory the starter at quarterback, with Jimmy Carpenter at left half, Chuck Colvin at right half and Bill Sides the fullback. Senior Bufford Carr started at offensive left tackle for the hobbled starter Murphy.

ABOUT 8,000 SHOWED UP at Fair Park Stadium for the unusual 2 p.m. Friday kickoff and saw the Eagles stall on their first offensive series, wasting excellent field position when a Ysleta punt into a brisk wind died at the Indian 41. Ysleta took over on downs at the 32 and penetrated all the way to the Eagle 29 before being stopped on fourth down.

Gregory, at quarterback, with the wind behind him, threw for right half Chuck Colvin running in the flat but missed him. Bill Sides went straight ahead for two and it was third and seven at the

Eagle 32. Then Gregory called a play, "90-41 in," with which he was very familiar as a receiver. He took the snap, faked to both Sides going straight ahead and Colvin crossing behind. Carpenter, from Gregory's usual left half position, simply ran straight into the line and took off upfield. Gregory carried out the fake to Colvin, took a step, turned, and launched a high, arching spiral that carried almost 50 yards in the air. Carpenter, five yards behind the safety Glen Adams, took it in full stride with a classic over-the-shoulder catch at the Ysleta 27 and sped into the end zone, 68 yards for the Eagles' first score. Before that play, Carpenter had caught three passes all year for a total of 46 yards. *Reporter-News* photographer Don Hutcheson caught the play just as the ball was arriving over Carpenter's shoulder. The paper used the photo on the front page Saturday morning with the caption writer comparing Carpenter's play to the famous 1954 World Series catch by New York Giants center fielder Willie Mays off Cleveland's Vic Wertz.

On the field and in the stands, the play broke tension. With Wells and Hayseed Stephens watching from wheelchairs on the sidelines, the Eagles scored the next four times they touched the ball and led, 35-0, at the half. Gregory engineered four scoring drives, then Gervis Galbraith guided the offense to its fifth touchdown. The final score was 42-6, and the hero of the day was not Gregory or Carpenter, but third-string fullback Reyes Diaz. Playing in the second half, he finished as the game's leading rusher with 68 yards in 10 carries and he scored a touchdown. But it was the way the 5-4, 172-pound Diaz ran that always endeared him to the crowd.

"I just duck my head and go," grinned Diaz, who brought cheers every time his No. 27 entered the game. Diaz, or "Dizzy" to his teammates, liked to run over defenders and literally went out of his way to do so, even in an open field. "I don't have much speed, so I just try to run over them," he said.

~

THE EAGLES WENT TO THE locker room thinking they would no doubt play Amarillo next, in the new quarterfinals bracket created by the addition of new districts in the realignment after the 1955 season. If they were to repeat as state champions, the Eagles would have to defeat four playoff opponents instead of three. The Sandies of 3-AAAA were a huge favorite over Fort Worth Paschal of 4-AAAA in a Saturday bi-district game, having beaten Paschal, 36-7, early in the season. Moser told the Eagles to enjoy the weekend and told them tickets were arranged for them to see the Hardin Simmons-Texas Tech game at the stadium Saturday afternoon.

Abilene assistants Wally Bullington, Blacky Blackburn and Tommy Morris drove to Amarillo to scout the teams. Moser told Bullington and Blackburn to concentrate on Amarillo, and Morris to watch Paschal. By the half, Blackburn had switched over to help Morris because it had become evident that Paschal needed watching. The Panthers in fact upset the Sandies, 13-7, with a terrific defensive effort. The Sandie faithful also wondered if Amarillo coaches and players weren't looking past Paschal to Abilene.

"The visitors seemed ready and the Sandies weren't," wrote Putt Powell in the *Globe-News.* "That was the whole story. Many fans stayed away waiting to the see Sandie-Abilene game which would have been at Amarillo Stadium. But, the Texas Interscholastic League playoffs are sudden death."

That development necessitated a coin toss, which Paschal authorities won. Abilene would meet the Paschal Panthers in the state Class AAAA quarterfinals at 2 p.m. Saturday, Dec. 8, at Farrington Field in Fort Worth.

Abilene 42, Ysleta 6
Nov. 30, 1956

Dec. 8, 1956

"WHEN WE LOST HAYSEED, I thought we were shot," said Chuck Moser. "The kids didn't, but I did."

The coach kept the thought to himself, of course, and reacted officially to the circumstances as any good coach would whose offense had been crippled.

"We started concentrating on defense," he said.

Long runs and passes and lots of touchdowns were what attracted attention to a team; most fans and sports writers will always love offense. As Moser said, "Most of the time, the fans just watch the ball carrier and let it go at that." In reality, however, in their unbeaten 1956 season, the Eagles would have had to score only a single touchdown to win seven of those games. In two games, they would have had to score twice. In only one game, against Waco, would the Eagles have needed three touchdowns to win. Had the first teams played the entire game, those totals certainly would have been lower. Only twice did the Eagle first-team defense surrender a touchdown in the 10-game regular schedule.

Tactically, a strong offense served its purposes. When a team played all-out, like Abilene did, and it already had a two or three-touchdown lead in the second quarter, the effect on the opposition could be demoralizing. But when the question simply was winning a football game, to a good coach the solution was simple: a team can't win the game if it doesn't score.

So the Eagles started concentrating on defense, which was a scary though when one considered the San Angelo game. Moser had called that performance, "the best defense of any team I've coached since I've been here. Our defense won it, and I think the team winning the championship will do it on defense."

~

NOW THE COACH'S FOCUS became placed on making such a defense even better. Depending on the game situation and the other team's tendencies, the Eagles lined up in one of three basic defenses: a 5-2, with five linemen, two linebackers, two cornerbacks and two safeties; a 4-3, with four linemen, three linebackers, and the same secondary; or a gap-8, a short-yardage defense used mainly near the goalline. The Eagles' most celebrated defenders were end Stuart Peake and linebacker Jim Rose, though the entire unit was so strong that after the San Angelo game, *Reporter-News* sports writer Fred Sanner was at such a loss that he just listed numbers: "74, 23, 66, 60, 86, 53, 70, 72, 29, 64." Rufus King, Charles Bradshaw, Ervin Bishop, Guy Wells, Stuart Peake, Jim Rose, Boyd King, Bufford Carr, Gervis Galbraith, John Young.

"Here it was gang tackling that accomplished the task," wrote Sanner, "there it was a single tackler knifing through, but always it was a pressing band of black and gold chewing up the blue and orange runners." Sanner didn't mention 21 and 71, Glynn Gregory and Jimmy Carpenter at the safeties, whom Chuck Moser argued were actually better on defense than offense.

"Since Gregory and Carpenter have been playing safety," Moser said, "there has never been a run made against us for over 20 yards, and there's never been a pass completed over their heads."

Moser was as surprised as anyone to be preparing his team for Fort Worth Paschal and not Amarillo. After five games, Paschal was 1-4, with losses to Amarillo, Highland Park, Dallas Adamson and Class AAA power Cleburne. But then district play opened and the Panthers were unbeatable. In the Fort Worth loop, they played strong defense routinely and strong offense when they had to (in a 47-33 shootout with speedy Harry Moreland and Arlington Heights).

Paschal coach Bill Allen, a 20-year veteran in schoolboy coaching circles, said he had been "experimenting" during the early losses. "We accidentally found the right boys and now we've got sort of a Cinderella outfit."

Like Moser, Allen believed in defense as the real difference between two teams.

"The only secrets left in football any more are your defenses," Allen said, "and I just hope we can run one or two that Chuck hasn't seen before. We've got one that I know Abilene hasn't ever played against."

Maybe not. Each week Moser had assistant coach Bob Groseclose teach the junior varsity at least 10 defenses the opposition might use. In the ensuing scrimmage, the JV would run a different defense on every down as the varsity offense worked on recognition and reaction. If the Eagle offense in a game always seemed to know what was coming, it was because of that mental workout.

~

PASCHAL'S OFFENSE WAS A strange run-and-shoot affair, with the quarterback and both halfbacks possessing significant statistics both running and passing. Halfback Dan Gurley had gained 493 yards rushing, had completed eight passes for 133 yards and three touchdowns, and was the team's leading receiver with 10 catches for 139 yards. The other halfback, David Erwin, had 650 yards rushing and had completed an incredible eight of nine passes for 119 yards and a touchdown.

"We run well and pass awfully well," Allen said. "And, the thing I like the most," he added, alluding to the upset of Amarillo, "is that we've got a lot of spirit. Our kids have come along awfully well and have good size and good overall speed."

On Friday, as the Eagles left for Fort Worth, there were two threatening reports. One was from the weather bureau, forecasting cloudy and cold weather Saturday afternoon. The other was from Columbia, Missouri, and it said that Chuck Moser was a candidate to replace retiring head coach Don Faurot at the University of Missouri. Moser denied a report in *The Dallas Times-Herald* that he had actually interviewed for the job.

"I have talked to Faurot on the phone," Moser said. "He wanted to know if I'd come up and talk with them about it. I told him as long as my team is in the playoffs I didn't see how I could. I haven't applied. I won't go until after the playoffs, and I'm not sure if I'll go then." Faurot confirmed to the *Reporter-News* that Moser was "under consideration" but had not been interviewed. Faurot said there had been more than 50 applications for the position and that Moser had been one of 10 or 12 coaches contacted.

On Saturday afternoon, the clouds and cold in fact materialized, along with a misting, miserable rain. That the Abilene coach and his team were able to retain their focus—concentrate on defense—soon became apparent. What happened at Farrington Field served as a measure of what can happen when a coach believes his accomplished defensive team can play even better. In the game, played on a slick, wet field, the Panthers didn't run a single play in Abilene territory. Paschal's deepest penetration was its own 47. Abilene held the Panthers to 41 yards rushing and 33 passing on only three completions in 13 attempts, with two Abilene interceptions.

Moser was pleased, though he admitted field conditions may have been a factor. The field had received a routine heavy watering early in the week, but then the expected evaporation didn't occur as hard rain fell on Thursday, followed by the cold, wet norther.

TO WIN THE GAME, THE Eagles would have needed only one touchdown. They got two, both scored by Gregory against Paschal's multiple defensive sets. Peake and center Jim Rose said the Paschal defenses kept changing but that the Eagles were not surprised by them, nor did they present very much trouble.

Playing quarterback in the first half, Gregory put Abilene on the board with a 25-yard burst. In the second half, Moser inserted Gervis Galbraith at quarterback, and the junior, in the coach's estimation, played well, particularly in the conditions. By the fourth period, snowflakes had begun to fall. Gregory scored again on a 19-yard run, and the final score was 14-0. Gregory was the leading rusher with 102 yards on 20 carries, and the Eagles amassed 259 yards on the ground. Abilene didn't complete a pass. Gregory missed on five attempts and Galbraith on two.

Watching play in the second half, Moser made a decision.

"Gervis is our quarterback next week," Moser told the team in the locker room.

In Dallas, Thurman "Tugboat" Jones had made a good career decision. In his first year at the Highland Park helm after leaving Midland, Jones saw his Scotties win a district championship and advance into the playoffs. He was denied a shot at the Eagles, though, when the Scots fell to Wichita Falls, 19-7, in another cold, wet quarterfinals game that Saturday. In the Farrington Field pressbox, Wichita Falls assistant coach Hunter Kirkpatrick correctly called the coin toss, placing the Abilene-Wichita Falls semifinals game in Coyote Stadium at 2 p.m. Saturday, Dec. 15.

Abilene 14, Fort Worth Paschal 0
Dec. 8, 1956

Dec. 15, 1956

"They run single wing left and right. They have waited to play us for two years. They are great on defense—they have lost one game in two years. Be ready."

UPSTAGING THE EAGLES IN ABILENE wasn't easy, but Bobby Morrow did it easily. An American Cold War hero with his three gold medals from Melbourne, Morrow flew on a private plane into Abilene Municipal Airport on Tuesday and landed in the middle of a huge civic celebration. The *Reporter-News* estimated that 25,000 people paid Morrow tribute at some point during the day, at the airport red-carpet reception, during an hour-long parade through the city, and at a banquet that evening at Catchings Cafeteria.

Morrow was the star of an Abilene Christian College track team, coached by Oliver Jackson, that in participation at invitational events such as the Texas and Drake Relays, and in the NCAA championships, brought even more national publicity to Abilene than the Eagles did.

Praising the 21-year-old Morrow as an American icon were baseball legend Tris Speaker (a native of Hubbard in Hill County), champion golfer Byron Nelson, Texas A&M all-American "Jarrin'" John Kimbrough from Haskell, presidents of all three Abilene colleges, civic leaders and military brass from Dyess Air Force Base, and Abilene mayor C.E. Gatlin, who presented Morrow the key to the city.

Morrow and Chuck Moser were easily the two most famous men in the city. Interestingly, both had come to Abilene from towns deep in the Rio Grande Valley just miles apart: Moser from McAllen, and Morrow from San Benito.

∽∽

ABILENE AND WICHITA FALLS WERE only 144 miles apart. The cities were about the same size, same economy (Wichita Falls hosted the schoolboy all-star "Oil Bowl" game annually), same working-class ethic that produced hard-nosed football players who in the 1950s played for their city's only high school. Abilene and Wichita Falls could have been stupendous natural rivals, and Abilene, San Angelo, Midland, Odessa and Wichita Falls could have been a dream district for football.

But Wichita Falls was a shade too far east. The city was only 144 miles from Abilene, but 300 miles from the Midland-Odessa area, farther even than Amarillo from Abilene. So Wichita Falls was aligned by the University Interscholastic League with cities in the Fort Worth area north to the Red River. It was a rare opportunity, then, when the state playoffs brought the Eagles and Coyotes together.

Wichita Falls in 1956 was a great team, with speed and size and athleticism, and the Coyotes literally had a natural advantage: they ran the single wing.

The single wing was a backfield formation that was a throwback clear to the birth of football. In old black-and-white movies about Knute Rockne and Jim Thorpe, Notre Dame and Carlisle were running the single wing. By the 1950s, practically all football teams from high school to professional were running some version of the T formation, with the quarterback "up under" the center. Teams never practiced defending the single wing, because they didn't have to. Until they played Wichita Falls. If Moser wanted to give his defense a test, this was it.

In the single wing, the tailback lined up five yards directly behind the center. To one side of the tailback was the fullback. In front of the fullback, very close to the line of scrimmage, was the blocking back. Split just outside the end was the wingback. There were many variations off that standard formation.

Plays began with a direct snap from the center to either the tailback or the fullback. What ensued was a series of "spins" and criss-crossing backs that was very deceptive because the spin concealed the ball from the defenders. The fullback could spin and fake to the tailback going one direction, the wingback going the other, then spin again and take off directly into the line of scrimmage. Further confusing the situation was the single wing team's habit of running behind an unbalanced line, that is, two linemen to one side of the center and four to the other. With four linemen, the blocking back and the fullback all tightly grouped, it focused blocking power in one area, which was another feature of the single wing.

A defender's instinct was to follow motion, particularly if the motion was convincing. The defensive coach drilled his players to "stay at home" until the ball carrier appeared out of the pack. It wasn't easy. A classic example was a played called the "keybreaker." Defenders routinely "keyed" on the actions of offensive linemen and backs. For example, against a T-formation team, the linebacker would watch the guard. If the guard pulled, the linebacker followed him, because that's where the play was going. But Wichita Falls ran a "keybreaker" play, in which the guard pulled, pulling the linebacker with him, and the tailback or fullback then carried the ball through the vacated hole. In nine years, running the single wing at Wichita Falls, coach Joe Golding had guided the Coyotes to five district championships and two state titles, in 1949-50.

∞

THE EAGLES, CONCENTRATING ON DEFENSE anyway, spent a lot of time in practice "staying at home." Complicating the situation was the unfamiliarity of the scout team with the essential spins and deception of the single wing. Probably the week's toughest assignment fell to the coach getting the scout team ready to run the Coyotes' offense against the varsity defense. The Eagles did get one big break. Starting tailback David Allred, the Coyotes' leading rusher with 901 yards, was out with a broken collarbone suffered in the Highland Park game.

Offensively, Gervis Galbraith worked all week with the first team. Moser had decided he wanted Gregory's running, receiving and blocking talents at his natural left halfback position. On Thursday, two doctors examined injured guard and defensive end Guy Wells. Both concluded that Wells should not risk his injured kidney to any more contact. He was through for the season, and it was a blow. "Wells was one of our four best defensive men," Moser said. Moving in at right guard was 151-pound Hubert Jordan, with 158-pound junior John Young taking over for Wells at defensive end.

Eagle cheerleaders each week tried to think up a clever way for the Eagles, with their traditional "Eagles" chant, to beat that week's opponent. At the Friday morning pep rally, they unveiled one of the season's best: "Eagles, Eagles, Withdraw Wichita." The Eagles bussed to Wichita Falls Friday afternoon and headquartered at the Kemp Hotel. Stephens, Wells, Butch Adams and Mike Bryant joined the team for the pre-game meal Saturday morning and a place had been made for them to watch the game from the sideline.

Wichita Falls had scored 393 points in its undefeated season while allowing 65. Only Amarillo and Arlington had scored more than once against the Coyotes. Abilene had scored 462 points and allowed 52, including an amazing 18 points in its last six games. Wichita Falls had rushed for 3,125 yards but now was missing its best runner Allred. Abilene had 3,833 yards rushing but a still untested junior at quarterback. Taking over for Allred at tailback was David West, sort of a "fifth back" who had rushed for 597 yards. Fullback

Harold Morgan was the passer and had thrown for 724 yards and eight touchdowns.

~

THE GAME WAS A SELLOUT, 15,000 people counting standing room only. Aesthetically it was a beautiful spectacle in Coyote Stadium, under blue sky and golden December sun. Wichita Falls wore its home jerseys, red with white numbers and black trim, black pants and white helmets, while the Eagles wore the white jerseys, black pants and gold helmets.

But it was windy, and with his emphasis on defense winning the game, when the Eagles won the toss, Moser told his captains to take the wind. Wichita Falls chose to receive and very quickly Moser's strategy paid off. Abilene's defense stuffed the single wing and on fourth down and six, the Coyotes punted to the Eagle 39. It took 11 plays to drive the 61 yards.

With Gregory and Carpenter alternating carries, the Eagles drove into Coyote territory, then came up against fourth down and one at the 31-yard-line. Gregory slammed for two yards but the ball popped loose. Eagle tackle Bufford Carr saved the drive with his recovery at the 28. Two plays later, after a five-yard loss, the Eagles faced third and 14. Gregory got the call and appeared to be stopped but bolted forward for 12-plus yards. He was pulled down short of a first down, but Coyote coach Joe Golding thought it was the turning point in the game.

"We had Abilene on third down and 14 yards to go," he said. "We even had Gregory stopped, but he just seemed to squirt out of our hands." Now it was fourth down and inches. Galbraith handed to Carpenter, who found a hole Carr and guard Hubert Jordan had created in the Coyotes' short-yardage defense. Once through the hole, Carpenter was in the clear and he sped 19 yards for the Eagles' first touchdown. Gregory's PAT made it 7-0.

Abilene had a golden opportunity moments later when cornerback Charles Bradshaw recovered Harold Morgan's fumble at the

Coyote 22. Abilene reached the eight, but penalties and the Wichita defense stopped the threat. The Eagle defense, meanwhile, was having little trouble with the single wing, with linebacker Jim Rose, end Stuart Peake and tackle Rufus King, in Golding's estimation, doing the most damage. For the afternoon, the Wichita Falls offense would gain only 152 yards, 133 of that on the ground. But the Coyotes made it 7-6 midway through the second quarter when halfback Fritz Land turned in the day's most exciting play, faking out one tackler after another as he returned a Gregory punt 56 yards for a touchdown. Wichita had a bad snap from center on the point-after. Morgan tried to run it across but was tackled by Gregory.

THE WICHITA THRONG WAS AROUSED, but not for long. The Eagles' Chuck Colvin returned the kickoff to the 29. Carpenter ran for a first down to the 49. Gregory ran for 27 yards in two plays, the second a double reverse that carried to the Coyote 31. Carpenter carried twice and Gregory once for a first down at the 19. Galbraith threw incomplete, then Gregory ran to the 14. Galbraith called a modified draw play that sucked in the middle of the Coyote defense. Galbraith slipped Gregory the ball and the halfback stormed 14 yards to the end zone.

"Glynn Gregory," said Joe Golding. "Take him off the field and there would have been a world of difference." Gregory's kick made it 14-6 with a minute left in the half. The drive had taken 12 plays, but its pace was relentless and convincing, coming as it did immediately after the shock of the Coyotes' quick touchdown. If Wichita Falls were going to win the game, something unusual would have to happen.

It didn't. Abilene scored a third touchdown on a 60-yard drive in the third period, Carpenter getting his second TD from five yards out. Wichita Falls once drove to the Abilene 22 before losing the ball on downs. Gregory led all rushers with 131 yards in 26 workhorse carries, and Carpenter added 84 yards on 17 tries. The Eagles didn't complete a pass. David West led Wichita Falls with 59 yards on 21 carries. Morgan completed only one of four pass attempts for 19 yards, and Golding was asked why the Coyotes didn't throw more.

"Any man who would throw with defenders like Gregory and Carpenter ought to have his head examined," Golding said. "We couldn't afford to pass."

"The Eagles were the hardest to block I ever saw," said Coyote tailback West. "They wouldn't stay down but would get up and come back at you."

Wichita starting tackle Larry Dellinger, a senior, had had an interesting afternoon. In junior high he lived in Abilene and played on the unbeaten ninth grade team at South Junior with Gregory, Carpenter and others. "You can't forget old friends," was all he would say.

Down south, unbeaten Corpus Christi Ray won a 13-6 battle over Baytown to get into the championship game. On Sunday morning, Abilenian Rusty Crownover flew Moser, schools superintendent A.E. Wells, and schools ticket manager Neil McLeskey to Austin, where the group met a Corpus Christi delegation that included schools superintendent Dr. R. L. Williams and Ray head coach Bill Stages. The parties agreed to play the championship game in Austin, at Memorial Stadium on the campus of the University of Texas, at 2 p.m. Saturday, Dec. 22. Abilene won a coin toss for home team and chose to wear gold jerseys. Ray, whose colors were red and white, would wear white. There was an agreement about footballs. Ray used Wilson footballs, Abilene favored the Spaulding J5V. Each team, on offense, could use its football of choice. Dr. Williams, a graduate of Hardin-Simmons University in Abilene, was so moved by the camaraderie in the meeting that he later phoned Don Oliver at the *Reporter-News* and said he wanted it in the newspaper that he had "never worked with such a wonderful group of men." He said that "the Abilene group was most cooperative in every respect in setting up the state championship game."

Moser and Stages knew each other from South Texas coaching circles, but they had never coached against each other. Now that they were, Stages' interest in the game became personal. He was the man who had coached Hull-Daisetta to its 43-game winning streak.

Abilene 20, Wichita Falls 6
Dec. 15, 1956

Dec. 22, 1956

"This is it. I know you will all do your part every day this week. They are the best team you have played for 3 years—We can beat them if we are sharp and tough."

CHUCK MOSER WAS RIGHT about championship teams, and he was wrong. The Abilene Eagles were about to prove it.

The Eagles rolled into Austin on Friday, Dec. 21, with two streaks and a record on the line.

Their streak of consecutive games won stood at 36. They were playing to become only the third high school team in Texas to win three straight state championships, after Waco (1925-26-27) and Amarillo (1934-35-36). And by winning, the Eagles would become the school with the most state championships—six—in Texas schoolboy history. This was a passel of glory to pack into three short years, particularly after prolonged mediocrity. "What is it now?" wondered Don Oliver in his column. "Win No. 37? Championship No. 6? We'll take 'em all."

Twenty of 23 Texas sports writers picked Abilene to beat Ray, which was in a state title game for the first time. The margins ranged from one point to "no doubt." Amarillo's Putt Powell thought it was reasonable to suppose the Eagles would score more touchdowns than Ray made first downs. An opposing view, sort of, was filed by Tom Murray of the *Baytown Sun and Times,* who had just watched Ray beat Baytown, 13-6, in a classic semifinals struggle. "If Abilene can beat this rugged ball-control Ray team," Murray said, "I'll go along with Abilene as being the greatest in schoolboy history." Murray saw it as Ray 20, Abilene 14, as did Louis Anderson of the *Corpus Christi Caller-Times*. "The Texans have an outstanding ball club and great desire," Anderson said. Most writers picked Abilene by 21-7. The cumulative guessing was Abilene 22, Ray 9.

~

MOSER PUT HIS TEAM THROUGH a light familiarization workout at Memorial Stadium and the team overnighted at the Driskill Hotel. Such expenses came out of revenue from gate receipts, which of course went up when Abilene began winning so regularly. "Since taking over as athletic director here in February, 1953," Don Oliver wrote, "Moser has added some $98,121 into the athletic fund of the public school system through his winning ways on the gridiron. When Moser took over, the athletic fund showed a balance of $2,769.28. Through November of this year the balance was $74,621 and when the gate receipts of the four playoff games are thrown in, this figure will move well over the $100,000 mark."

Among the equipment brought to Austin were several white helmets, borrowed by Moser from Abilene Christian College. The Eagles had enhanced their reputation for breaking helmets, even the new Riddell molded plastic models that weren't supposed to break.

The team ate its pregame meal at 11 a.m. and later bused to the stadium a few blocks away. It was another beautiful Texas December afternoon, the first full day of winter. The teams, Abilene in gold and Ray in white, came onto the field at 1:15 for warm-ups. Some of the Ray players looked like collegians. Center Max Christian's program weight was 218. End Sonny Davis was 196, tackles Walter Beck and Dick Hulbert 203 and 191 respectively, guard Frank Eddleman 187. Quarterback Arthur McCallum, 175, was touted as one of the best quarterbacks in the state. All three running backs were averaging more than five yards a carry. The two teams' only common opponent was Waco. Ray had beaten the Tigers 33-6 in bi-district. The Texans ran a multiple offense that included almost 30 variations of the basic

T formation. "The main thing is that our kids know how to adjust when they go into these various formations," Moser said. "If we get confused, they're gonna hurt us."

Defensively, Stages liked to crowd the line of scrimmage, placing eight Texans within a foot of the offensive line, with an "umbrella" of two halfbacks and a safety to watch for the pass. "We've used the umbrella a lot this year," Stages said. Ray had allowed 13 opponents a total of 93 points. The defense almost dared the opposition to pass, something that would show up in a scouting report. Moser had said passing was vital in a big game. "We know you can't win tough ball games without it," he said. Leaders in the Texan defense were Christian, Davis, guard Floyd Brown and tackles Hulbert and Beck.

ABOUT 25,000 WERE IN the stadium for the 2 p.m. kickoff. Abilene won the toss, received the kickoff and returned it to the 39. The Abilene offense and Ray defense trotted onto the field. The Eagles formed their military huddle, facing the defense, interior linemen in front, ends and backs behind, the quarterback facing them. They looked at Gervis Galbraith, he looked at them. They had practiced the first play many times during the week. Now Galbraith called it and it was official. The game was under way. Galbraith told them the snap count, repeated it. They clapped and broke the huddle and came up to the line. Sure enough, the Texans were in the umbrella. End Kenny Schmidt took off deep. The Eagles were going for the home run on the first play of the game. Schmidt was clear and Galbraith threw, but the pass fell short.

It was a shot worth taking, and it might have worked, but now the surprise was gone. The Eagles shifted into what they did so well. Gregory gained eight on second down and fullback Bill Sides ran for four and a first down at the Eagle 49. Jimmy Carpenter picked up three more, into Texan territory, but then a Galbraith-Gregory pitchout misfired. Ray's Frank Eddleman recovered the fumble at the 50-yard line.

The Texan offense came to the line breathing fire. In five plays they had gained the Eagle 19 and looked like a team that could beat the Eagle defense. Then end Stuart Peake broke through and hit quarterback Arthur McCallum. The ball came loose and bounced all the way back to the 44 before McCallum could fall on it. Unperturbed, McCallum threw to end Sonny Davis at the Abilene 21. He threw again to Davis, this time to the Eagle 4. Abilene was very much a team in trouble. McCallum kept on a quarterback sneak to the 2. Sub halfback Bart Shirley rammed to the one. McCallum tried another sneak and was piled up at the one-foot line.

On fourth down, the two teams massed at the goalline, Abilene in its gap-8 defense. The center Christian snapped the ball, the lines charged, and suddenly the ball was in the air above the tumult, floating free, describing a lazy parabola toward the left end of the Texan line. It landed directly in front of Eagle linebacker Gerald Galbraith, who smothered it at the 3 as fans on both sides screamed. The ball appeared to have simply squirted through McCallum's hands at the snap. McCallum couldn't say what happened. Stages, obviously, thought it made a big difference in the ball game. "We don't want to take anything away from their team," he said, "but if we had scored, that would have helped our cause."

~

THE EAGLE BACKS LINED UP in the end zone. Gregory improved things somewhat with a three-yard dive to the 6. Austin sports writers were familiar with Gregory and Carpenter. Gregory had made the all-state team as a junior, but there was something more recent. In June, Abilene had won the Class AAAA baseball tournament in Austin, beating Highland Park, 13-0, in the championship game at nearby Disch Field. Gregory was the catcher on that team, and Carpenter, an all-state outfielder, in the three-game tournament got eight hits in 11 at-bats, a .727 average, and he scored nine runs, all records that were still standing at the end of the century.

Now Carpenter was about to give them something else to remember. Ray was still in its umbrella defense. In the huddle, Galbraith looked at right tackle Boyd King. "I asked old Boyd if he could take that old boy out (tackle Walter Beck)," Galbraith said. "Sure, run that old 4-play," King told him. It was the right halfback dive play straight ahead, with straight-ahead blocking and a quick count, a good strategy against a defense massed on the line of scrimmage. If a halfback could pop through....

Galbraith called it: "4 Straightaway, on Set, on Set." The Eagles in their gold jerseys, standing in their end zone, broke the huddle with a clap of hands, trotted to the line of scrimmage at the 6, fell into the hands-on-knees "ready" stance, looked across the line at the looming Ray defenders. Boyd King and Hubert Jordan, the right guard, found their men and took their splits to get the best blocking angle. "Down," Galbraith called, with the downward inflection. The team dropped into its three-point stance. "Set," Galbraith yelled, but without time for the rising, anticipatory inflection, because the Eagles had charged. Galbraith took the snap from Jim Rose, pivoted right, handed to Carpenter going by, and going by so fast that Galbraith barely got the ball to him. Boyd King got position on Walter Beck, just like his coach had taught him, and knocked Beck outside. Jordan blocked Floyd Brown inside.

Carpenter, all 153 fleet pounds of him, hit the hole in a flash and burst into the clear on the other side. A Ray halfback came up. Carpenter spun to the outside, flaring slightly toward the right sideline, and in a couple of strides was in high gear. It was a footrace with the Ray safety that Carpenter won easily, 94 yards to the end zone. His teammates sprinted all the way down the field after him, and after Gregory's kick, Abilene led, 7-0.

Men who have played football, for the rest of their lives may refer to a particular kind of traumatic event as "a 14-point turnaround." A team is on the goalline, about to score, when something happens—an interception runback, or a fumble and a 94-yard run. Not only has the team lost its seven points, the other team has scored seven, more or less in the same breath. It is a terrific "what if" shock, and it had happened to the Ray Texans.

~

"THEY'RE JUST KIDS," said Bill Stages. "They can't take that kind of shock and recuperate." On the Abilene side, Chuck Moser was in kind of a shock of his own. "What would you have given for our chances when they were down on our one-yard line?" he said. Stages wouldn't blame the umbrella but credited Carpenter's speed for the play's success. He was through the hole and gone before Ray could close it down. "They've got fine speed," Stages said of Carpenter and Gregory. "The speed of those two halfbacks was the difference in the ball game," said Ray assistant Dan Purcell.

The 14-point turnaround works both ways. After Carpenter's run, the energized Eagles took control of the game. The game settled into Ray's end of the field, but fumbles hurt both sides. Abilene lost three, killing good drives, including one in the second quarter when Carpenter fumbled at the end of a 38-yard gain. He was straining for more when he was hit hard and the ball came free at the Ray 24. Later Abilene had a fourth down at the Ray 25, where Galbraith missed Gregory with a pass.

The Texans became conservative. "We couldn't do otherwise," Stages said, astutely; he had seen what happened to other teams who felt forced into the gamble against Abilene. "At that stage of the game we certainly didn't have any business gambling. If we had tried some of those fancy handoffs or passes there in our end of the field and they had backfired, the whole game might have blown up and turned into a runaway. We felt like with ball control maybe we could get the ball into a position where we could open up. We felt that if we could get the ball in position, we could get back in the ball game."

But the Eagle defense wouldn't allow it. Big fullback Bobby Myers was the leading Ray ball carrier with 37 yards. After his two strikes to Davis in the first drive, McCallum didn't complete another pass.

Abilene scored an insurance touchdown on its first possession of the second half. Ray received the kickoff, gained six yards, and punted. The Eagles came to the line at their 36 and gained only two yards in two plays against a Texan defense that appeared to have made halftime adjustments. Then on third and eight, Galbraith looked at Boyd King again. He called 4 Straightaway. King and Jordan opened the same hole and Carpenter was gone again, this time 62 yards. "The closest Ray defender couldn't have hit Carpenter with a rock," wrote Don Oliver.

It was 14-0, and the Eagles were more than in control. In the second half, Ray gained only 26 yards rushing and none passing. Jim Rose finished the game in a white helmet. Carpenter finished with 227 yards rushing and two touchdowns, and defensively he intercepted McCallum twice. The Austin sports writers would get to see him one more time, in the spring, when Abilene repeated as the Class AAAA baseball champion. Gregory added 71 yards in 20 carries, and Abilene finished with 332 yards rushing.

Even more dominant than Carpenter in the game was the Eagle defense. Ray finished with 105 yards rushing and 40 passing, and Moser had been right. The team with the best defense won the championship. But then someone reminded him of his claim that it takes a passing attack to win the big games. The Eagles didn't complete a pass against Ray. They only tried two. In fact it was the third game in a row that the Eagles didn't complete a pass. They beat Fort Worth Paschal, Wichita Falls and Corpus Christi Ray totally by running the ball.

"That belief of mine was sure proved otherwise," Moser said. But it was proven by an unusual team. "They are by far the best football team that we have ever played," Stages said, arguing, as Carl Price had surmised, that the 1956 Eagles were better than the '55 squad. "They've got better offensive stability in their running game this year," he said, "and more team defense, better team defense than any high school team I've ever seen, and have a lot more poise than the '55 bunch."

~

AT THE END OF THE GAME Hayseed Stephens was jumping up and down on his crutches. Line coach Hank Watkins, who had a nickname for just about everybody, came up and hugged "Old Poker Face," his name for Jimmy Carpenter. "Hate to lose you, Jim," Watkins said. "Hate to leave, Coach," Carpenter said. "Wish I could play two more years." The players let the coaches strip to their underwear before throwing them in the showers. Teen music issued from the Eagle bus as it rolled out of a silent Memorial Stadium. Stuart Peake on guitar, singing "Never Felt More Like Singing the Blues," a Guy Mitchell radio hit. Peake sat in the back of the bus with the seniors: Rufus and Boyd King, Jim Rose, Kenny Schmidt, Charles Bradshaw, Jimmy Carpenter, Glynn Gregory, Bufford Carr, Hubert Jordan, Ervin Bishop, 21 seniors in all.

"The juniors and sophomores sat in the front and talked about next year's team," said Moser of the ride home. "Those young kids are ready to go. John Young came up to me and asked when spring training would start. I told him I didn't know, and he answered, 'I wish it was starting Monday'."

Abilene 14, Corpus Christi Ray 0
Dec. 22, 1956

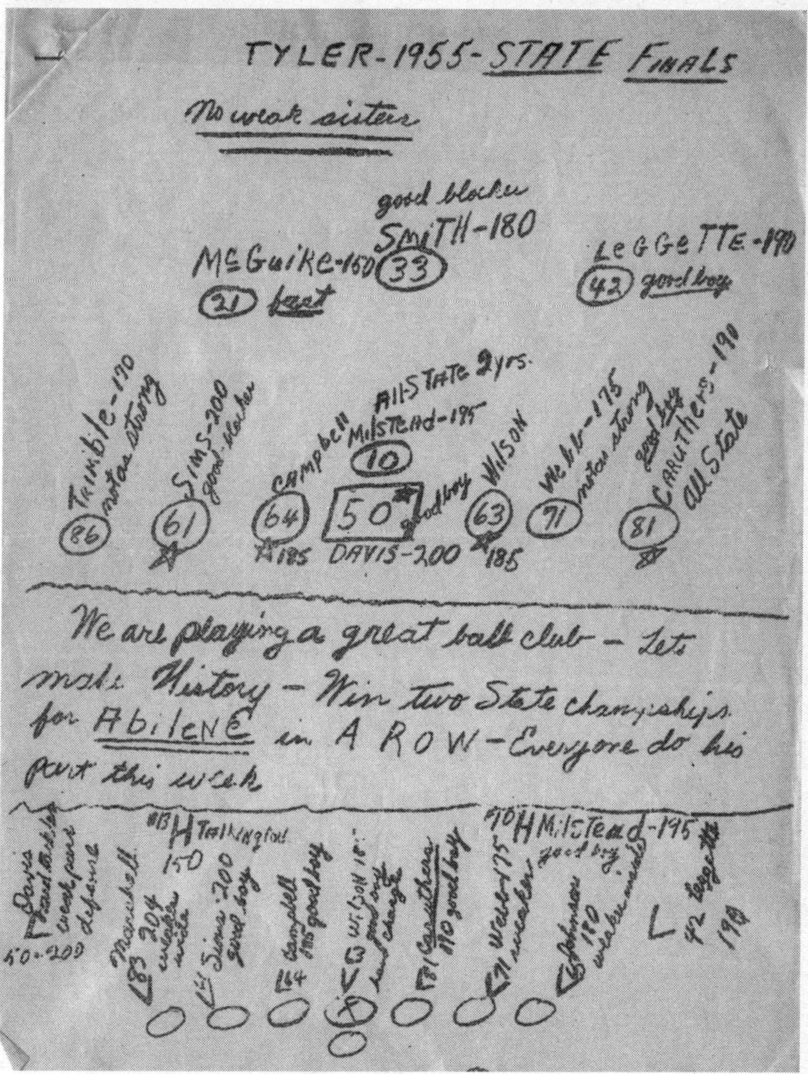

The scouting report for the state championship game in Fort Worth in 1955. Moser almost always drew up the entire scouting report, but this cover page was created by an assistant.

Photos and documents courtesy of Abilene High School, Gerald Galbraith and Gervis Galbraith.

Fullback James Welch breaks through on the trap play for Abilene's first touchdown against Tyler. Nobody could quite believe what they had seen after that first drive.

Rufus King hit Tyler's great Charlie Milstead with a block that knocked him five yards backward and to the ground.

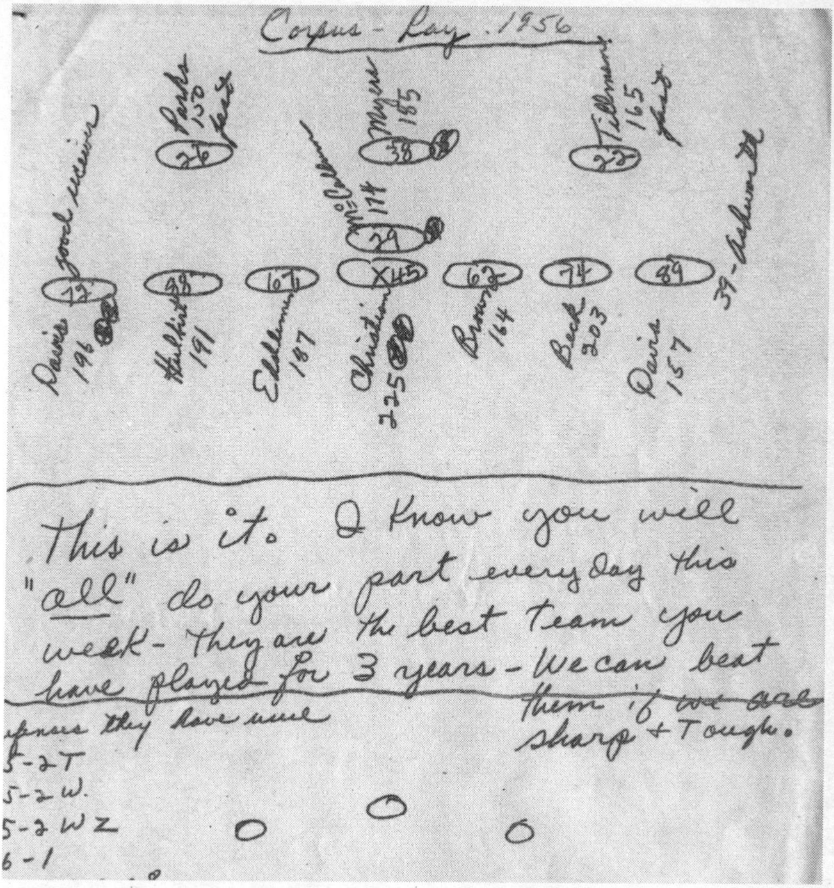

Corpus - Ray. 1956

This is it. I know you will "all" do your part everyday this week - They are the best team you have played for 3 years - We can beat them if we are sharp + Tough.

Defenses they have used
5-2T
5-2W.
5-2WZ
6-1

The scouting report for the 1956 championship game against Corpus Christi Ray in Austin.

Gervis Galbraith (29) quarterbacked the Eagles against Ray after Hayseed Stephens broke his leg. His cousin, Gerald Galbraith (51) recovered a fumble just outside the Eagle goalline that was the biggest play in the game.

Gregory breaks loose for yardage against Ray, but the day's star was the other halfback, Jimmy Carpenter, with two long touchdown runs.

A Friday morning pep rally always preceded the games. If the Eagles were going on the road, the crowd followed them outside to the colorful Eagle Bus and cheered as motorcycle patrolmen escorted the bus to the edge of town.

The 1957 Abilene High Cheerleaders. Mascot is Temple Lindsey. Top of stairs to bottom: Lynda Renfro, Mary Gene Bradshaw, Judy Jones, Sylvia Blackley, Christie Smith.

Bill Sides up the middle in "the Amarillo game."

The Eagles with Eagle bus driver Bert Berry ready to head home after their 49th straight win

1957

Sept. 13, 1957

CHUCK MOSER KNEW what graduation had done to his football team. As president of the Abilene Kiwanis Club, it was Moser's responsibility to sign off on the club's schedule of events before it went to press. In the summer of 1957, he looked at that schedule and saw the club's annual banquet scheduled for Tuesday evening, Dec. 10. If the Eagles were in the playoffs, Moser would be routinely scheduled to address the Eagle Booster Club that night. But he let the banquet stand.

Glynn Gregory and Jimmy Carpenter went back to Austin one more time, in May of 1957, to lead the Eagles to a repeat Class AAAA state baseball championship. Then they graduated, along with Stuart Peake, Jim Rose, Hayseed Stephens and the others who in their three years saw five state championship trophies deposited in the Abilene High School trophy case. They were a dazzling cohort.

What was left for 1957 was one offensive starter and three defensive starters.

"I still think we will be tough to beat," Moser said, "but we don't have any of those super boys like we have had, and we will get beat some time." He was only being realistic. In his mind, Moser had already formed the points of a Sunday school lesson he knew he would have to teach, on a Sunday morning after the Eagles had lost.

The biggest returning player, among the players anyway, was the streak. Moser and his coaches only thought about the next game. The players thought about the streak. It was a legacy, and they took it into their possession, and with it a number: 43.

With the Big Spring victory in 1956, The Eagles had secured the record for large-classification schools at 30 straight, eclipsing Lubbock's old record (1951-53) of 29. Now, in 1957, six more victories, and the Eagles would tie the all-time state schoolboy record of 43 consecutive wins, set by Corpus Christi Ray coach Bill Stages' own Hull-Daisetta Bobcats in 1937-40.

"It's good and it's bad," said Stages about winning streaks. "It's good that it builds up an element of pride in the kiddos, but that pressure builds up, too."

It changed the importance of every game. In 1957, Abilene opened the season against San Antonio Jefferson, which would have been just another non-district game except for the streak. The game received considerable attention in the statewide media.

"When we had that streak going," Stages said, "all the writers came around and gave us big spreads. And it was good copy. But that pressure got pretty tough on the kids."

Now the 1957 Abilene kids had this record, this possession, this pressure, passed into their hands with nary a Gregory or Carpenter in sight to help them protect it. While not exactly a liability, success had taken on weight. "With the burden of three consecutive state championships on their back," wrote *Reporter-News* sports writer Jimmy Browder in his Jefferson game advance, "the Abilene Eagles will put their 1957 wares on display at 8 p.m. tonight against a big eleven from Thomas Jefferson High School in San Antonio."

At Abilene High, Chuck Moser did what he always did. He told his players they had but one goal, and that was to beat San Antonio Jefferson. When two-a-days began, for the first time, the Eagles reported to new training facilities at the southeast corner of the high school grounds. A field house fronted North 6th Street with locker rooms and showers for the varsity, junior varsity and B teams, a first-class training room complete with whirlpool, an equipment room, and a laundry room. Beyond the field house was a regulation-sized football field inside an eight-lane running track. This was the varsity practice field; the other teams practiced on adjacent unmarked fields. The field house was paid for with revenues from the athletic fund.

TWO-A-DAYS WERE HOT and miserable. Nobody worried about the streak during two-a-days. The second day was the worst. No matter how conditioned a player was, the first contact left everyone stiff and sore, particularly in the neck and shoulders. When you hit someone like Chuck Moser wanted you to hit someone, you felt it in the neck and shoulders for a few days. Dull headaches were not uncommon. The Eagles pulled on pads, pants and jerseys, carried their high-top cleats outside into the heat and sat on benches or on the ground. With tongue depressors they slathered Vaseline from big cans onto their feet, pulled on white sweat socks over the Vaseline, showered talcum powder onto the socks, pulled on their cleats and laced them high and tight, like Moser instructed, while the Vaseline squished around inside.

It never rained in August and afternoon temperatures routinely topped 100 degrees. Workouts were two hours or a little less, with breaks scheduled not for water, but for a pepperminty solution squirted by managers into the players' mouths. It didn't do much for thirst, but it kept players hydrated as sweat poured out by the pound. The solution was also supposed to cut through the "cottonmouth" effect created by steady exertion in such heat. Workouts ended with 10 or more sideline-to-sideline (53 yards) wind sprints. Players ran as hard as they could because they knew Moser was right, that this kind of conditioning would pay off in the first game, and that if they didn't run hard, Moser would make them run some more. In the training room after practice were lined up tall cans from which managers had emptied rolls of adhesive tape, to tape players' ankles before practice. After practice, the cans became wonderful tall containers of ice and water, gulped down by players who didn't care if it tasted like adhesive tape.

Two-a-days typically lasted a week or a little longer until, mercifully, school started. On the players' class schedules, "Athletics" was their last-period class, and practice was always under way before the last bell rang. Students poured out of the building and got in cars and drove away, truly not knowing what they were missing. By the first day of school, about 110 boys were practicing on the three teams at Abilene High.

FOR THE FIRST TIME since 1954, Abilene was not the state's top-ranked team in the pre-season Class AAAA poll. Amarillo was No. 1, then Corpus Christi Ray, then Abilene. From the team that was surprised by Fort Worth Paschal in the 1956 playoffs, Amarillo returned five starters on offense, including three in the backfield.

Fullback Bill Sides was the only returning Eagle starter on offense. Gervis Galbraith had gained invaluable experience at quarterback after the Hayseed Stephens injury. Right halfback Chuck Colvin had speed, was a hard, talented runner and had as much if not more playing time than any of the Eagle backs in 1956. But he would always be second-string to either Gregory or Carpenter. Right half was up for grabs. Getting the start against Jefferson was compact speedster Stan Cozby, a junior up from the B team.

John Young, a 165-pound guard, and center Gerald Galbraith, Gervis's cousin, would be the leaders in the line. Both had extensive playing time in '56, and Young played as if he had been wired by Stuart Peake. The other guard was newcomer Truman Bridges. The tackles were big and talented Mike Bryant (194) and Ronnie Alldredge (185). Jimmy Perry and Mike McKinnis were the ends.

Defensively the picture was a little better, with Young and both Galbraiths returning starters. Moser's biggest concern was in the deep secondary. "We'll miss Gregory and Carpenter's defensive play more than anything," he said. Jim Perry, who was 6-5, and substitute end Bob Swafford, 6-3, would be the safeties.

IF THE STREAK COULD BE a liability, Moser said it also had to be counted as an asset. "We have a group of kids," he said, "who were substitutes on some great football teams." There was a legacy of spirit and determination that came with playing on the same team as Stuart Peake and Jim Rose, and a confidence that had become ingrained by constant success. Indeed the seniors and juniors on the team literally didn't know how to lose. Coaches across time have acknowledged the importance of "learning how to win." The 1957 Eagles had been taught to win by masters.

The most important returnee was Chuck Moser. After the December, 1956, story linking him with the coach's job at the University of Missouri, the reports started to flow. Moser was going to the University of Texas. He was going to SMU. He was going to Texas Tech, at a salary rumored to be $25,000 a year. None of these reports panned out, and Moser didn't talk much about them. In 1957 he was the most famous football coach in Texas. But he stayed at Abilene. He said several times during those months that he loved working with high school athletes and didn't know whether he would get the same enjoyment from coaching college kids.

The high school athletes knew that was a true statement. They knew Moser's love for them was genuine.

"I just can't put my finger on where his greatness comes from," said Bobby Jack Oliver, the all-state tackle in 1953, "but I can tell you from my own personal experience, we all worship him and would do anything in the world for him."

"During my senior year in high school I would watch him and just hope that I could pattern my life after his," said Twyman Ash, "Old Glue Fingers." "He not only taught the boys football, he taught them to look to the future. He helped each boy realize what an education would mean. In his own words, you can't eat that football when you get out of school and have to make a living."

"We used to have to carry eligibility slips around to the teachers each week," said Sammy Caudle, the 1955 all-state guard, "and how we hated them. We knew if the teachers put anything bad on them it meant a little extra running after practice. It made better students out of us, though."

"While playing under Coach Moser I learned much more than I could have ever learned by not being associated with him," said David Bourland, the '55 quarterback. "I am not only talking about learning football, but just learning how to be a man of respect in everyday life."

"One thing he taught me was to have confidence," said Jim Millerman, who in 1953 scored the first touchdown by a Moser-coached Eagle team. "Another thing that I consider important is that I learned not to worry about things. He always said that instead of worrying, you should think your problems out."

"Coach Moser wants more than good football players, he wants gentlemen who know how to act no matter where they are," said H.P. Hawkins, who promised Moser the winning TD in the '54 state championship game. "Having played for Coach Moser is something that I will always be proud of. He is the type of person and coach that any father should want his son to be associated with."

CONSCIOUSLY OR NOT, MOSER provided his 1957 team with an identity all its own. Since 1953, his Eagle teams had worn either white or gold jerseys. On Friday night, Sept. 13, 1957, the Eagles filed out of the stone field house and walked across the track to the field wearing black jerseys. The sleeve stripes were white, the numbers were gold with white piping. Pants were still black, helmets were gold. It was a classy look, the look of a champion.

On the field, the Eagles did a nice job establishing their identity. They beat San Antonio Jefferson, 26-13. It was not intimidating, like 47-0, but it was still 1-0 in the won-lost column. And the Eagles did develop a 26-0 lead, before Jefferson scored two late touchdowns.

The Eagles started the game in their old customary fashion, driving 88 yards in 11 plays, all rushes. Colvin and Sides bit off chunks of yardage, and the Eagles overcame a 15-yard penalty. The new left halfback, Stan Cozby, got the TD on a 16-yard run on fourth down. "My idea of a good quarterback is one that takes the ball club all the way," Moser said. "On that first drive, Gervis Galbraith took them 88 yards, or actually 103 when you count that 15-yard penalty, and that's a fine job when you're that consistent."

Abilene scored again in the first quarter after recovering a Jefferson fumble at the Mustang six. Colvin scored on a sweep from two yards out. Gervis Galbraith kicked the PAT for 13-0. Moser let strong-armed junior quarterback Freddie Martinez run the team for two series, and on the second one the Eagles went 82 yards to score. Sides picked up 22 yards on one carry and Martinez hit end Mike McKinnis for 14 in the drive. Colvin bulled six yards for the TD and Galbraith missed his second PAT to make it 19-0 at the half. Galbraith came back in to direct a third-period scoring drive, during which Galbraith hit McKinnis for 13 yards, end Bob Swafford for 16, and halfback Eddie Woods for 10. Sides finished the drive with carries of five and four yards. Sides finished with 83 yards in 14 carries and Colvin, still bothered by the effects of strep throat, added 71. Gerald Galbraith, junior 200-pound tackle Frank Aycock and the safeties Swafford and Jimmy Perry led an Eagle defense that limited Jefferson to 161 total yards. For a first game, Moser said his team did "a real fine job."

Abilene 26, San Antonio Jefferson 13
Sept. 13, 1957

Sept. 20, 1957

"They will be one of the 4 best teams we will play all year. They are conditioned and tough. We must be 'really' ready mentally for a real hard 4-quarter game."

FLORISTS IN ABILENE KNEW they had four regular events that would sustain their businesses: weddings, funerals, Valentine's Day and the Abilene Eagles.

The Eagles gave the florists a big fall season. On average they would play five games at home and in recent seasons a playoff game could be counted on.

To the games, the girls wore "mums." They were huge chrysanthemum globes, either white or yellow, arranged with black and gold ribbons dangling down, and on the mum itself was fixed, in black pipe cleaners, an "AHS," and gold glitter was applied over all. They were real creations, which the girl's date ordered (the florists delivered them on Friday afternoons) and she wore like a giant corsage.

If the girl were dating a football player, the "AHS" would be replaced by the player's number. Sometimes girls would wear more than one mum, one from a player and one from parents or other friends. Cheerleaders almost always wore two, sometimes three. There might be 300 such mums in the student section every Friday night for home games, meaning 1,500 mums for the season, and business was always better when the team was winning. The mums, according to the degree of grandeur, cost around $6.50. Florists loved the Abilene Eagles.

IN ABILENE, THE DEFINITION of "respectable season" had changed. In 1953, it meant six or seven wins and the others losses. In 1957, it meant contending for a state championship. After the Jefferson game, Abilenians were talking animatedly about another respectable season.

"Football fans are funny," said Chuck Moser at the Tuesday night meeting of the Eagle Booster Club. "They judge a bunch of kids on the first five plays. I don't think you could say we've got a great ball club on just one game. Wait four or five games at least."

The Eagles did "a real good job" in their opening game, but he reminded the boosters that Jefferson was a "real weak" team. He said Sweetwater, on Friday, would be "a four to five touchdown better ball club" than Jefferson.

"It takes a lot out of a bunch of kids when you talk about our getting in the playoffs when we're trying to get ready for Sweetwater," he said.

Players, coaches and fans in Sweetwater were certainly aware of the improvement in their chances with Gregory and Carpenter gone to places like SMU and Oklahoma. Sweetwater had tied heavily favored Breckenridge, 14-14, in the season opener and as ever was pointing for Abilene. "All they have to do over there is mention Abilene and they get fired up," said JV coach Blacky Blackburn, who had scouted the Mustangs against Breckenridge. Blackburn said the Mustang offense was "solid, one that's based on power," and that the defensive line from tackle to tackle was "very big and very strong."

On Tuesday afternoon the Abilene JV ran Sweetwater plays against the first-string defense. It was a spirited 15 minutes, the *Reporter-News* observed, "and when Moser whistled the end of the scrimmage, the spirited Eagles asked for more." But there was another foe during the week against which spirit didn't count. Several players, including fullback Bill Sides, missed the Wednesday practice with the flu. Reserve tackle Ronnie Luckie was still in bed Thursday, and halfback Stan Cozby and defenders Bob Swafford and Frank Aycock had sore throats. Then during warm-ups before the game, second-team quarterback Freddie Martinez pulled something in his back. He was supposed to share time with starter Gervis Galbraith, but now it was a matter of what would Moser do if Galbraith got hurt? Martinez tried to work out the pain but couldn't. "In the second half, he couldn't even bend over far enough to take the ball from center," Moser said.

Fumbleitis was also in the air. The Eagle defense was doing its job early in the game, but first Gervis Galbraith and then Chuck Colvin fumbled Mustang punts. Bob Swafford saved the second situation when he recovered the fumble at the Eagle 36. Finally with its hands on the ball, the Abilene offense went to work. Sides carried three straight times for 18 yards, to the Mustang 46. Then Galbraith called a counter play, faking to Sides straight ahead and handing to Colvin cutting across. John Young and Mike Bryant had a hole waiting for him, Colvin raced through, and sped to the end zone untouched.

∽∽

SWEETWATER CAME RIGHT BACK, going 80 yards in seven plays, including a 27-yard left-handed pass from 192-pound fullback James Parker to right half Eddie Scott. It was the first time since the 1954 Midland game that a pass had been completed over the Eagle secondary. A play later, left half Glen Reed got the ball on a reverse, got around the corner, and scored from 33 yards out. "That reverse play was the longest run from scrimmage against us in 30-some ball games," Moser said, "and I'll bet you we worked on stopping that play a hundred times in practice." The key block in the run was thrown by quarterback Ardis Gaither. It was common for quarterbacks to become blockers in the T formation as run by high schools. David Bourland had been one of the best, and Gervis Galbraith was a good blocker.

Moser's game plan was to run Sides and Colvin at the right side of the Sweetwater defensive line. Colvin finished the game with a whopping 192 yards on 17 carries, and Sides had 107 in 24. Scouts had noticed the Mustang linemen and linebackers "stunted" a lot, a stunt being a defensive technique that sent defenders into specific motion patterns at the snap of the ball. Sometimes the best thing an offense could do was run right at the stunts. After the kickoff it was almost exclusively Sides and Colvin clipping off gains from 10 to 12 yards. Finally Colvin, who only weighed 155, got his second touchdown of the night on a 10-yard burst, dragging two tacklers with him, to make it 13-7 midway in the second quarter. The Eagles scored again before the half, and it was Colvin all the way. From the Abilene 11, Colvin ripped off 20 yards on a sweep left. On the next play, he got the ball on the belly play at left tackle and went all the way, 69 yards, outrunning Gaither to the end zone. Galbraith kicked the point and it was 20-7 at the half.

Sweetwater did its best to get back into the game in the third quarter, with a big assist from Abilene backs, who lost three fumbles in the quarter. Sides lost the first one, Sweetwater recovering at the Abilene 26. Somehow the Eagle defense made the Mustangs run 12 plays to cover the 26 yards, but on the 12th play Gaither scored on a sneak from the half-yard line. The missed PAT made it 20-13. Seconds later Sides fumbled again, and Sweetwater recovered again, at the Abilene 45. The 1,000 Sweetwater fans in the crowd of 12,000 perked up. But then Swafford, the safety, broke up a fourth-down pass to end the threat.

It was Swafford, in the opening minute of the fourth period, who set up the touchdown that gave the Eagles breathing room. Swafford intercepted on the Abilene 33 and returned it to the 49. Galbraith faked to his fullback, then threw to end Jimmy Perry for 35 yards to the Mustang 16. A clipping penalty pushed the Eagles back, but then Galbraith found sub halfback Tim Walter all alone at the goalline and hit him for the touchdown. The Eagles added an insurance touchdown after a fumble recovery at the Sweetwater 29. Colvin scored his third touchdown through a big hole at the four-yard line. Junior guard Don Hughes came in to kick the final PAT.

"The game reminded me an awful lot of our game with Amarillo in 1955," Moser said. "We got them down 14-0, then they came back and made it 14-13 in the third quarter before we won it 35-13. As a fan, I really enjoyed the Sweetwater game. Both teams played real hard. You just won't see better high school games than that."

Moser said the defensive line of Joe Ward, Frank Aycock, Truman Bridges and Ronnie Ingle did a "fine job" of stopping the Mustang rush, and that Gerald Galbraith and John Young played well defensively. "The kids have been doing real well on defense," Moser said. "I'm proud of them. But they've been making too many real big mistakes. Take out just four plays and Sweetwater would have had a hard time scoring on us."

"The Eagles proved one thing," wrote Don Oliver. "They're going to be tough to beat down the line, if they continue to show as much improvement as they did Friday night."

Abilene 34, Sweetwater 13
Sept. 20, 1957

Sept. 27, 1957

AFTER TWO VICTORIES, ABILENE still was third-ranked statewide behind Amarillo and Corpus Christi Ray. Amarillo had walloped Dallas Adamson, 57-0, and then exacted revenge, 34-7, against Fort Worth Paschal, for its 1956 playoffs disappointment.

The week's big news, particularly in southern newspapers and dominating the front pages of the *Reporter-News,* was President Eisenhower's order sending paratroopers of the 101st Airborne, the "Screaming Eagles," into Little Rock, Ark., to enforce implementation of a desegregation order there. The focal point was Little Rock High School. Texas Gov. Price Daniel sent a telegram to the president saying, "I am shocked at your action in Arkansas." Sen. Lyndon B. Johnson said, "There should be no troops from either side patrolling our campuses." Arkansas Gov. Orval Faubus claimed the president sent in the troops "without proper authority" but otherwise declined comment.

History was pending in Los Angeles, where the city council was divided over a proposal to move the Brooklyn Dodgers to L.A. At issue was an agreement between the city and the team. Dodgers' president Walter O'Malley said the council had only four days to decide. Los Angeles Mayor Norris Poulson said he will "put up the fight of my life" to see that Los Angeles got the Dodgers.

There was a national flu epidemic. Many college football games had to be canceled, and flu seemed to be part of the preparations week in and week out for the Eagles, and for the team the Eagles were playing. Moser did the best thing he knew to do. Over the weekend, all the players, managers and coaches got flu shots.

THE EAGLES WERE HOSTING Lubbock Monterey, which was 0-2 after playing very strong teams from Fort Worth Paschal and Highland Park. "Wally Bullington says they've got the best passer he's seen since Vince Matthews of Houston Austin," Moser said. "They've thrown an awful lot of passes in their games so far, and we think they'll probably throw 30 or more against us." The Monterey quarterback, Fred Parson, was dubbed "the passin' Parson" by the *Reporter-News,* which apparently couldn't see the Plainsmen as much of a threat to the Eagles' streak. "Bill DuBose, their coach, is one of the best coaches in the state," Moser argued. "They've lost both of their games, so they'll probably throw everything they've got against us."

At least it would be good experience for Jimmy Perry and Bob Swafford in the Eagle secondary. After the long pass play by Sweetwater, Moser devoted extra practice time to pass defense but wouldn't say what the effect might be. "That's something that's hard to tell," he said. "Pass defense is the hardest thing to coach."

The Eagles beat the Plainsmen, 58-0, and the streak reached 40. Monterey was not a very good team, but with this victory, nevertheless, a certain nobility began to emerge. Mal Elliott of the *Reporter-News* said the Eagles "appear to gain more prominence every time they walk on the field." Against Monterey, he said the Eagles "outdid themselves," and called the team "ambitious." While the team on the field was Lubbock Monterey, the Eagles were also playing the 1956 Eagles, and the '55 team, against whom, regardless of their talents, the 1957 Eagles were determined to measure up. "They were a group of kids that were willing to give everything they had," said coach Wally Bullington, who in 1957 succeeded Hank Watkins as line coach. "They probably accomplished more than the championship teams with what they had."

~

WHAT THEY HAD AGAINST Monterey, even more than an offense that produced 58 points, was a defense. In the 1956 playoffs, when his first-string quarterback was lost, Moser made defense his first focus. In 1957, with nowhere near the offensive talent that the championship teams had possessed, Moser made defense an everyday focus. "You can't have a consistent winner without good defense," he said. "We've been spending about half our time working on defense since Aug. 31."

It was starting to show. Monterey's farthest penetration in the game was its own 43-yard line. The Plainsmen finished the game with four first downs and 67 yards of total offense. Abilene had 27 first downs, 302 yards rushing, and 95 passing. Fullback Bill Sides was the leading rusher with 118 yards and junior halfback Stan Cozby scored three touchdowns. Junior quarterback Freddie Martinez, who had become essentially an alternate quarterback with the starter Gervis Galbraith, led the team on a 93-yard scoring drive with pass completions of 25 and 15 yards. In the second half, Martinez threw a touchdown pass to end Bob Swafford, who caught the ball at the 15, spun out of two tackles at the 10, and scored standing up. Halfback Chuck Colvin returned a punt 60 yards for a touchdown, the Eagles' first scoring kick return of the season, and 137-pound junior halfback Tim Walter scored twice on short runs. Sophomore quarterback Charles McCook scored his first touchdown as an Eagle late in the fourth quarter to make it 58-0.

"Only thing bad about the Abilene performance," Elliott wrote, "was the extra point kicking. They made good only four of eight tries, two by Galbraith and two by guard Don Hughes."

With the victory, the Eagles gained a game on the University of Oklahoma. The Sooners of coach Bud Wilkinson had won 41 straight games. On this weekend the Sooners had an open date, which let Chuck Moser's team edge nearer in local and state media stories that had begun to refer to the Abilene Eagles as "Little Oklahoma."

Abilene 58, Lubbock Monterey 0
Sept. 27, 1957

Oct. 4, 1957

DON OLIVER IN HIS Oct. 1 column invited *Reporter-News* readers to "turn back the pages of time to Oct. 1, 1954, the night that the Abilene Eagles lost their last football game.

"The Warbirds, beginning to have the Chuck Moser look, had beaten Highland Park, 40-0, and Sweetwater, 13-0, and there was talk that the Eagles might be a state title contender.

"However, a green-shirted band of Breckenridge Buckaroos were on their way up, too, and with their magnificent backfield of Bennett Watts, Jakie Sandefer, Clyde Harris and Dick Carpenter and a line backed by Jerry Payne, Sonny Everett, Tom Beasley and Jerry Cramer, blasted Abilene, 35-13, before a stunned crowd of 10,100 at Fair Park Stadium. That '54 Breckenridge club was, in our opinion, one of Texas' all-time great elevens."

Now, suggested Oliver, the Eagles, in order to maintain their winning streak, were going to have to beat a Breckenridge team "that some folks in Stephens County say is a better club than the '54 outfit."

It wasn't a bad angle. It had a nice symmetry. If the streak had to end, wouldn't it be romantic if the team to end it was Breckenridge?

The Buckies had been tied, 14-14, by Sweetwater in their season opener, a team that Abilene had beaten soundly. But then eyes popped when Breckenridge whipped Class AAAA power Wichita Falls, 20-6, and then shut out Gainesville, 26-0. Buckaroo quarterback Bobby Goswick, to those who had seen him play, looked like the second coming of Bennett Watts, if not Sammy Baugh.

"Offensively, we're a definite scoring threat this year," said coach Emory Bellard. "We've got pretty good speed, good quarterbacking and we block well."

"I'll say one thing," said Chuck Moser, "if they're as good as that '54 ball club, we don't have a chance. That ball club was one of the best teams I've ever seen. I just don't know whether they're that good this year or not."

∽∾∽

SHOTS OR NO, RESPIRATORY INFECTIONS still were visiting the Eagle fieldhouse. This time it was end Mike McKinnis, who missed school on Thursday with a sore throat and a temperature of 100. He was given penicillin. Taking his spot in the starting lineup was Joe Ward, a regular on defense.

It was the Eagles' first road game of the season, 31 miles up State 351 to Albany and then U.S. 180 24 miles to Breckenridge. After their last practice on Thursday, Moser said the Eagles "had more zip and life today than at any time this season. The team is coming along real good. As good or better than we expected."

"Last year Abilene trounced Breckenridge, 41-0," wrote Jimmy Browder of the *Reporter-News,* "but no such score is indicated for Friday night. In fact a defensive battle is indicated, and the total score may not be 41."

In front of 9,000 people in a 6,500-capacity stadium, Abilene beat Breckenridge, 41-20. This was 41 points scored on a team that had allowed Wichita Falls a single touchdown. Metaphors started to change. The team that so recently "outdid itself" now was striking "with the quickness and deadliness of a rattlesnake." This was starting to sound like the 1956 Eagles.

Actually, the score didn't indicate the battle. Abilene shocked the Buckies, scoring two long touchdowns in their first three plays of the game, but Breckenridge battled back to tie and never was out of the game until the fourth quarter.

The Eagles won the toss and received the opening kickoff. Speedy, intense Breckenridge sprinted down the field and cut off the return inside the 20. Moser as usual had sent the first series of plays into the game with his quarterback, Gervis Galbraith. The first play was a run to set up the second play, which was a play-action pass to a halfback downfield, the same play on which Glynn Gregory had so many long receptions. The first play went off as ordered, and the pass was due on second down. But the Eagles were too deep in their own territory, at their 18-yard line, so Moser sent in a messenger calling it off. Instead, Galbraith ran a counter play in which he faked to the fullback and handed to right half Chuck Colvin crossing behind.

Colvin ran 82 yards to a touchdown. The Breck linebackers and secondary over-pursued to the fullback fake, as scouts had seen them do, and Colvin had clear sailing. Bellard was crestfallen. "Failure of our secondary to react quickly enough," he said. Galbraith missed the conversion. Abilene kicked off, Breckenridge ran three plays, and punted to the Eagles at the Abilene 41.

This was acceptable field position. Moser told Galbraith to run the pass play on first down. It went 59 yards for a touchdown. Galbraith took the snap, made the play-action fake and threw down the middle to left half Stan Cozby. Cozby made a pretty catch, stumbled, recovered his stride, and ran to the end zone, and Abilene was ahead, 13-0, with hardly three minutes gone in the game.

THE BRECKENRIDGE CROWD MAY HAVE been stunned, but Bobby Goswick was merely motivated. The Buckaroo quarterback led his team on a freewheeling 81-yard drive to get back into the game. In the drive, Goswick ripped off a 25-yard run through most of the Eagle team. He hit Ronny Payne with an 18-yard pass. He ran 16 more yards to the Abilene nine. From there, the Bucks were slapped twice with 15-yard penalties. But Goswick kept the Buckies coming and then hit Payne again, this time for 27 yards and a touchdown.

Abilene couldn't move, and early in the second quarter Breckenridge cranked up a 78-yard, 18-play drive that ate up most of the period and tied the game at 13-all. With 2:15 left in the half, halfback Joe Ed Pesch scored from four yards out on a sweep right, but the conversion was wide.

After the kickoff, Moser sent junior quarterback Freddie Martinez into the game and told him to throw. After a pair of runs netted 15 yards, Martinez threw two straight completions, the second good for 35 yards and a touchdown to end Bob Swafford, who made a circus catch in the end zone. He and Breck defender George Wragg both went high for the ball, wrestled for it, and Swafford fell on his back to the ground with the ball in his arms. "I knew I wanted it the worst," he said. Galbraith hit the PAT, and with a minute left in the half Abilene was back out front, 20-13. Moser and others thought it was the turning point in the game. "If we hadn't got that one before the half, we'd of had us a ball game," said Colvin.

Moser had wanted to score quickly, and early, as a hedge against a Breckenridge team whose speed empowered them to score quickly, at any time. In the second half, the Eagles started to wear the hosts down. The Eagles opened the second half with a 14-play, 74-yard march to a touchdown. The big play in the drive was Galbraith's 36-yard completion to end Jimmy Perry, who carried to the Breck 14. Fullback Bill Sides got the score from three yards out.

The Eagles were quickly back in business when Larry Parker was hit hard on the kickoff runback and fumbled, Abilene's Don Hughes recovering at the Buckie 31. Sides, then Cozby, then Colvin, carried, for a total of 24 yards. Then it was Sides' turn again, and he ran up the middle to the end zone for the TD that made it 34-13 with 2:10 left in the third period. Both teams added a touchdown in the fourth quarter, and Abilene had an important victory, but it was a last-minute defensive stand that was the hot topic after the game. A Breckenridge score would have meant six more pushups before practice the following week. Twenty was bad enough.

Abilene 41, Breckenridge 20
Oct. 4, 1957

Oct. 11, 1957

THIS WAS QUIRKY. Here were the Abilene Eagles, poised to break another record for consecutive victories, and the same three teams stood in the way.

In 1956, the Eagles were going for most consecutive wins by a Class AAAA team, a record held by Lubbock High at 29. To tie the record, the Eagles first had to defeat that very Lubbock Westerner team, and then Waco. Then to set a new record, Abilene had to beat Big Spring.

In 1957, the Eagles were going for most consecutive wins by a Texas high school team irrespective of classification, held by Hull-Daisetta at 43. Hull-Daisetta was a consolidation of students from Hull and Daisetta, tiny communities west of Beaumont. A few thought the big-school record was the one that really counted, as opposed to victories by a tiny school playing other tiny schools on scrubby fields. Most, though, thought that 43 in a row was 43 in a row, whether it was muny softball or Hull-Daisetta or the Oklahoma Sooners. To tie the record, the Eagles had to defeat Lubbock, then Waco. To win its 44th, Abilene had to beat Big Spring.

In 1957, as in 1956, it was not the stuff of which Cecil B. DeMille movies were made. Against the '56 team, it didn't matter much who the Eagles had to play. In 1957, Waco appeared to be the only team with any sort of chance to stop Abilene short of the record.

Of course Chuck Moser didn't see it that way. "They're a better defensive ball club than we are," he said of the Lubbock Westerners. "They're well-coached and real tough tacklers and blockers."

"Defense," wrote Mal Elliott in the *Reporter-News,* "is expected to be the key word when the two teams clash at 8 p.m. Friday night at Jones Stadium."

It was true that after four games, the Westerners had allowed only 26 points, 13 to Odessa and 13 to Plainview, while Abilene had surrendered 46. But the Westerner offense had scored only 38 points, and 13 had been enough for both Odessa and Plainview to defeat Lubbock, 13-0 and 13-6 respectively. Lubbock's two shutout victories were over Dallas Wilson, 9-0, and Fort Worth Northside, 23-0.

∽∘∾

ABILENE'S OFFENSE, MEANWHILE, had hammered out 159 points and appeared to be getting stronger with every game. Still, Moser harped on defense.

"I'm disappointed," Moser said, his players reminded of his displeasure 20 times before every practice, with every push-up they did. "Breckenridge scored more points against us last week than any time since the Breckenridge loss in 1954." He was still concerned that his defense was making "big" mistakes: long pass plays and long runs. Breckenridge had achieved both.

Offensively, the Westerners were undistinguished. To find interest there, Mal Elliott had to point out that Westerner quarterback DeWitt Weaver was the son of the Texas Tech football coach. "Weaver," Elliott said, "is a dangerous passer," but statistics were not provided. The Westerners ran the Wing-T, he said, and had five offensive starters back from 1956.

Abilene was supposed to be without junior left halfback Stan Cozby, injured in the Breckenridge game. Tim Walter, another junior, who only weighed 137 but had speed, would start for Cozby.

It was only 6-0 after one quarter at Jones Stadium. Linebacker Gerald Galbraith intercepted a Weaver pass at midfield. On third down and five, Chuck Colvin took a pitchout on a sweep to the left. Fullback Bill Sides threw the key block, and Colvin ran 34 yards to the Westerner 11. Walter gained five and Sides did the rest, on two carries. The point-after was wide. Moser had tried both Gervis Galbraith and junior guard Don Hughes as placement kickers, a chore handled for two years by Glynn Gregory, but neither had established any consistency.

ABILENE MOVED INSIDE THE 20 again in the first half but was turned back by the Lubbock defense. Then the Westerners had to punt from the one, and Abilene had a first down at the Lubbock 43. Stan Cozby, playing despite injury, got the TD from the three, and Galbraith's placement was wide again. The Westerners fumbled the kickoff return, giving Abilene the ball at the 39. Alternate quarterback Freddie Martinez scrambled for 15, Sides ran 20 yards on the draw play to the four, and Colvin got the score from there. A Lubbock penalty gave Galbraith two tries at the PAT. He missed both. Abilene scored once more before the half, set up by a 46-yard punt runback by Colvin. Reserve fullback Tony Martinez got the TD, and Galbraith finally made good on a PAT.

That made it 25-0, and the Eagles sent in the subs after the half. Second-half touchdowns by Tim Walter and third-string halfback Eddie Woods made the final score 39-0. Abilene had 399 yards rushing and 92 passing, completing an amazing nine of 11 passes. "The only thing I was really pleased with was our passing," Moser said. "It has improved more than anything else." Lubbock managed only four first downs and 87 yards of total offense and only once was able to cross its own 47-yard line. Now the Eagles were going to play Waco to tie the record. And they didn't have to do any pushups.

Abilene 39, Lubbock High 0
Oct. 11, 1957

Oct. 18, 1957

IF THE EAGLES WERE GOING to tie the record against Waco, and then break it against Big Spring, then the fans at home would get to see it. Both games were at Fair Park Stadium.

As the Waco game approached, the Tigers were having trouble getting ready for Abilene, and the Eagles were having trouble getting ready for Waco. In Waco, it rained six inches on Sunday and Monday, and the high school practice field was flooded. Coach Carl Price had to move his practices into the gymnasium. "Unless key personnel get the flu or hurt themselves falling down on the gymnasium floor this week," wrote Don Oliver, "the Waco Tigers are going to be in the best condition of the season for the Abilene Eagles here Friday night."

In Abilene, two starting linemen missed Tuesday practice with the flu. "If we don't get Gerald Galbraith and Mike Bryant ready, I wouldn't be at all surprised if we get beat Friday night," Chuck Moser said. Making things worse, Galbraith's substitute, Alan Peake, was also down with the bug. Third-stringers Johnny Garner and Don Reese were working at center during offensive drills and scrimmages. Also out were sophomore guard Rip Thomas and junior end Charles Flynn. All of these cases might in fact have been caught during the game in Lubbock. "The Westerners had a lot of flu last week that we didn't find out about until after the game," Moser said. "We traditionally play well against them, but I don't feel that this was a real test since they were weakened by the flu."

In his column, Don Oliver did an analysis of the streak and also printed the streak's game results, year by year, "for posterity, and to settle a few friendly arguments down the line.

"Twenty-five different schools have contributed to the winning skein, which won't change if the Eagles make it 43, since the Tigers bowed to the Warbirds last year and are already on the list," Oliver wrote. "The Eagles recorded 14 shutouts in the string and in 39 of the games scored over two touchdowns while only nine teams scored more than one touchdown against Abilene."

THE TEAM FARING WORST IN the streak was Lubbock. The Westerners had played Abilene four times and lost the four by a cumulative score of 185-21. No other team had lost four, but in 1957 the Eagles had yet to play Odessa, Midland and San Angelo. Only two teams, Breckenridge and Sweetwater, had scored more than two touchdowns in any one of the games, Sweetwater scoring 20 points in 1955 and Breckenridge 20 in 1957. There were 10 playoffs victories included in the streak, with a cumulative score of 338-44.

Overall, Oliver wrote, Abilene had averaged 36.9 points per game in the streak, and the opposition 6. If the Eagles were to complete an undefeated season in 1957, "something we won't even think about at this time," Oliver wrote, the streak would stand at 51, "far behind in national standings. According to the October issue of 'Teen' magazine, Bedford County Training School of Shelbyville, Tenn., won 78 straight from 1942 to 1950, and Tallahassee, Fla., High, ran up 57 straight wins from 1942 to 1947."

A crowd of 10,000 showed up at Fair Park Stadium to see if the Eagles could make it No. 43. Waco had lost only once, 26-20 to San Angelo, a game that Waco coach Carl Price thought the Tigers should have won. Waco quarterback Tom Stollenwerck had completed 31 of 53 passes for 406 yards and two touchdowns. Left half Dickie Vitek, a converted quarterback, had completed five of 10 for 111 yards and a touchdown. Vitek was also the team's leading rusher with 281 yards on 51 carries, and the other two backs, Freddie Lamb and Melvin Trousdale, had 433 yards between them. Waco was averaging 370 yards of offense per game. The Tigers were big, averaging 183 in the line, and they were tough on defense, having allowed only 44 first downs in five games. *Waco Times-Herald* sports writer George Raborn said the best things about the Tigers were their offensive versatility and their aggressiveness and gang tackling on defense.

WACO HAD WARMED UP FOR the Abilene game by beating Arlington Heights, 40-0. Price called it his team's "best game of the year." A year before, Arlington Heights had upset Waco, and people said the Tigers had been looking beyond Arlington Heights to the Abilene game. Not so in 1957, apparently.

With 3:37 remaining in the third quarter at Fair Park Stadium, Freddie Lamb, the fullback, crashed one yard into the end zone for a Waco touchdown. The point after made the score 13-7, Abilene. The Eagles had controlled the first half with strong defense, the runs of Chuck Colvin and fullback Bill Sides, and two touchdowns on short runs by Colvin. Waco ran only eight plays in the first half. But with their first possession of the second half, the Tigers had stormed 75 yards and trailed Abilene by only six points. All the Eagles were in uniform after the flu, but would they have the second-half stamina to deal with a very threatening situation?

After the Waco kickoff, Abilene moved from its 29 to the Waco 46 in eight plays. Then Colvin got loose for 21 yards to the 25. Stan Cozby picked up three, then Gervis Galbraith on a quarterback keeper added 10 more. From the Waco 12, Colvin smashed for two yards and then the trap play sprang fullback Bill Sides to the three. Sides got the call again and battled through tacklers to the end zone. The 71-yard drive had consumed more than seven minutes. Don Hughes kicked the point after with 8:25 remaining to play, and at 20-7 the Abilene faithful breathed easier, but still had that last Waco drive fresh in their minds. They really breathed easier when Abilene stopped the Tigers after the kickoff. The difference was pass defense. At one point the Tigers had completed five straight passes. But late in the game, they managed only one completion in six attempts.

The Eagles, starting from their 44, mounted a quick 56-yard drive for their last touchdown. Colvin got 48 of it all at once before being pulled down at the Waco three. Sub fullback Tony Martinez, Freddie's brother, ran the final three for the score. Hughes converted the PAT and it was 27-7. Waco didn't quit, driving against the second string into Abilene territory one last time, but the Eagles had their 43rd victory to tie the Hull-Daisetta record. Colvin finished with 160 yards on 24 carries and Sides had 92 on 19. Waco totaled 170 yards of offense and Moser told his team, "You played your best defensive ball game of the year tonight."

Abilene 27, Waco 7
Oct. 18, 1957

Oct. 25, 1957

IT WAS A DIFFERENT RECORD, but the same sense of anticlimax. There was no way in the football universe, or even the general universe, that Big Spring was going to beat the 1956 Eagles and stop them from setting the Class AAAA record for consecutive victories.

Nor were the 1957 Steers going to beat Abilene and deny them the Hull-Daisetta record, even if the entire Abilene first string missed the game with the flu. In its second year in District 2-AAAA, the Steers' non-conference schedule still consisted entirely of Class AAA teams: Andrews, Levelland, Snyder, Sweetwater, Lamesa and Kermit. Against this competition, the Steers had won two and lost four, scoring 79 points and surrendering 97. Against a sterner schedule, Abilene had scored 225 points and allowed 53. Against the common opponent, Sweetwater had beaten Big Spring, 26-6, while Abilene had handled the Mustangs, 34-13. In the statewide rankings, Abilene was climbing. Amarillo was still No. 1. Abilene was No. 2.

Clearly, then, a record about to be broken was the only interesting thing about this game. It was the first game in District 2-AAAA play, but the 60-point headline in the *Reporter-News* shouted, "Eagles Seek Record 44th Against Big Spring Tonight." It was enough to bring a crowd of 9,000 to Fair Park Stadium on a cold, 40-degree night. They could say they had been there, then go home as early as the half.

The Eagles wore their 1957 black jerseys for the occasion. Fullback Bill Sides was scheduled to rest a leg badly bruised in the Waco game. Shifting over from left half to take his place was junior Stan Cozby. Filling in for Cozby was 137-pound Tim Walter. With this lineup, the Eagle backfield averaged only 150 pounds per man. The Steer backfield averaged 184, thanks in large part to the presence at right half of all-district basketball player Jan Loudermilk. A 6-6, 210-pound halfback was interesting. "There was just so much of him to hit," said Eagle tackle Frank Aycock.

IF YOU LAID NINE Jan Loudermilks end-to-end, it would more than represent Big Spring's total offense in the first half. The Steers had managed 19 yards and no first downs. Big Spring coach Al Milch did hit upon a successful strategy for moving the ball down the field.

Milch called for the quick kick four times. A quick kick, that is a punt on second or third down, was designed to catch the defense without a deep man to return the kick and ordinarily was used to correct poor field position. It was not a category for which records were kept, but it is likely that Big Spring, like Abilene, set a new record that night.

The Eagles had an early long touchdown run called back, then scored on their second possession, dashing 63 yards in four plays. Right half Chuck Colvin got 40 yards of it all at once before being pushed out of bounds at the Big Spring five. Colvin came right back with a five-yard run for the touchdown and, once again, the point-after kick failed.

Big Spring took the kickoff, ran two plays, and quick-kicked. With no one to retrieve it, the kick, by fullback Wayne Fields, rolled all the way to the end zone, 75 yards. The touchback gave the Eagles the ball at the 20. Abilene drove all the way to the Big Spring six, but Cozby fumbled and Steer tackle Chubby Moser recovered at the two. On third down, Fields quick-kicked again, the Eagles this time taking over at their 49. On the first play of the second quarter, from the Big Spring 38, Gervis Galbraith dropped back and found Colvin open at the 15. Colvin made the catch, spun out of the grasp of safety Benny McCrary, and scored. This time the PAT was blocked, and Abilene was up, 12-0.

The Eagles scored a third touchdown before the half, at the end of a 69-yard drive. Tim Walter got 16 yards, then threw the halfback pass to Colvin for 15 yards, to highlight the drive. Galbraith got the score on a six-yard run with only 15 seconds remaining before intermission. The Eagles finally got a point-after, off the toe of guard Don Hughes, and it was a misleading 19-0 at the half. At that point Abilene had 230 yards rushing, 67 passing and 16 first downs. It was enough to send many folks streaming for home and hot chocolate.

BIG SPRING TOOK THE KICKOFF after the half and immediately posted its first first down on two Loudermilk runs and a long fall.

The Steers moved all the way to the Eagle 17 before stalling. A fumble, a blocked punt, and an interception followed as both teams became sloppy in the cold weather. At the end of this, Big Spring had the ball but soon was resorting again to the quick kick. But the magic had gone out of this strategy and the kick traveled only eight yards, presenting Abilene the ball at the Steer 23. Walter worked the half-back pass again to Colvin on the first play, then Cozby popped through cleanly on the fullback trap and scored. Hughes' kick made it 26-0 with 20 seconds remaining in the third.

The Steers tried the quick kick one last time, this one by Loudermilk that traveled 49 yards. But by now the Eagles were watching for it, and safety Bob Swafford was able to get back, field the ball, and return it 24 yards to the Steer 39. From there the Eagles scored in four plays, sub fullback Tony Martinez getting the TD on a 13-yard run. The PAT failed, it was 32-0, and subs scrimmaged the last 10 minutes into the history book.

In the Eagles' end of the fieldhouse, the number 44 was not to be seen or heard, anywhere. To Moser and his team, Big Spring was simply "Number Seven." On the blackboard, as was customary, was a chalked message focused on the next opponent: "Bash the Bronchos."

"Winning 10 games this year has always been more important to us than the record," Moser said. "We'll still win our games one at a time." He did give his players a small reward on the occasion. He got up on a bench and said, "How about staying out til 12 tonight," giving the Eagles a 30-minute extension on their regular curfew.

The game that broke the record would be the last one in which the streak would be the biggest news. Beginning with Odessa, the games would count not so much against the streak, as against when the season would end.

Abilene 32, Big Spring 0
Oct. 25, 1957

Nov. 8, 1957

"This is one game we MUST win. We need to sacrifice this week in order to be mentally and physically prepared. Odessa is real quick, alert, and play much like we do except they throw lots."

AFTER BIG SPRING, THE EAGLES had an open date in which to bask in the attention brought by their new record. It was an opportune time to receive a reporter and photographer from *Time* magazine, who put together a short story and photo (of the Eagles at practice) to recognize the feat nationally. Other reporters arrived from around the state, as Bill Stages had predicted, and the publicity was nice, but Moser didn't want anybody's head turned. He would have been more comfortable if he thought you could beat Odessa with stories in *Time* magazine.

While the Eagles relaxed with the open date, Odessa played Big Spring and beat the Steers, 27-13. The Bronchos had already beaten San Angelo, 27-6, and going into the Abilene game actually held first place in the District 2-AAAA standings with their 2-0 record. Abilene was made a two to three-touchdown favorite, but Odessa coaches, players and fans realized they had a chance, against an Abilene team without Glynn Gregory, Jimmy Carpenter and Stuart Peake on it. The Eagles were unbeaten, but at least they were human, and the Bronchos were playing them at home, for Homecoming. It was also the first return of the Victory Bell to the Odessa stadium since Abilene had taken it away after the 1954 season. There were 15,000 tickets sold for the game, including the usual Abilene allotment. The Eagle Booster Club sold 565 tickets on the special train to Odessa. Whatever the foundations for expectations on either side, in the five-team district this was a crucial game. Both teams had beaten Big Spring, Odessa had beaten San Angelo, and both the Bobcats and Midland Bulldogs were in rebuilding seasons. The winner of this game, either Odessa at 3-0 or Abilene at 2-0, would be the clear favorite to win the district championship and advance to the playoffs.

∽∾∽

THE BRONCHOS HAD ONLY LOST twice in seven games and they had been beaten badly only once, 35-0, by top-ranked Amarillo, a team people were openly comparing to the 1956 Eagles. According to the *Amarillo Globe's* Putt Powell, not Odessa or any other team had even been a test for the Sandies. Odessa's coach was the very creative, pass-oriented Hayden Fry, and that worried Moser, particularly since rains during the week kept the Eagles in the gym, where it was difficult to practice pass defense. The Bronchos ran multiple formations off the basic T, and quarterback Gerald Erwin had completed 36 of 87 passes for 555 yards. Buddy White, a 157-pound fullback, was the leading Odessa runner with 423 yards and six touchdowns.

By contrast, Abilene's Chuck Colvin went into the game with almost 800 yards rushing and 13 touchdowns, and fullback Bill Sides, whose bruised leg kept him out of the Big Spring game, was back at full speed after the open date. And the Eagle defense was showing signs of becoming dominant. After allowing 46 points in the first four games, Abilene had surrendered just a single touchdown in the last three. After an earlier than usual pep rally, the Eagles left at 9 a.m. for the long ride on U.S. 80 to Midland, where they set up headquarters at the Scharbauer Hotel, ate their pre-game meal, and continued on the 20 miles to Odessa for the game.

Abilene took the opening kickoff and quickly drove 64 yards to score, but Odessa fans were hopeful when the Bronchos stormed upfield after the kickoff. When it was a push-and-shove game, one side wasn't dominating. From its 35, Odessa drove to the Abilene 6, including a 24-yard pass from Erwin to halfback Ronnie Goodwin. But on first and goal at the six, Goodwin met a solid wall, then Eagle nose guard Joe Ward cut down the fullback White after one yard. Erwin tried the air on third and fourth down, but both passes were incomplete.

It took Abilene only 11 plays to cover the 96 yards, and the game's complexion was changed. Colvin, who ran for 189 yards in the game, and Sides, who had 131, clipped off one good gain after the other behind signature Eagle blocking. Sides got the score on a 13-yard fullback sweep around right end. Hughes missed the PAT and it was 13-0. If it was going to be a game of serve-and-volley, Abilene was up a break serve.

BUT THIS TIME, ODESSA'S OFFENSE stalled, against an Eagle defense, led by the intense John Young, that was becoming more accomplished by the week. Odessa had to punt, and the Eagles set up shop at their 13-yard line. Again, they set out four and five yards at a time, and in the middle of the drive Sides broke a trap play for 24 yards to the Broncho 37. The Broncs once again forced Abilene into a fourth-down situation, but Colvin slashed for short yards to sustain the drive. He also got the touchdown, on a short halfback sweep around the left side. Again the PAT failed, it was 19-0, the Eagles had scored on three straight possessions, and the big Odessa crowd was starting to let its thoughts wander to who would be crowned Homecoming queen.

As it turned out, the second half was entertaining. Odessa received the second-half kickoff and immediately drove toward the Abilene end zone. But at the Eagle six, on third and four, a pitchout lost yardage and then an Erwin pass fell incomplete. Odessa came back with a second strong drive minutes later, but the same sequence—a botched pitchout and a poor pass—again stopped the Broncs, this time at the Eagle 15. Back they came, after holding the Eagles, driving to the Abilene 13. But Abilene junior linebacker Charles Harrison smothered an Odessa fumble at that point, and all the gas was gone out of the Broncho effort.

Of 58 Abilene offensive plays, Colvin and Sides carried on 41, accounting for 310 yards rushing between them. The Eagle defense procured its third shutout in four games, the Victory Bell rang out celebration of a second District 2-AAAA triumph, and it was Abilene, winner of 45 straight, in the driver's seat for its fourth straight district championship.

But the Eagles suffered one big loss: middle guard Joe Ward, a mainstay in the defense, suffered a separated shoulder in the game and would be out indefinitely.

Abilene 19, Odessa 0
Nov. 8, 1957

Nov. 15, 1957

SENIORS ON THE 1957 Abilene Eagle squad were Truman Bridges, Ronnie Ingle, Bill Sides, John Young, Eddie Woods, Tony Martinez, Dale Graham, Ronnie Luckie, Robert McKissick, Chuck Colvin, Gervis Galbraith, Rikki McPherson, Leldon Kelso, Gerald Galbraith, Jimmy Perry, Mike Bryant, Mike McKinnis, Bob Swafford, Ronnie Alldredge, Alan Peake, Jack Reese, and Joe Ward.

They played their last home game at Fair Park Stadium against the Midland Bulldogs on Nov. 15. They were the seniors on the team that was supposed to settle back into respectable mediocrity after the glory years of 1954, 1955 and 1956. Instead, they were the leaders of a team that was unbeaten in eight games, was ranked second in the state behind mighty Amarillo in Class AAAA, and was a three-touchdown favorite to beat Midland and clinch its fourth straight "Little Southwest Conference" district championship. They had scored 276 points and in their last four games, against Lubbock, Waco, Big Spring and Odessa, had allowed only seven points. Their coaches said that as a team, they did more with what they had than any of the three state championship teams. Now only the Bulldogs and the San Angelo Bobcats stood between them and a third straight unbeaten regular season.

In 1954 and '55, the Abilene-Midland collision had been the pivotal game in district play. In 1956, Midland after the departure of

Wahoo McDaniel and Tugboat Jones had slipped to a record of 6-2 by the time unbeatable Abilene arrived. In 1957, the Bulldogs had faded some more from greatness. They had been beaten by two Class AAA teams, Snyder (40-14) and Lamesa (7-6), had been tied by rebuilding San Angelo, 0-0, and barely squeaked past Big Spring, 7-0. Overall Midland was 4-3-1. Still, Midland fans chartered a T&P special train to Abilene, because the feeling persisted that the 1957 Abilene Eagles could be beaten.

JOE WARD'S INJURY COMPELLED Chuck Moser to shuffle his defensive lineup. End John Young moved into Ward's middle guard spot, junior Don Hughes took Young's end position, and tackle Dale Graham took over on defense for Mike Bryant, who was an offensive starter.

It was the last time in 1957 that the Eagles would play at Fair Park Stadium, and it was Homecoming, and they made it memorable. Victory No. 46 in the winning streak was a 41-0 pounding of Midland, and it was reminiscent of so many of the victories that had gone before. Midland won the toss, took the kickoff, ran three plays and punted. Abilene promptly drove 56 yards in nine plays to score. Quarterback Gervis Galbraith, who gained good yardage on the quarterback bootleg all night long, gained 24 of the yards in one run, and left half Stan Cozby got the score on a one-yard dive. Guard Don Hughes missed the point after, the only one he would miss all night long.

Again Midland couldn't move. The Bulldogs didn't pick up a first down until midway in the second quarter. After the punt, the Eagles started from their 21 and moved the 79 yards in nine plays. Right half Chuck Colvin, breaking tackles, got the TD on a 37-yard pass from Galbraith on the first play of the second quarter. Minutes later Colvin caught another pass, this one from Freddie Martinez, and raced 74 yards to the end zone, but the touchdown was nullified by a clipping penalty downfield. Colvin got loose again before the half, this time on the Statue of Liberty play, and was touchdown bound when he was pulled down from behind as the half ended. In the game, Colvin broke the 1,000-yard mark, collecting 82 yards in 11 carries, giving him 1,054 yards in nine games. Colvin also caught four passes in the game, for 71 yards and a touchdown.

The Eagles scored again on a 63-yard march to open the second half, Cozby carrying 12 yards on the belly play for the score. When Galbraith scored again moments later, on another 24-yard bootleg, Moser sent in the second and third teams to practice for 1958. Fullback Tony Martinez scored a second-half touchdown on a one-yard run, and halfback Rikki McPherson closed out the scoring on a 28-yard sweep around the right side.

~

MIDLAND FOR THE GAME MANAGED 143 yards rushing and didn't pick up a single passing yard. The Bulldogs' deepest penetration was the Eagle 31. In their last home game, the Eagle seniors led the team to its 46th victory, its fourth straight district championship, and its ninth straight win in an undefeated season. Of all that, only "No. 9" meant anything to Moser and his team. On the blackboard went "Beat San Angelo."

The Midland game also meant something else to Moser. His defense, continuing to improve, apparently had worked through its vulnerability to the long pass play, and the Eagles missed only one of seven PATs. This was encouraging. Maybe not against Midland, but in big games every point was crucial.

The next day, Saturday, Nov. 16, at Norman, Notre Dame halfback Dick Lynch took a fourth-down pitchout from the three-yard line and scored the day's only touchdown with 3:50 left in the game as the Irish upset the Oklahoma Sooners of coach Bud Wilkinson, 7-0, and stopped the Sooners' winning streak at 47 straight. In a week, at San Angelo, "Little Oklahoma" would have its chance to catch up.

Abilene 41, Midland 0
Nov. 15, 1957

Nov. 22, 1957

SPORTS WRITERS ARE HUMAN. Yes, they are journalists, and compelled by professionalism to be objective. And they remain objective, for the most part, when the story is "hard news," such as the account of the game itself.

But they bubble or bleed with the home team. Sports writers regularly take a loss as hard, or even harder, than the players or the coaches. And there are times when they can't help themselves and actually allow themselves to become part of the team.

It happened all the time, in West Texas newspapers in the 1950s, in columns written by sports writers like Putt Powell of the *Amarillo Globe,* Bob Milburn of the *San Angelo Standard-Times,* Ted Battle of the *Midland Reporter-Telegram,* and Don Oliver of the *Abilene Reporter-News.*

A column was different from straight news coverage. A column was a reporter's personal window on the world, where he could get things off his mind in the first person or, more commonly in the 1950s, in the third person, what was called in the trade the "editorial we."

And so *Reporter-News* readers, the week of the San Angelo game, had Don Oliver's worst fears on view. His column, "Oliver's Twist," began:

> "With Notre Dame ending Oklahoma's win skein at 47 straight, the Bobcats of coach Bob Harrell would like nothing better than to be the heroes this week and stop the Eagles at 46 straight.
>
> "The thing that worries us, and coach Chuck Moser," Oliver continued, "is that the Eagles apparently are looking more towards their trip to El Paso for the bi-district clash with Austin High, than they are the San Angelo fracas. True, the Eagles have already clinched the playoff spot. But, we fear that a loss to San Angelo would have terrible after-results on the team. It would take away the

> element of pride that has kept the youngsters playing much better than was anticipated all year long. And, without that pride, Abilene is just another good high school football team."

That last sentence may have risen in part from some wise strain of realism cruising in his blood. But Oliver's main intention was to provoke the players, to make sure they played their part in defeating San Angelo.

> "If the Eagles believe that San Angelo is just going to roll over and play dead, they've got a lot more thoughts coming," he wrote. "We have the utmost confidence in the Abilene Eagles of 1957, and certainly in Moser and his staff. We believe that the Warbirds can uphold the tradition that has carried them through 46 straight victories and three state championships. But, they are going to get their severest test of the season Friday night, and we just hope they'll be ready.
>
> "We'd rather lose in the playoffs, if we've got to lose. Certainly not to our San Angelo neighbors."

AND THERE, IN THE LAST SENTENCE, was the human Oliver revealed. Lose? Fine. Bound to happen. Lose to San Angelo? Please, God, no.

Oliver had reason to be afraid. Every week, fans in the opposing city compared the 1957 Eagles to the 1956 version and made the very reasonable argument that this team was mortal and could be beat. This week, the fans were in San Angelo. Additionally, grudges were stacked up in San Angelo like firewood, going back to 1953.

"With the game being played in San Angelo," Oliver observed, "where the Bobcats and their backers are being constantly reminded of the 'commando tactics' charge made last year by the Abilene school board, we fear that Abilene is going to have to put out maximum effort all the way if they are to protect their record."

Of course the constant reminderer of the "commando tactics" charge was Bob Milburn of the *Standard-Times.* It was an objective recollection—the charge had in fact been made and had become part of history—but Milburn's real objective was to provoke the Bobcats to play passionately and beat Abilene.

At game time, though, the sports writers had to go sit in the pressbox, while down on the field the players and coaches decided who was going to bubble, and who was going to bleed, the next morning.

And it was the field that turned out to be the biggest problem for both teams. At the kickoff, it had four inches of snow on it. Traditionally, the Eagles and Bobcats always met on Thursday, Thanksgiving Day. And Thursday had been a nice autumn day. But it wasn't Thanksgiving Day, which was not until the following week. In one of those occasional quirks of the calendar, Thanksgiving fell very late in the month, Nov. 28. So Abilene and San Angelo played on Friday night. Overnight from Thursday to Friday, a cold, wet front passed through West Central Texas and in San Angelo it snowed most of the day. In Abilene, 3,000 tickets had been sold for the game. At the kickoff, a total of 3,500 fans were huddled in San Angelo's new 15,000-seat stadium, with the temperature below freezing.

BY GAME'S END, THE TWO teams had fumbled a total of 18 times. Abilene lost an astonishing six fumbles, including one on its own one-yard line and another on the 26.

Yet Abilene won, 12-6, the Eagles' 47th straight, to complete a third straight unbeaten regular season. Fullback Bill Sides and the Abilene defense were the frozen heroes. Sides scored two second-half touchdowns, on runs of 29 and 27 yards, and picked up 105 of Abilene's meager 133 yards rushing. The Eagles attempted three passes, all incomplete. The Eagle defense, meanwhile, held San Angelo to 25 yards rushing and seven passing.

The fumbles made it interesting. Eagle tackle Frank Aycock recovered a fumble at the San Angelo 27 to set up what turned out to be the winning touchdown in the fourth period. On the first play, Sides burst through on the fullback trap and slogged straight ahead to the end zone. The PAT was wide and Abilene had a 12-0 lead with 7:02 left in the game.

San Angelo couldn't move after the kickoff, but Mac McCoulskey's 50-yard punt died at the Abilene one. Quarterback Gervis Galbraith fumbled then, and Bobcat guard Ken Milliken recovered his third fumble of the night, setting up the Bobcats at the Abilene two. On third down, quarterback Bobby Lowrey found end David Senter in the end zone for six points. Lowrey bobbled the PAT snap, was smothered by the Eagles' John Young, and it was 12-6 with 3:11 remaining. Hearts went into throats when Galbraith lost another fumble, this time at the Abilene 35, but the Bobcats could do nothing against the Abilene defense.

Moser said the game was his "worst job of coaching."

"I learned more lessons than anybody," he said. "It's been a long time since we played on a wet, cold, muddy field or had to punt on third down. I guess I should have alternated Freddie Martinez more with Gervis Galbraith at quarterback. Gervis was playing defense too, and he never had a chance to come out and warm his hands. That makes a difference on a night like that. We've never had a game where we made so many mistakes and still won. That defense is a wonderful thing."

The Eagles already knew who, and where, they would be playing in the bi-district round of the Class AAAA playoffs. They would fly west to play El Paso Austin on Thanksgiving Day.

Abilene 12, San Angelo 6
Nov. 22, 1957

Nov. 28, 1957

EL PASO AUSTIN WAS THE SECOND ITEM on the agenda at the weekly Eagle Booster Club meeting on Tuesday night.

The first was a new 15,000-seat stadium for Abilene. School Superintendent A.E. Wells talked about where the stadium might be built, what it might cost, and what it would look like.

Wells said the board was considering six sites for the $750,000 stadium, three on the north side and three on the south side. One of the south side locations would place the stadium on the grounds of a second high school east of Buffalo Gap Road, that was in final planning stages. The board had visited high school stadiums in Tyler, San Angelo, Andrews, Odessa and Midland, and also Rice Stadium in Houston, Memorial Stadium in Austin, and North Texas State Stadium in Denton.

"By building the new stadium on the site of the proposed second high school," Wells told the Booster Club, "taxpayers will save between $150,000 and $175,000."

Architects had not yet been hired, but Wells said the "present thinking" of the school board was for "an excavated stadium where the playing field is below the ground level and that persons entering the stadium from the ground level would be about halfway up the structure."

In December, there was not much hope of having the new stadium ready for the 1958 season, but even if it were, Wells said, Fair Park Stadium would still be needed for junior high games. There were 38 games played on the stadium turf in 1957.

Eagle assistant coach Bob Groseclose told the Boosters that El Paso Austin "was a much better team" than usually represented El Paso in the playoffs. It had been three years since the El Paso school board fired or reassigned all the high school coaches, after Abilene's 61-0 pounding of this same Austin team in 1954, and the fans there were hopeful.

"People there think that Austin has the best team El Paso has had in many years," Groseclose said, "and that it will be a different story when Abilene comes to town this year."

~

AFTER THE TOUGH, SNOWY San Angelo game, the Eagles had only two real practices to prepare for the Panthers. On Wednesday, they flew west in two chartered planes, held a short practice at the Austin field to acclimate themselves to the high altitude, and retired to the Hilton Hotel to wait for the Thanksgiving Day Kickoff.

Austin had won eight games, lost one (to Odessa, 39-20), and tied Albuquerque Highlands, 7-7. They had good size and some speed and in fact were judged to be the best El Paso football team in the playoffs since the 1949 Panthers shocked a heavily favored Lubbock team. They had scored 213 points and allowed 122. Abilene, with its defense that had allowed only 59 points, including only 13 in its last six games, was favored by four touchdowns. Nevertheless, hopes were high as the teams lined up under cool, clear skies for the 2 p.m. kickoff. Those hopes sagged a bit when on the first play after the kickoff, Abilene's Chuck Colvin cleared the line of scrimmage on the power play at right tackle and ran 64 yards to the El Paso 12-yard line. The Panther defense rose up and held Abilene to five yards on two running plays, but then right half Stan Cozby ripped seven yards into the end zone to put Abilene up, 7-0, after Don Hughes' PAT.

The first of five Abilene pass interceptions stopped Austin's first drive, but this time the Panther defense held and forced a punt. But Eagle safety Bob Swafford, who had grabbed the first interception, did it again on the second El Paso series and Abilene was in business at its 41. It took three plays, the big one a 50-yard sprint on a fullback trap by Bill Sides to the Panther five. From there Colvin scored on the next play and it was 14-0 with 4:35 remaining in the first period.

By the end of the period, it was 27-0. He didn't mean to, but end Jimmy Perry, kicking off after Colvin's touchdown, drove the ball low and it ricocheted off a Panther lineman "like a line drive," Don Oliver wrote, and into the grasp of the Eagles' Joe Ward at the 50. A minute later, Cozby caught a 33-yard pass from alternate quarterback Freddie Martinez and was dropped at the four. The Panthers tried, holding Abilene out of the end zone for three downs, but on the fourth, Martinez sneaked into the end zone for the TD and it was 21-0 with 1:08 left in the quarter.

El Paso went for the bomb after the kickoff, but Swafford, a busy defender, intercepted his third pass of the game, returning it from the Eagle 29 to the Panther 35. Martinez came back onto the field with the Eagle offense and promptly hit Colvin with a short pass that the halfback took all the way to the end zone. Hughes missed the PAT, and it was 27-0 at the end of the first quarter, pretty much playoffs business as usual between Abilene and El Paso. The Eagles obviously were going to collect their 48th consecutive victory, and El Paso parents and fans were wondering who they were going to have to fire next—the school board?—before the black and gold scourge from the east could be beaten, or even kept up with.

THE NEXT THREE PLAYS WERE SCRIPTED as if to make the point. After the kickoff, the Eagle defense drove the Tigers backward to their one-yard line, third down. El Paso coach Pug Gabriel, a former Odessa High star, called for a quick kick, the ball to be snapped through the quarterback's legs to the fullback, who would kick it. But the ball didn't make it through the quarterback's legs and caromed around until the Eagles' Carlton Gunter fell on it in the end zone for the touchdown that made it 33-0, Abilene.

At the half, it was 41-0. Reserves used the second half to practice for 1958. The final was 60-0, the team stopped at a restaurant for its Thanksgiving dinner, and flew back to Abilene with Friday night on everyone's mind. On Friday, top-ranked Amarillo would play at Fort Worth Paschal, the winner to meet Abilene in the quarterfinals.

Everyone supposed the winner would be Amarillo, and the Sandies did polish off Paschal, 26-6. In fact, Moser and the Eagle coaches had spent most of their time before the San Angelo and El Paso Austin games peering at films of the 1957 Amarillo Golden Sandies.

In these films, they saw a team with which they were familiar: the 1956 Abilene Eagles.

Abilene 60, El Paso Austin 0
Nov. 28, 1957

Dec. 7, 1957

> *"This is an important one. We must win this one and still be ready the next week. They hit hard but we will hit harder. I know every one will be ready. 'Study and know'."*

NO. 1 AMARILLO VS. NO. 2 ABILENE.

The biggest game of the season in Texas high school football. "The headliner of the year," proclaimed the Associated Press. "This is the one everybody has been waiting for." Harold V. Ratliff of the AP, the dean of Texas sports writers, called it "a Homeric struggle in the Panhandle. With a crowd of more than 20,000 looking on, Amarillo will make its greatest bid for a state championship in a decade. To do it, the Golden Sandies, coached by Joe Kerbel, a fellow who has become accustomed to state titles, will have to stop the longest winning streak in high school football."

Kickoff was set for 2 p.m. Saturday in Amarillo's Dick Bivens Stadium. Amarillo was made a 6 1/2-point favorite, and knowledgeable people thought that was conservative. "You line those two ballclubs up on the field, and personnel-wise, there isn't an Abilene player, maybe with the exception of fullback Bill Sides, who could make that Amarillo starting lineup," said Fort Worth Paschal coach Bill Allen, whose team had just lost to Amarillo and who had lost to Abilene in the 1956 quarterfinals.

In Abilene, Chuck Moser picked up his clipboard Monday afternoon, walked out of the coaches' office in the field house and down the corridor to the varsity locker room. As he did before every practice, he stood at a blackboard just inside the locker room door. The

Eagles, dressed out in practice whites except for cleats, fell silent, and Moser looked at them and told them he didn't think they could beat Amarillo.

"I made the statement that I didn't think we could beat Amarillo, *but…*," Moser said. "So when we were going out on the field to practice, three of the seniors came up and said, 'Coach don't you ever say you don't think we can beat Amarillo.' We did have a group of kids who had been substitutes on some great football teams, and they were extremely determined to do as well as we'd done in the past."

The Sandies' victory over Fort Worth Paschal had avenged Amarillo's bi-district loss to Paschal in the 1956 playoffs, a game in which the Sandies were solid favorites. The '57 win was particularly sweet to five starters returning from the '56 team: quarterback John (Soapy) Sudbury, halfback David Russell, fullback Ken Kendrick, guard Billy White, and end Joe Ted Davidson.

SO MANY RETURNING STARTERS off a very strong team was only one way the '57 Sandies resembled the 1956 Abilene Eagles. Amarillo had roared through 11 games, scoring 456 points to an amazing 36 for the opposition. No team on its schedule scored more than one touchdown against Amarillo, and five didn't score at all. *Amarillo Globe* sports writer Putt Powell, who had been around about that long, said this was the best Sandies team in Amarillo High history.

"They're the only ones to go through the entire season completely untested," Powell said.

The Sandies were big and fast, superb in the fundamentals, ferocious on defense and they didn't stop running until the whistle blew. Halfbacks Russell and Dickie Polson were compared throughout the season to Glynn Gregory and Jimmy Carpenter, and Amarillo coaches said Billy White was better than Stuart Peake. The Sandies ran the belly offense and the "Oklahoma" 5-2 and 4-3 defenses, just like Abilene. And the Sandies' coach was Joe Kerbel. It was Kerbel, at Breckenridge, who had last defeated Chuck Moser and the Eagles, 48 games before.

The winning streak was important to Moser and the coaches, but clearly secondary to their goal. The Midland victory had secured the district championship with one district game left against San Angelo, and then there was El Paso Austin in the first game of the playoffs, and no matter what Bob Groseclose told the Booster Club, the Abilene High coaching staff didn't see any threat there. Their next big game, Moser knew, would be Amarillo. In the week after the Midland game, it was worth risking a loss to San Angelo, which nearly happened, to start focusing on Amarillo. Eagle coaches had already scouted the Sandies twice, and Moser and his staff spent many hours studying those reports, and Amarillo game films. After the San Angelo game, Moser and his staff flew to Amarillo on Saturday to watch the Sandies against Amarillo Palo Duro in their last regular season game.

"They have a great football team," Moser said. "They are big, fast, and have great desire. We've scouted Amarillo three times and have not yet found a weakness."

Not a weakness, maybe, but of course what Moser didn't say was that the coaches had found several tendencies in Amarillo's style of play that became a crucial part of their planning for the Sandies.

Once on the practice field, the Eagles were intense. Not all the helmets in the Moser era got broken in games.

"Each day during the week, all our coaches developed more confidence," Moser said, "and I think the confidence came from the boys rather than the coaches."

But the Eagles were not at full strength. Starting center and linebacker Gerald Galbraith's right knee was so painful from calcium deposits that he had to watch most of the practices. All week Moser wasn't sure if he could start, or even play. It was a blow, playing against a great offense like Amarillo's, because Galbraith called the defensive signals.

~

THE COACHES, MEANWHILE, TAUGHT the players the things the scouts had seen about Amarillo. For example, the Sandie defenders "stunted" on almost every play, defenders criss-crossing from their set positions, trying to confuse blocking schemes. In a typical stunt, the outside defender would slant inside, and the defender next to him on the inside would loop behind him to the outside. Eagle coaches taught the linemen to double up (called a "double team") on the defender going inside, while a back coming up to block would take the defender going outside.

"Another thing," Moser said, "Amarillo had the best gang tackling we'd ever seen." During practice, the Eagles worked on a special play that might take advantage of that Sandie strength. Scouts had also seen that Sandie defensive halfback David Russell, a tremendous football player, always came up quickly to the line of scrimmage against running plays.

Lastly, Abilene coaches thought they saw something useful in the way the Amarillo defenders lined up against a team's punt formation.

There was one other thing. It involved Eagle safety Jim Perry, who got a lot of specialized work during the week.

"Our two safeties were Bob Swafford, who was about 6-3, and Perry, who was 6-5," Moser said. "They were both fast, both track men. They were tall, fast, and tough—tremendous high school safeties." Swafford and Perry were taught a new defensive technique that the coaches thought might slow down Amarillo's terrific quarterback option featuring Sudbury, a very smooth and deceptive quarterback, and the halfbacks Russell and Dickie Polson, both with 10-flat speed. Time after time in defensive scrimmages during the week, they practiced this new technique, with Moser watching closely. He was apprehensive about using this strategy, but he thought he had no choice.

There was an interesting mental wrinkle. In all 48 games the Eagles had won, they had never been behind in the score and had only been in a tie situation twice. Moser said he couldn't be sure what might happen if Amarillo opened up a lead.

"I have enough faith in the kids that I know they will do their best if they get behind," Moser said. "I notice that when we have been tied, they really went to work and went ahead. This year's Breckenridge game is a good example. We scored in two minutes after they tied the score."

ON THURSDAY MORNING, THE LAST 15 of 4,600 tickets were sold in Abilene. On Friday morning after the pep rally, the Eagles boarded the Eagle Bus for the long ride to Amarillo where they would headquarter at the Herring Hotel. Saturday morning at 5, a special train left the Texas and Pacific Depot downtown, carrying hundreds of Abilenians who paid $8.70 each for the trip. Thousands more traveled by car, most following U.S. 83 to Childress and then U.S. 287 to Amarillo.

In the locker room, Moser consulted with team physician Dub Sibley and made a decision. Sibley took Gerald Galbraith into a corner, inserted a needle into his knee, and injected two vials of painkiller. It would let Galbraith play, but only at about 70 percent.

At the kickoff, the sky was clear with temperatures in the 40s and a wind strong enough to affect the kicking game. Dick Bivens Stadium was built to seat 15,000, but there were steep dirt banks behind either end zone and those were carpeted with fans. In all, 23,000 people saw the game. Amarillo wore gold jerseys, the Eagles their signature '57 black jerseys with gold numbers. Elsewhere in the state that afternoon, San Antonio Jefferson was hosting Austin, Port Arthur was at Houston Bellaire, and Dallas Highland Park was at Wichita Falls in the other AAAA quarterfinals.

The Eagles' starting offensive lineup: left end Jim Perry, 176; left tackle Mike Bryant, 192; left guard John Young, 166; center Gerald Galbraith, 172; right guard Truman Bridges, 163; right tackle Ronnie Alldredge, 167; right end Mike McKinnis, 184; quarterback Gervis Galbraith, 153; left half Stan Cozby, 158; right half Chuck Colvin, 162; fullback Bill Sides, 167.

Abilene accepted the opening kickoff, couldn't move, and with a bad punt into the wind gave Amarillo great field position at the Eagle 38. It was not a good start against a team as powerful as the Sandies. But then the Eagle defenders, by now instinctively, did as they were coached. The first hit was very hard. Dickie Polson fumbled and Truman Bridges recovered for Abilene. But the Eagles gave it right back on Cozby's fumble—the Sandies knew something about hitting—and Amarillo marched 54 yards for the game's first touchdown, on Russell's halfback pass to end Joe Ted Davidson. For the first time since Oct. 1, 1954, the Eagles were behind.

Gold and black jerseys flew against each other. Abilene was having trouble moving the ball while Amarillo, with Sudbury running the belly option smoothly, looked like a threat to score every time it came to the line of scrimmage. But they didn't. Something always seemed to happen to stop the Sandie runners just as the play was about to develop. It was the Eagle safeties, playing as they had been coached.

"We were playing a 4-3 with four defensive backs," Moser said. "Just before the ball was snapped, the safety away from the sideline would come up on the line of scrimmage and crash. His only job was to stop the quarterback. The end away from the sideline would then cover wide—contain—and the cornerbacks would sit back and wait for a flat pass. The other safety had coverage deep both ways."

Moser called it the "Mud Defense." Years later, coaches in the National Football League would call it the "safety blitz."

"I was afraid to run it except in bad weather," Moser said. "If anybody had sent two men deep, we'd had it. Our name would have been mud. But if we hadn't had that defense, I don't care how many touchdowns you score, we couldn't have stopped them."

EVEN WITH THE DEFENSE, Moser knew the Sandies could score again at any time. The Eagles needed to score before Amarillo got a two-touchdown lead. "If we had gone to the dressing room at halftime trailing 14-0, there's no telling what might have happened," he said. At the end of the first quarter, Moser took Gerald Galbraith out of the game. Alan Peake went in on offense at center, and the fullback, Bill Sides, took over for Galbraith at linebacker.

In the second quarter, the Eagles suddenly got a break. Amarillo had to punt into the wind and Abilene took over at the Sandie 45. Moser called a play that the Eagles had worked on so hard in practice. Freddie Martinez, in at quarterback, gave the ball to Sides on the fullback power play at right tackle. Sides made five yards, then was about to be gang-tackled. There were nine gold jerseys within three feet of him. Sides looked outside and there was Martinez, trailing him, just as they had practiced. Sides flipped the ball to Martinez, who ran untouched the final 40 yards to tie the score, 7-7, with 9:10 remaining in the half.

It was a very big play. After the kickoff Amarillo roared 82 yards to score again, on Sudbury's one-yard run with 3:34 left in the half. Instead of 14-0, it was 14-7, and Abilene got that touchdown back immediately, on another special play.

This one was called the "Russell Special," based on safety David Russell's tendency to come forward aggressively against the run. The Eagles returned the kickoff to their 39, then Martinez, still in at quarterback, ran the belly option to the left side. Perry, the left end, stayed in to block but he was watching Russell. The coaches had told him to wait until Russell was within three yards of the line of scrimmage, then break deep. When he did, he was the only receiver out, and he was all alone.

Martinez hit Perry at the Sandie 38, the lanky end eluded a defender, and completed the 61-yard play to tie the score again only 24 seconds after Amarillo had taken the lead. In back-to-back plays, the Eagles had scored two long touchdowns against a Sandie defense that had not given up more than a single touchdown in a game all year. At the half, it was 14-14, and Moser sensed that Abilene had gained the momentum. For the second half, Amarillo naturally chose to receive. Moser chose to take the wind.

It worked. Amarillo had to punt into the wind, and Abilene had the ball at its 42. Running the belly series against the stunting Amarillo defense, the double-team blocking scheme started to open holes. Colvin got 27 yards, Cozby 19 and Sides seven as the Eagles marched goalward. Finally, on fourth down, Sides got the touchdown from the one. The PAT was no good, but Abilene had a 20-14 lead in the third period and the 1957 Amarillo Golden Sandies were at last being tested.

IT DIDN'T HELP THAT RUSSELL, the Sandies' leading rusher, had been injured and was on the sideline in the second half. Without him, and against determined Eagles playing the Mud Defense, the Amarillo offense slowly deteriorated. The Sandies would pick up only 70 yards rushing and 19 passing in the second half.

Abilene held on to its 20-14 lead into the fourth period. Then came the game's biggest play. It was another special play the Abilene coaches thought would work against the Amarillo defense. But this time Moser didn't call it. Sophomore quarterback Charles McCook called it, and Moser nearly had a heart attack.

With seven minute left in the game, the Eagles faced a fourth-and-nine at the Amarillo 40. Eagle scouts had seen that Amarillo left a sizeable hole in the middle of their alignment against punts. In practice, McCook had been instructed to tell Charles Flynn, the punter, to run a fake punt any time the Eagles had a fourth down near the 50 with less than five yards to go. In the excitement, McCook told Flynn to run the fake punt, even though there were not five, but *nine* yards to go for the first down. McCook told Moser what he had done and Moser tried to call time out.

Too late. Flynn was playing the nervous-punter role so well that on the sideline *Abilene Reporter-News* photographer Don Hutcheson framed Flynn, thinking something bad was about to happen. But the snap went directly to Colvin, the blocking back in punt formation, who burst through the unguarded middle and ran 14 yards for a first down at the 26.

Kerbel said that play broke the Sandies' backs. "Until that point," Kerbel said, "we were still in the ball game. We still had a chance."

Quickly the Eagle offense took the field against the rattled Sandie defense. Colvin got the call on the first play, a power play at left tackle, and went the 26 yards to put Abilene in control of the game 26-14, with 5:05 remaining. Now the Sandies were out of balance, and over-pursuing on defense, trying to make a play. Kerbel said it was the over-pursuit that made the Eagles' last score, a Cozby run with three minutes left, look so easy.

It was about that time that a dark smudge appeared in the north, a horizontal brown line above the flat Panhandle horizon. Everyone who saw it knew what it was. It rose quickly above the horizon like the dark roof of a convertible being pulled into the sky. By the time the game's last seconds were ticking down, it had become a wall, five miles away, coming hard, then one mile, then a couple of city blocks. And just as the game ended, with theatrical timing, it hit. A howling dust storm engulfed the stadium of the Amarillo Golden Sandstorms.

Here at last was the scene out of Cecil B. DeMille, God himself believing that Amarillo would win and so in the morning hours stirred his finger in the winds over Kansas and Nebraska to get this big valedictory cloud headed southward to arrive just at the moment of the Sandies' triumph, hoping an Amarillo sports writer would recognize the high drama and write a story worthy of Grantland Rice, God, and Cecil B. DeMille.

Only the wrong team won.

The valediction belonged to the 1957 Abilene Eagles, "substitutes on some great football teams," who now knew they were pretty great themselves. "I'll tell you the truth, I didn't think you could do it," Moser told his team. The Eagles had beaten a team that had been directly compared to the 1956 Eagles, and they had beaten them badly. Pound for pound and heart for heart, the 1957 Eagles were arguably the best team of them all. Dirt outlined the tracks of the Sandies' tears and stuck to the teeth of the roaring Abilenians. Tyler in 1955 might have been the best, but the greatest game anyone had ever seen the Eagles play was this one, the 49th straight.

Abilene 33, Amarillo 14
Dec. 7, 1957

End of the Road

Living by the Rules

Contrary to Don Oliver's earlier reports, some weekend research by The Associated Press "definitely established," said a short boxed story on the front page of the Monday morning *Reporter-News,* "that Abilene has the longest winning streak in high school football history.

"The only school with a record anywhere near Abilene's is Massena, N.Y., which managed 45 games without a loss or tie. This school went through 55 straight games without a loss but a tie prevented it from being a record. Massena finally lost in September of this year. Massilon, O., once had a 47-game winning streak."

The game was talked about for days. Fort Worth Paschal coach Bill Allen, who had said only Eagle fullback Bill Sides could crack Amarillo's starting lineup, said he had never seen anything like the 1957 Abilene Eagles. "That ball club is a tribute to the greatest coach in the history of Texas high school football, and to that terrific desire that he instills in those boys."

"We know this," wrote Don Oliver Monday morning, "the Abilene Eagles of 1957 are just as much a credit to Abilene as were the state championship teams of 1954, 1955 and 1956, if they don't win another game."

The triumph over Amarillo vaulted Abilene into the No. 1 ranking statewide and made them 12-point favorites over Highland Park. It also created a couple more office chores for Chuck Moser on Tuesday. First, he had to run off more eligibility slips to give his players that day after practice.

On Wednesday, just as they had the 12 previous weeks, the players would carry the slips with them through the day, presenting them to the teacher in each of their classes. There were blanks for a grade and for comments, in accordance with Moser's first three "General Rules" for his players: "1. You must be enrolled in four subjects and passing three subjects in order to be eligible to play; 2. Show your teachers and school the highest kind of respect; 3. Turn your eligibility slip in to coach's gym office by Thursday 8:30 a.m."

If a player wasn't passing three subjects, he didn't play. If a player received three negative comments regarding deportment, he didn't play. (If he received one or two deportment comments, he ran extra sprints after practice. Players hated the eligibility slips. But they all agreed the slips were effective.)

Next, Moser sat down and made a tape recording. That night, assistant coach Blacky Blackburn set the recorder on a table, pressed "Play," and out came Moser's voice to an overflow meeting of the Eagle Booster Club at the Coca-Cola auditorium.

"Last summer," said the coach's voice, "I didn't think we had a chance against Amarillo."

Of course that was why Moser wasn't at the meeting.. In August he had approved the Abilene Kiwanis Club banquet date—Dec. 10—because he didn't think the Booster Club would be meeting that night. And so as president he was presiding at the annual banquet, and it gave a nice glimpse into his priorities. His underdog team had just won a sensational victory, the biggest game of the year in Texas high school football, but on Tuesday night, Dec. 10, his greater civic responsibility was elsewhere in the city.

"When we set the date for the banquet," said the voice from the recorder, "I never once thought we would be in the playoffs."

Before the season began, Moser had said, "We will get beat sometime." Twelve times his team had proved him wrong. The team without any super players had played its way into the state Class AAAA semifinals against Highland Park. After Moser's comments, Blackburn told the Booster Club the Scotties were a great football team, and very fast.

"They ran out of backfield positions for their 10-flat boys, and had to make an end out of one of them," Blackburn said. "We've got some boys in Abilene who can catch them. Bobby Morrow, Woodhouse and those other ACC sprinters."

His reference was to Bobby Morrow, the Abilene Christian College sprinter who had won the three gold medals at the 1956

Olympics, and to Morrow's ACC teammate Bill Woodhouse, who joined him on ACC's NCAA champion sprint relay teams.

On Thursday morning at 8:30, Moser received eligibility slips from all his players. Two of them, defensive regulars, turned in slips that, according to Moser's rules, disqualified them for the Highland Park game. The Eagles would play Highland Park without them, and without injured starting linebacker Gerald Galbraith.

Dec. 14, 1957

WITH 3:36 LEFT IN THE GAME, the state Class AAAA semifinals at the Cotton Bowl in Dallas, the Highland Park Scots broke the huddle and trotted up to the line of scrimmage.

Waiting for them were the gold jerseys of the Abilene Eagles. The line of scrimmage was the Highland Park 42, where the Scots faced third down and nine. Abilene, with its great defense, was leading the Scotties, 20-14. The Scots, with great team speed, lined up in a formation they hoped would take the Eagles by surprise. It was a short punt formation, but the Eagles had worked against it, recognized it, and shifted their defense against what they knew was going to be a pass. As they did, one Eagle struggled to remember, with the shift, what he was supposed to do: rush the passer, or cover.

Scottie quarterback Bobby Reed took the direct snap from center and looked for Jack Collins, a senior 180-pound halfback with 10.1 speed. Collins was looking for an open area in the Abilene secondary and found one about 20 yards downfield not far from the right sideline. The defender responsible for that area had decided he was supposed to rush. Reed threw. Collins made the catch and outraced the Eagle secondary 30 yards to the end zone.

With the bowl in near pandemonium, Collins, as versatile and valuable to the Scots as Glynn Gregory had been to the Eagles, kicked the extra point. But the Scots were whistled for illegal motion, and Collins had to kick again. This time he missed, and the score remained tied, 20-20.

But the Scotties, two-touchdown underdogs, had taken the lead anyway. In 1957, the winner of a tied playoff game was determined statistically. The first tiebreaker was penetrations. A team scored a penetration any time it ran a play inside the opponents' 20-yard line. In the game, Highland Park had five penetrations. Abilene had three.

Freddie Martinez, the better passer of Abilene's two rotating quarterbacks, tried to bring the Eagles back. He hit halfback Stan Cozby for 20 yards to the Highland Park 43 with 2:10 remaining, but then four straight passes fell incomplete. The clock hit 0:00 and the Cotton Bowl turf disappeared beneath a swarm of purple and gold. There were two reasons for hysteria. One, the Scotties were going to the state championship game. Secondly, the Scots had ended the Abilene Eagles' winning streak at 49. Hard to tell which the Scottie players and fans considered the bigger feat. That night, a Dallas man who identified himself only as the parent of a Highland Park player, telephoned the *Reporter-News* to praise the Eagles' sportsmanship even in the shock of a loss such as this. The caller said he saw an Eagle player run across the field and shake the hand of the Highland Park coach.

The coach was Tugboat Jones. There was no doubt in his mind what had been accomplished.

"That's what I came here for," said Jones in the chaotic Highland Park locker room, "to beat Abilene. If anybody was to beat Abilene, I think I deserved to do it. After all, I had some fine teams at Midland in 1954 and '55, didn't I? I worked awfully hard but never could win."

This was the same Tugboat Jones who had sat in press boxes in Lubbock and Amarillo, glumly watching the Eagles, who he would have to play in a couple of weeks, dismantle the Westerners or the Sandies. After the 1955 season Jones had seen enough of Sammy Caudle and Elmo Cure and David Bourland and Stuart Peake and Glynn Gregory and Jim Welch and the King boys and all the rest of the Abilene Eagles, and he resigned as coach of the Midland Bulldogs. Jones, an alumnus of Abilene Christian College, did have great teams at Midland in 1954 and '55 but couldn't even get out of the district.

"We never had enough speed," he said. "We could gain ground, and we had fine lines, but not enough speed."

In 1956, in his first team meeting at Highland Park, he told his team he wanted "some kids on my team that can beat Abilene. I left Midland because we didn't have enough good boys to beat Abilene, but I think you are the ones who can do the job."

~

IN THE EAGLE LOCKER ROOM, Chuck Moser faced a challenge for which even he was unprepared. He raised his voice above the strange and intense din of disappointment and told his players, "There's no sense in crying." But his voice broke and they cried anyway, most of them. You never forget how to do that. Fans outside waited and cheered as if they had won, but it didn't help. All the Eagle seniors had been in the ninth grade the last time the Eagles lost a football game. This was a first they could not have dreamed of. It didn't matter that Highland Park had had the better athletes and terrific team speed. It didn't matter that starting center and linebacker Gerald Galbraith was injured and couldn't play, or that two-way all-state tackle Mike Bryant played hurt. It didn't matter that Moser had benched two defensive starters when they turned in unacceptable eligibility slips from their teachers on Thursday morning.

"We made five serious mistakes," Moser said, "and you can't win with that many. Highland Park only made two. We made two serious mistakes that we hadn't made before all year. I just guess we were supposed to get beat."

The Eagles ate their post-game meal in a completely foreign environment and settled into the Eagle Bus for the unique ride home. Falling in behind, as the bus skirted Fort Worth on the Northwest Highway and moved onto U.S. 80 toward Weatherford, were a few Abilene cars, proud for once of their pace behind a bus through Parker County.

It was after 9 when the bus crossed the little divide at Baird and coasted down to the flat plain for the last 20 miles. Clyde slid by, and then Elmdale, and up ahead were the faint lights of Abilene. Then there were other lights. Car lights. Multiple dozens of cars, lining the north shoulder of the highway, reaching from the city limits three miles to the east toward the approaching Abilene Eagles.

The bus reached the line and the cars fell in behind, raising a ruckus of honking and yelling and cheering that the jackrabbits out in the serene West Texas December darkness could hear for miles.

"I've never seen such a traffic jam," said officer J.E. Luten of the Abilene Police Department. Many of the cars followed the bus all the way to the field house at the corner of North Sixth and Shelton.

"There a great mob gathered to speak a word, give a pat on the back, or just catch a glimpse of their battle weary idols," wrote David McPherson in the Sunday morning *Reporter-News,* in a story stripped across all eight columns above the mast on Page One under the headline, "The End of the Road—You Just Can't Win 'em All."

By 11 the mob had dispersed. The last of the Eagles had exited the field house, greeted friends and parents, hugged girlfriends, and gone off in cars to do whatever high school football players in Abilene did at the end of an era, on a Saturday night, with no midnight curfew and the thought of Highland Park meeting Port Arthur for the state championship curling through their minds.

CHUCK MOSER TAUGHT HIS end-of-the-road lesson to his Sunday School class at St. Paul Methodist Church Sunday morning. The usual class size was 22; this morning there were 32 junior high students tucked into the classroom, and one sports writer. Moser told the class that the end of the winning streak would "help us have a better team next year. It will make us appreciate winning more."

At a final team meeting on Monday, Moser told his team, "You voted at the start of the season to win all 10 of your games, and you did. You had two goals to attain, and you got one of them. I can remember back before I came to Abilene that a 12-1 record would have really been something. I have never seen a town that likes a bunch of kids like Abilene does you boys. The people love you all."

Technically the Eagles completed the season unbeaten, with a record of 12-0-1. But that didn't mean anything to anybody on a quiet Saturday, Dec. 21, in Abilene, the Eagle Bus parked in the motor pool, the black jerseys folded and put away, the gold helmets lined side-by-side on shelves in the equipment room, while on the radio Highland Park beat Port Arthur, 21-9, in the state championship game.

IN 1958, MOSER'S EAGLES won 10 games and lost two, to Sweetwater in the second game of the season, and to Wichita Falls in the state quarterfinals at Abilene, the last Eagle game played at Fair Park Stadium. In 1959, the Eagles moved into the new stadium out by the airport, Shotwell Stadium, named for the coach whose late-life career decision opened the door to the Moser era. The Eagles defeated San Antonio Thomas Jefferson, 14-12, in the first game played at Shotwell Stadium, keeping intact Moser's record of never losing a season opener. In 1959 the Eagles again went 10-2, losing at last to hated San Angelo, 13-0, in San Angelo, and again to Wichita Falls in the state quarterfinals.

Moser left Abilene High after the 1959 season to become the city schools athletic director.

"I was burned out," he said. "I went to the office every day but Christmas."

The player pool also told him it was time to move on. There were no more Gregorys and Carpenters and Peakes coming up. Then, in September, 1960, the city's second high school, Cooper, opened, and in its first season played a junior varsity schedule. The

1960 Eagles, under new head coach Wally Bullington, won seven and lost three, two of those district games, to Midland and Odessa Permian. At the end of the season the Abilene High Bell Team towed the bell to Odessa and presented it to the new district champion, Permian High School. It was a time for joy in El Paso. The team coming to play El Paso Ysleta in the bi-district round of the playoffs was from Odessa, not Abilene. When Ysleta beat Permian, 31-21, there was near delirium in the city, and the school board breathed a huge sigh of relief.

Moser had college offers but he declined them. He had often said he always preferred working with high school kids because at that level he was a true teacher. A man echoing that belief was Gordon Wood, who created his own legend coaching the Stamford Bulldogs and the Brownwood Lions. The words belonged to Wood, but they could have come from either man. At the high school level, Wood said, "You have to work with the players you get, the students."

Moser remained as Abilene athletic director for 14 years. On January 14, 1974, at a regular meeting of the Abilene Independent School District Board of Trustees, Dr. Herman Schaffer moved to accept the resignation of Charles Moser, "who has been in the system for 21 years, with regret." And that the Board send a letter commending him for service rendered in the Abilene ISD. Mrs. Margaret Rutledge seconded the motion. The motion carried. When he resigned, he was making $17,000 a year.

Moser moved to College Station to become an assistant coach at Texas A&M University under old high school adversary (Breckenridge and San Angelo) Emory Bellard. He remained in that area after retirement and was a regular at frequent reunions of his Eagle players. The first such reunion, in 1979 in Abilene, attracted more than 100 people and most of the famed players. But the most popular man at the reunion, other than Moser, was a slight, balding dentist from Lubbock. Billy Jack Rudd, the student manager in 1953-54 who Moser said was so gung-ho "that he made me more gung-ho. I'm not so sure that Rudd didn't start the whole thing." The star halfback

Glynn Gregory said, "I think that if you picked the most valuable player on all these teams, that it would be Billy Jack Rudd." Of course the reunion was Rudd's idea.

Moser died on May 7, 1995, at the age of 76. At Abilene High in the 1990s new athletic offices were built adjacent to the locker rooms and practice fields and the complex was named the "Chuck Moser Field House."

Fair Park Stadium continued to be the site of junior high games. When Fair Park was renamed "Oscar Rose Park" in memory of an Abilene construction pioneer, the stadium became Rose Park Stadium. The old stands eventually were removed and replaced by just a low tier of bleachers but at the end of the century the field was there still, surrounded by a chain link fence. Its name now is "Curly Hays Field," after an Abilenian famed for officiating high school and Southwest Conference football games, and Pop Warner games are played there. The stone field house underwent renovation that left it looking like any other framed building except for the south exterior, where the renovators leftmost of the old stone wall standing.

In 1999, *The Abilene Reporter-News* named Chuck Moser the "Abilenian of the Millennium" in sports.

Abilene boys played in two more state championship games in the century, in 1967 when Austin Reagan mounted a classic goalline stand in the last minute of the game to defeat Cooper, 20-19, and in 1996, when Austin Westlake pounded Cooper, 55-15.

Abilene High did not make the state playoffs again until 1999. The Eagles' longest winning streak in that time was nine.

Epilogue

SUNDAY MORNING, DEC. 15, across the top of the *Reporter*-News sports section above the Highland Park game stories was a huge headline in bold capitals.

"IT WAS INEVITABLE"

It was a good headline, probably conceived by an editor weeks or months before the editors needed it, as early as September, certainly before the Amarillo game.

It was inevitable. When the hands of the game clock on the Fair Park Stadium scoreboard reached 0:00 shortly before 10 p.m. on the night of Oct. 8, 1954, it became inevitable that the Abilene Eagles would lose a football game.

They had just beaten Borger, 34-7, an important district-opening victory after the 35-13 loss to Breckenridge the previous week. Up next was Odessa, the defending district champion and state Class AAAA finalist.

The Eagles beat them, too, 21-7, but that wasn't inevitable. Odessa came to play, and to win, and the Bronchos did their best to do so. Nor was it inevitable the following week that Abilene would beat Pampa, but the Eagles did.

Nothing that the Eagles accomplished in 48 straight games after Borger was inevitable. Every time, two teams showed up, coached by men who had worked hard to give their team its best chance to win. On each team were players who didn't play the game to lose. The players were talented and tough, so much so that this district with Pampa and Borger and Amarillo and Lubbock and Midland and Odessa and San Angelo and Abilene earned a nickname in the statewide press: "the Little Southwest Conference." Tugboat Jones, the Midland coach, said it best: "For two years we had a great football team and couldn't get out of district. We figured if we could beat Abilene, then we were going to win state. Beat Abilene and you're going to be state champion."

Beyond the district in the playoffs were other champions who knew they either had to win or go home to basketball season. Arguably the El Paso teams were outgunned, but in Texas high school football even a donkey can find a diamond. Certainly, lining up for the opening kickoff, they didn't believe their defeat was inevitable just because it was Abilene across the line.

What happened on Nov.25, 1954, or Dec. 18, 1954, or Oct. 14, 1955, or Dec. 17, 1955, or Sept. 28, 1956, or Nov. 22, 1956, or Sept. 13, 1957, or Dec. 7, 1957, was not inevitable. Eleven adolescent boys on either side, on a tide of their own physical and emotional growth, swept along by confusing new forces arriving with the dawn of a new culture that was both exhilarating and dangerous and all about them, eleven racing teenaged minds breaking the huddle and coming to the line of scrimmage to engage eleven like minds across the line, with variables of preparation, injury, illness, unrequited love (girlfriends were Moser's great fear), courage, determination, upbringing, instinct and Texas weather thrown in. Then the ball was snapped and luck and plain old fate kicked in.

NOT A SINGLE ONE of these games did the Eagles win inevitably. They were talented and fundamentally and wonderfully prepared, but the only thing inevitable about the 1954-1957 Abilene Eagles was that sooner or later they would lose a football game.

Finally they did, on Dec. 14, 1957, and Tugboat Jones got what he wanted. He gave up in Midland, moved to Dallas and Highland Park High. There he beat Abilene and finally got to play another week and his Scotties in fact won the 1957 Class AAAA state championship, beating Port Arthur, 21-9. Just like he had said: beat Abilene, and you win the state championship.

But Jones only accomplished the inevitable. The Eagles accomplished something else. At the end of the 20th century, the media locally, statewide and nationally, busied itself with making lists of "the century's biggest and best," in every kind of category.

In Texas, *The Dallas Morning News* undertook a complete weeklong series of the state's "best of the century." Naturally the editors recognized high school football's place in the Texan culture, and they named a "Team of the Century." That team was the Abilene High School Eagles, 1954-1957.

In a long story with several photos, the News recalled what the Eagles and Chuck Moser had accomplished in winning 49 straight football games. Nowhere in the story, in the morning newspaper in Highland Park's home town, the town where the streak ended, was there any mention of the Highland Park Scotties, or of Tugboat Jones. It was the Abilene Eagles who achieved history, to which Jones is lucky to be a footnote.

Another footnote: In that same end-of-the-century poll, the *Morning News* selected Gordon Wood, winner of two state championships at Stamford and seven at Brownwood, as high school "Coach of the Century." In February, 1953, Wood was one of the 21 applicants for the Abilene job when the school board selected Moser.

IF YOU RAN HISTORY BACKWARDS, the scope of this history would continually narrow, as events disappeared just as they had appeared, one at a time, back through 1957, 1956, two state championships won, a streak of 23, then one championship won, back through 1954, funneling and arrowing in tighter and tighter focus toward some point where it all started until March, 1953, was reached, and the first days of this history streaking toward their February source until the first seconds flashed by and then disappeared, into a mimeographic "ditto" machine, knocking it with the force of brilliant, thunderous history high into the air, tumbling it over and over until it came back down, landing right side up and finally bouncing into stillness on an ordinary institutional desktop in a dark, silent ten-by-ten office in Eagle Gym at the corner of South Second and Peach in Abilene, Texas, waiting for Chuck Moser to walk through the door.

Then he does, and time starts forward and out of the machine on the first day emerge rules. Not rules of football, but of living. No smoking or drinking. Pass or don't play. Highest respect for school and teachers. No stealing. Home by 10 on school nights. No cussing. Act like a gentleman. Then come rules of football. Football Rule No. 1 on Chuck Moser's list: "The ball is never dead until the referee's whistle kills it. Play till you hear the whistle." Rule No. 2: "The horn or gun doesn't stop the play. Always finish the play."

Some of the players, all in their 60s in 2004, still have pages from that blue-ink ditto machine, that they have kept in file folders: rules, policies, plays, scouting reports, hundreds of pages each year, all given to them by their coach simply so they would play the game well and have the best chance to win.

They have clippings, too, so they want to always know what the scores were. But they also kept the pages of rules and policies. It's how they played the game. Invariably they will say they have lived their lives that way. And a feeling emerges, among the players but also among Abilenians of that generation. It is a feeling of being different from people their age who grew up in other cities. They saw for almost four years—almost the length of an entire high school education—what can happen when you live by the rules, know all the plays, and run till the whistle blows. Now they wonder if the message was so strong that they carried it with them, part of their education not available to others. They wonder aloud, if their lives have been different, because of a football team, the Abilene High School Eagles, 1954-57.

The Streak

No. 1 **Abilene 34, Borger 7**
at Abilene, Oct. 8, 1954

No. 2 **Abilene 21, Odessa 7**
at Odessa, Oct. 15, 1954

No. 3 **Abilene 41, Pampa 7**
at Abilene, Oct. 22, 1954

No. 4 **Abilene 47, Amarillo 0**
at Amarillo, Oct. 30, 1954

No. 5 **Abilene 35, Lubbock 7**
at Abilene, Nov. 12, 1954

No. 6 **Abilene 28, Midland 14**
at Midland, Nov. 19, 1954

No. 7 **Abilene 27, San Angelo 0**
at San Angelo, Nov. 25, 1954

No. 8 **Abilene 61, El Paso Austin 0**
at Abilene, Dec. 4, 1954

No. 9 **Abilene 46, Ft. Worth Poly 0**
at Ft. Worth, Dec. 11, 1954

No. 10 **Abilene 14, Houston S.F. Austin 7**
at Houston, Dec. 18, 1954

No. 11 **Abilene 34, Highland Park 0**
at Dallas, Sept. 9, 1955

No. 12 **Abilene 45, Sweetwater 20**
at Abilene, Sept. 16, 1955

No. 13 **Abilene 13, Breckenridge 0**
at Abilene, Sept. 30, 1955

No. 14 **Abilene 35, Borger 6**
at Borger, Oct. 7, 1955

No. 15 **Abilene 47, Odessa 0**
at Abilene, Oct. 14, 1955

No. 16 **Abilene 40, Pampa 12**
at Pampa, Oct. 21, 1955

No. 17 **Abilene 35, Amarillo 13**
at Abilene, Oct. 28, 1955

No. 18 **Abilene 62, Lubbock 7**
at Lubbock, Nov. 12, 1955

No. 19 **Abilene 28, Midland 7**
at Abilene, Nov. 18, 1955

No. 20 **Abilene 35, San Angelo 6**
at Abilene, Nov. 24, 1955

No. 21 **Abilene 61, El Paso High 0**
at El Paso, Dec. 3, 1955

No. 22 **Abilene 33, Dallas Sunset 6**
at Abilene, Dec. 10, 1955

No. 23 **Abilene 33, Tyler 13**
at Ft. Worth, Dec. 17, 1955

No. 24 **Abilene 41, San Antonio Edison 6**
at Abilene, Sept. 14, 1956

No. 25 **Abilene 39, Sweetwater 7**
at Sweetwater, Sept. 21, 1956

No. 26 **Abilene 41, Lubbock Monterey 0**
at Lubbock, Sept, 28, 1956

No. 27 **Abilene 41, Breckenridge 0**
at Abilene, Oct. 5, 1956

No. 28 **Abilene 49, Lubbock 7**
at Abilene, Oct. 12, 1956

No. 29 **Abilene 45, Waco 14**
at Waco, Oct. 19, 1956

No. 30 **Abilene 42, Big Spring 6**
at Big Spring, Oct. 26, 1956

No. 31 **Abilene 47, Odessa 6**
at Abilene, Nov. 9, 1956

No. 32 **Abilene 41, Midland 6**
at Midland, Nov. 16, 1956

No. 33 **Abilene 20, San Angelo 0**
at Abilene, Nov. 22, 1956

No. 34 **Abilene 42, Ysleta 6**
at Abilene, Nov. 30, 1956

No. 35 **Abilene 14, Ft. Worth Paschal 0**
at Ft. Worth, Dec. 8, 1956

No. 36 **Abilene 20, Wichita Falls 6**
at Wichita Falls, Dec. 15, 1956

No. 37 **Abilene 14, Corpus Christi Ray 0**
at Austin, Dec. 22, 1956

No. 38 **Abilene 26, San Antonio Jefferson 13**
at Abilene, Sept. 13, 1957

No. 39 **Abilene 34, Sweetwater 13**
at Abilene, Sept. 20, 1957

No. 40 **Abilene 58, Lubbock Monterey 0**
at Abilene, Sept. 27, 1957

No. 41 **Abilene 41, Breckenridge 20**
at Breckenridge, Oct. 4, 1957

No. 42 **Abilene 39, Lubbock 0**
at Lubbock, Oct. 11, 1957

No. 43 **Abilene 27, Waco 7**
at Abilene, Oct. 18, 1957

No. 44 **Abilene 32, Big Spring 0**
at Abilene, Oct. 25, 1957

No. 45 **Abilene 19, Odessa 0**
at Odessa, Nov. 8, 1957

No. 46 **Abilene 41, Midland 0**
at Abilene, Nov. 15, 1957

No. 47 **Abilene 12, San Angelo 6**
at San Angelo, Nov. 22, 1957

No. 48 **Abilene 60, El Paso Austin 0**
at El Paso, Nov. 28, 1957

No. 49 **Abilene 33, Amarillo 14**
at Amarillo, Dec. 7, 1957

The Team of the Century

The Abilene Eagles, 1954-1957

Players

Bob Youngblood, Jack Self, H.P. Hawkins, Twyman Ash, John Thomas, Jim Millerman, Bob Hubbard, David Howle, Gene Colvin, Ronny Cearly, Jack Crumpler, Glenn Woods, Jim Briggs, Stuart Peake, Cullen Hunt, Freddie Green, Rufus King, Guy Wells, Hubert Jordan, David Steinman, Maurice Cook, Jim Busby, Don Beall, David Bourland, Homer Rosenbaum, John Barfoot, Frank Scarborough, Phil Bailey, Elmo Cure Jr., Jerry Henderson, Teddie Jack Key, Jimmy Carpenter, Glen Belew, Hollis Swafford, Weldon Moore, Pat Bland, Glynn Gregory, James Welch, Sam Caudle, Joe Taylor, Henry Colwell, Boyd King, Butch Adams, Jerry Avery, Pat Jones, Kenny Schmidt, Wayne Carpenter, Vance McFadden, Clint Murphy, Erwin Bishop, Charles Bottoms, Charles Bradshaw, Bufford Carr, Chuck Colvin, Reyes Diaz, Gerald Galbraith, Gervis Galbraith, Mike McKinnis, Mike Pelfry, Jimmy Perry, Henry Pinkston, Jim Rose, Bill Sides, Harold "Hayseed" Stephens, Joe Ward, Kim Winston, Frank Aycock, Ralph Bruton, Ronnie Alldredge, Tim Walter, Eddie Woods, Stan Cozby, Ronnie Ingle, Charles Harrison, Jerry Osborne, Freddie Martinez, Ronald Dale Conklin, John Young, Mike Bryant, James Brooke, Don Hughes, Truman Bridges, Jimmy Roberts, Bob Swafford, Alan Peake, Tony Martinez, Dale Graham, Ronnie Luckie, Robert McKissick, Rikki McPherson, Leldon Kelso, Carlton Gunter, Jack Reese, Johnny Garner, Charles Flynn, Charles McCook, Louis Adams, Ned Butler, Johnny Howe, Leroy Johnston, Charles Lacy, Rip Thomas.

Managers

Billy Jack Rudd, Don Bridges, Roy Reid, Bill Teague, Jimmy Johns, Charles Steinman, Charles Williams.

Coaches

Chuck Moser, Hank Watkins, Bob Groseclose, B.L. "Blacky" Blackburn, Shorty Lawson, Wally Bullington, Nat Gleaton, Tommy Morris.

About the Author

Michael Grant was a very slow fullback on Chuck Moser's last two Abilene teams in 1958-59. In 1969-71, he covered the Eagles as a sports writer for *The Abilene Reporter-News*, and in 1972 he was named the Texas High School Coaches Association "Sportswriter of the Year." He now lives in San Diego, California, where he is a journalist, an author and an educator.

Watkins, line coach; Bob Groseclose, backfield coach. Back row (l. to r.): Shorty ..., sophomore coach; Tommy Morris, B team assistant; B. L. Blackburn, B team coach; Nat Gleaton, soph assistant and head basketball coach. (Staff Photo).

Puss and Ronnie Ryan, John Whatley and Cowboy

...agles Eye 5th State Crown Against Tyler

...y JACK HOLDEN

...porter-News Editor

...WORTH, Dec. 16 —...
...age, at Houston's ...
...adium, one of the flash...
...ene Eagle teams ... to
...state finals ... ripped
...F. Austin 14-7, ... a
...state football ...

...y at 2 p.m. at TCU's
...ther Stadium ... another
...eam, in many respects
...ster and more ... the
...'54 champ, seeks a fifth
...s ... against Tyler.
...ose City's Lions, who have
... off 14 straight ...
...ears and own a ... record
...son, are a ... audie-
...ustin ... in 1954. That
...'54 was decided in the last

SEASON RECORDS

ABILENE — TYLER

[illegible]

... seconds on a scoring pass. If Saturday's game is anything like ... the 15,000 or more fans should get value received.

Weather forecasts indicate the game day will be clear and cool with temperatures around 50. There will be plenty of seats left for the customers in the 37,000-seat stadium, although there than 5,000 from Abilene and at least that many from Tyler have already bought tickets.

If the Eagles can take this one, they'll be the ... team in the history of schoolboy football in the state. Only Waco, with five championships and a tie for another, would be out front.

It's chapter three in the success story of Charles (Chuck) Moser, Abilene Eagle coach. The former star Missouri guard has had his team in the finals two of his three years in Abilene and has seen those teams win 34, lose three and tie one.

Moser's Warriors, who have had very little trouble running up a string of 32 straight conquests, are doped to win again Saturday. But this one isn't figured as any push-over. Tyler is big, it is fast and it has two of the state's finest players in quarterback Charles Milstead and halfback Joe Leggette.

Milstead, a 6-2 blond ... who weighs 180, is being hailed as another Walt Fondren, a Doyle Traylor or a Vince Matthews. He kicks, passes and runs and all of them well. He isn't Tyler's top ground gainer, but he has added 769 yards to the total, an impressive figure for a quarterback. He's also scored 1.. points.

Leggette is the top scorer with 120 points and the yardage leader with 980 yards and a 7.2 average. He weighs 188 and is a senior like Milstead. Rounding out the Tyler backfield are fullback Steve Smith, 175, and right half Kenneth McGuire, 150. The Tyler foursome averages 172 pounds to Abilene's 1.., in the line the Lions ... 185 to Abilene's 180.

Tyler has at least four stars in the line, end Byron Carothers, 185; center Jim Davis, 200; tackle Billy Sims, 20.; and guard Mauie W... son, 182.

Except for weight the Abilene line should match Tyler. The Eagles ...

...ger and ha... in the ...
... team.

The ... against T... have trouble ... Abilene. Nobody has ... and only ... have ... Abilene has ... points and ... Tyler has scored 331 ... ponents 87.

With the ... halfback Glynn Gregory ... halfback ... halfback Henry Colwell ... are figured ... as the ...

Whether ... with its ... Moser said ... we can ...

... Colwell ... who has ... Warriors ... Quarterback ... is a ...

Both teams ... but ... aerial ...

While Abilene ... Tyler ... the ... 1955 ...

...ead Holds Miami ...ead Despite 70

...ville, Fla., Dec. 16 ... The ... turned cold today and ... Snead's ... but The ... even ... to give him a ... stroke ... the halfway mark in the ... Sanford Open ...

... ... remained ... off the ... His second ... evening round gave Snead ... total of 1...

... in second place just one ... back of Snead were ... Biaggetti ... of ...

Biaggetti of Wilmington, Ohio, Jim Ferrie of Winston-Salem, N. C., and Marty Furgol of Lemont, Ill.

Ferree and ... shot 66—low score for the day. Biaggetti had a 67 and Furgol and Ferree fired 68s.

Field Reduced

The field of 125 was reduced to the 60 low scoring pros, plus ties, and 10 amateurs for the final five rounds. Pros shooting 144 or under qualified.

Gene ... of Bedford Heights, Ohio, tied for second place two strokes behind Snead after the opening round, matched Snead's 70 and finished in a ...-way tie at 1...

Others in that bracket were Mike Souchak of Grossinger's, N. Y., ... Cooper of Detroit and ... Doux Sanders of Miami Beach. Sanders had a 67, Cooper and Souchak a 69 each.

Ed Furgol of St. Louis and Ed (Porky) Oliver of Lemont, Ill., also grouped with six others at 137.

The sun shone brightly over the 6,208-yard, par 36-34—70 Mayfair Inn Country Club Course—but the temperature was in the chilling 40s and a biting wind ripped across the fairways.

Putting Troubles

Snead blamed the hand-numbing

High Game in Bowling

... Bridges ... a string of ... strikes Thursday night ... new season high game and ... Major League bowling ...

...ges' 2.. game ... nine consecutive strikes ... a new high in the Men's ... Association this year. His ... Co. team defeated Coca ...

PROBABLE OFFENSIVE LIN...

ABILENE			TYLER
Weight	Player	Pos.	Player
170	Freddie Green ...	LE	Byron Carothers
185	Rufus King ...	LT	...
180	Stuart Peake ...	LG	Mauie ...son ...
180	Elmo Curry ...	C	Jim Davis ...
170	Sam Caudle ...	RG	John Campbell
183	Homer Rosenbaum	RT	Billy Sims ...
193	Jerry Avery ...	RE	Mickey Trimble
141	David Bourland ...	QB	Charles Milstea...
175	Glynn Gregory ...	LHB	Joe Leggette ...
169	Henry Colwell ...	RHB	Kenneth McGui...
		FB	... Smith